COMMON
PRAYERS

BOOKS BY HARVEY COX

COMMON PRAYERS

❖

FAITH, FAMILY, AND A CHRISTIAN'S JOURNEY THROUGH THE JEWISH YEAR

Harvey Cox

HOUGHTON MIFFLIN COMPANY
BOSTON • NEW YORK
2001

For information about permission to reproduce selections from
this book, write to Permissions, Houghton Mifflin Company,
215 Park Avenue South, New York, New York 10003.

Visit our Web site: houghtonmifflinbooks.com.

Library of Congress Cataloging-in-Publication Data
Cox, Harvey Gallagher.
Common prayers : faith, family, and a Christian's journey
through the Jewish year / Harvey Cox.
p. cm.
Includes bibliographical references and index.
ISBN 0-618-06743-4
1. Church year — Prayer-books and devotions — English.
2. Christianity and other religions — Judaism. 3. Judaism —
Relations — Christianity. 4. Calendar, Jewish. I. Title.
BV30.C72 2001
263—dc21   2001024992
Printed in the United States of America

Book design by Robert Overholtzer

QUM 10 9 8 7 6 5 4 3 2 1

This book is lovingly dedicated to

MASHA TUMARKIN

1943–1993

SUZANNE TUMARKIN

1906–1994

RABBI MARSHALL MEYER

1930–1993

Also the sons of the stranger, that join themselves to the Lord,
To serve him and to love the name of the Lord, to be his servants,
Every one who keepeth the sabbath from polluting it,
And taketh hold of my covenant;
Even them will I bring to my holy mountain, and make them joyful.

— Isaiah 56:6, 7

Acknowledgments

The vigorous life of several Jewish congregations in which I have participated as a welcome guest have provided lively examples of living Judaism that both inspired me to write this book and sustained me while I was working on it. They include, among others, Congregation Eitz Chaim in Cambridge, Massachusetts, Temple Beth Zion in Brookline, Massachusetts, and Congregation B'nai Jeshurun in New York City. Generous rabbis and scholars of Judaica came to my aid when I found myself, as I often did, over my head. I think especially of Moshe Waldoks of Beth Zion, Irving ("Yitz") Greenberg, who is president of the National Jewish Center for Learning and Leadership, Cherie Koller-Fox of Eitz Chaim, and Professor Hillel Levine of Boston University. David Hartman, by inviting me to participate in conferences at the Shalom Hartman Center in Jerusalem, opened my eyes to a wider range of Jewish life than I had ever known before. At that thriving center of scholarship and spirituality Dr. Moshe Idell introduced me to the fascinating world of the Kabbalah. One rabbi, however, merits special mention. The late Marshall Meyer, who before his death was the spiritual leader of B'nai Jeshurun and for one memorable semester led a seminar with me at Harvard, taught me more about Judaism simply by being who he was than he could ever have known.

My editor at Houghton Mifflin, Eric Chinski, encouraged me from the first day we talked about the possibility of this book, and his friendly but exacting comments on the manuscript as it progressed have made it, I am sure, a better book than it would have been. Donald Cutler of Bookmark, my literary agent and friend for decades, made sage and good-humored suggestions at different stages. Luise Erdmann performed the demanding job of line editing with consummate skill.

My old friend and colleague Bishop Krister Stendahl, a New Testament scholar who has spent a lifetime deepening and improving relationships between Jews and Christians, carefully read the entire manuscript and offered indispensable comments and suggestions, most — not all — of which I have followed. My research assistant at Harvard, Andrea L. Anderson, skillfully searched out resources I needed, read chapters along the way, and made thoughtful suggestions. My faculty assistant for many years, Margaret Studier, made comments on the book as I wrote it, patiently printed out successive versions of the different chapters, and helped me in countless other ways.

My son Nicholas helped me a lot too. When we worked together preparing for his bar mitzvah, it was a wonderful education for both of us, affording us abundant opportunities to discuss the issues this book addresses. That discussion is still going on. Finally, my wife, Professor Nina Tumarkin, reviewed nearly every page with me more than once, took time from her own scholarly research in Russian history to read the entire manuscript, and continued to encourage me when I wondered if I had taken on something I could never finish. Besides, without the good fortune of my marrying her, the idea of writing this book would never have occurred to me. In addition, the many members of her extended family, both the living and the ones who are no longer with us, have always made me feel at home with them. In part, of course, this is a book about them, and I hope they enjoy it.

HARVEY COX

April 15, 2001
Last Day of Pesach, Easter Sunday
Cambridge, Massachusetts

Contents

COMMON
PRAYERS

Introduction

For my house shall be called
A house of prayer for all peoples.

— Isaiah 56:7

I N KEEPING WITH THE VISION of their prophets, the builders
of the ancient Temple in Jerusalem designed it to be a house of
prayer for all peoples. There was an inner area where only Jews
were admitted. Here stood the Holy of Holies, which only the
high priest was permitted to enter, and that only once a year, on the
Day of Atonement. There was also a section explicitly named "the
Court of the Gentiles." Throughout the ancient world, many gentiles
worshiped with Jews without ever converting to Judaism. The Jews
welcomed them as "God-fearers," and their presence in the Temple
reflected the age-old Jewish hope that one day all nations and peoples, including "strangers and sojourners," would join in praise of the
One who created them all.

The word "gentile" is not synonymous with the word "Christian."
Our English "gentile" is derived from the Latin term for "nation,"
and in Jewish usage it means anyone who is not a Jew. (I sometimes
enjoy informing my Jewish friends that among Mormons, "gentile"
refers to anyone who is not a Mormon, including Jews.) Of course,
the distinction between gentile and Christian meant nothing during
the years of Herod's temple, since the newborn Christian movement
was still a sect, among many others, within Judaism. But this changed
after 70 C.E. when, during the reign of the emperor Titus, the Roman

legions razed the Temple and expelled the Jews, including those Jews who were followers of Jesus, from Jerusalem. It was only after that catastrophe that the division between what we now call Judaism and Christianity began to set in. Decades passed before it became a complete rupture.

Today, only the famous Western Wall of the Temple remains. But I sometimes think of myself as one of those strangers or "sojourners" mentioned by the Jewish prophets. For a decade and a half, in addition to following my own spiritual tradition as a Protestant Christian, I have also lived and prayed with Jews. I have a special reason for doing so. Fifteen years ago I married a Jewish woman. Nina had been raised in a family of largely nonobservant Jews in New York City. As a teenager, partially (she now concedes) in a display of adolescent rebellion, she began attending activities at the Stephen Wise Free Synagogue. But when she left home for college and graduate school, she also became nonobservant. Later in life, however, after some painful personal experiences, she began to reclaim her Jewish heritage. She was still engaged in this quest when we met. Today her Jewish faith is deeply, and increasingly, important to her.

I was raised in a small town in Pennsylvania. My own parents were quite casual about churchgoing, but they dutifully dispatched my two brothers, my sister, and myself to the Baptist Sunday school next door. My grandparents attended it also but were not at all what I would call devout. Our family never said grace before meals, and as children we were never taught to say prayers before bedtime as some of our friends were. Nonetheless, as I grew older I became more involved in the church, first through the youth group and choir. I joined the church at thirteen; by then I was already fascinated with reading books about religion and theology. When I left for college I had decided I wanted to explore these fields further, perhaps even to become a minister. My parents did not disapprove but were somewhat less than enraptured. They advised, quite rightly, that a career in accounting would yield more financial security. As the decades passed, however, they reconciled themselves and eventually even seemed pleased with the direction my life had taken.

When Nina and I met we were both professors, she at Wellesley and I at Harvard. We had each suffered through the dissolution of a marriage and were slowly mending. I had three children, all grown. She had none. We had been introduced by mutual friends who thought we were well suited to each other, and we soon discovered we were. We recognized right away, of course, that our different religious paths constituted a factor we could not ignore. This led to many spirited discussions which made it clear that neither of us wanted either to convert to the other's faith or to find some in-between solution. Finally we both decided to stay what we were, to try to learn as much as we could about the other's religion, and to honor it and participate in it as far as our convictions would permit.

We have one child, Nicholas, who at the time of this writing is fourteen. We both agreed, before he was born, that we wanted him to grow up with some spiritual anchorage. But we also agreed that trying to raise a child in two religious traditions is almost always confusing and counterproductive. I am altogether satisfied with the decision we made. Since I recognize that Jews consider the child of a Jewish mother to be Jewish, that is the faith in which we are both nurturing Nicholas. We had also agreed, however, that this would not mean that I would delegate his spiritual tutelage to her. We have both shared in the process, and some of what the reader will find in this book consists of what I have learned in the fifteen years of study I have undertaken in order to equip myself to appreciate my wife's faith and to do my part in the guidance of our son. For me, indeed for all of us, it has been an intensely satisfying experience.

But most of what I have learned about Judaism during these years has not come from books. As anyone who knows how central family life is to Jews will recognize, our marriage entwined me in a maze of aunts and uncles, nephews, nieces, and cousins. As one of the family, I have been able to get a close-up of the Jewish world. It is important to me that the Judaism I have discovered is not quite the same as the one I have read about in historical accounts and theological works. It is a hands-on week-by-week and year-by-year Judaism of songs and scents and ups and downs, with both its comeliness and its homeliness clearly on display. Still, as a Christian, I experience Judaism from the perspective of a kind of metaphorical Court of the Gentiles, not as a complete outsider, but not as a full insider either.

Interfaith marriage is hardly unusual nowadays. Every year in America more Jews marry gentiles than marry each other. Despite the efforts of rabbis, priests, ministers, and, often, of parents and friends, the number of such marriages shows no sign of abating. We husbands of Jewish wives are hardly a homogenous group. We are

old and young, rich and poor, and in-between. We encompass journalists, policemen, computer engineers, psychiatrists, disc jockeys,
and a hundred other professions. Some of us are religious, some are
not. Very few of our number are what I am, a Christian theologian,
and I realize that this makes our marriage quite unusual (but, then,
are not all marriages in some sense sui generis?). We non-Jews who
marry Jews, though we may be a mixed company, inevitably get an
intensely intimate view of Judaism. This book is a kind of distillation
of what I have learned, during fifteen years of marriage, about Judaism, about my own faith, and about myself.

I have at least four reasons for writing this book. First, I want to
help my fellow Christians, especially those who might be curious but
puzzled about Judaism, to understand it better. Naturally I would
hope that anyone with a serious interest in Judaism would read primarily books by Jewish scholars. But in addition, these reflections,
written from my perspective of the Court of the Gentiles, might be a
helpful supplement for non-Jewish readers, if only because my angle
of vision is closer to theirs. As the husband of a Jewish woman I have
learned a lot, maybe even more than I originally bargained for, about
her tradition. I have now imbibed fifteen years of Jewish holidays,
Sabbaths, rituals, Torah studies, klezmer music, prayers, family gath-
erings, jokes, gossip, and gefilte fish. After several embarrassing faux
pas, I now know the difference between *mishugonah* and *mishpochah*
(an important distinction: the first means "berserk" and the second
refers to family), and between *kvetching* and *kvelling* (an even more
important one: the first means "complaining" and the second means
"taking pride in your children"). More seriously, I have fasted on
Yom Kippur, shivered at the blast of the shofar, sat *shivah* (the seven
days of mourning) when relatives have died, drunk the Sabbath wine
on Friday evenings, and prayed at the Wall in Jerusalem. In short, I
write from what I regard as a highly privileged position. I am a participant who is also in some measure an observer; an observer who is
also a participant.

I remain, of course, a sojourner in the Court of the Gentiles. My
perspective is not that of a full-fledged landsman. It never will be.
But neither is it that of a coldly objective analyst. The prayers I pray
when I am among Jews are Jewish prayers, but I have learned how to
make them my own as well. I have come to share some of the same
delights, hopes, and frustrations about Judaism that many Jews do,

though I feel them — as it were — in a different key. My knowledge of this ancient and complex tradition will never be more than that of a novice. But my unusual position as a Christian theologian who has taken an active part in Jewish life for a decade and a half enables me to draw some comparisons and contrasts most rabbis, priests, and ministers would not be able to make. For this reason, I hope this book can also serve, to quote the great Jewish sage Maimonides, as a kind of "guide for the perplexed" — in this case, perplexed gentiles.

My second purpose for the book is more personal. I want to explain how I have come to understand my own Christian faith better because of my marriage to a Jewish woman and my participation in the life of her faith community. Christians sometimes say that we need to understand Judaism because, after all, our religion is "rooted in the faith of ancient Israel." This is true as far as it goes. But what it overlooks is that there have been nearly two thousand years of Jewish history *since* Christianity came to birth. Little by little I have become quite uneasy with the "roots" metaphor. Thinking of Judaism in this way consigns it to the past. It makes living Judaism invisible. After all, we do not see the roots of a tree. They are hidden underground while the leaves blossom and the fruit ripens in full view. The roots analogy may even inadvertently contribute to the mistaken idea that Christianity has somehow superseded Judaism, a notion I completely reject. I want to understand Judaism, not just because of what it was, but because of what it is. Judaism is the tradition that sustains fourteen million human beings (many of them, it would seem, my relatives). And it is also a luxuriant repository of a spiritual wisdom available to anyone.

But Christians also have a special reason for understanding Judaism. Someone once defined Christians as gentiles who worship the God of Israel. I think this is correct, and therefore I also reject the dangerously deluded idea — still harbored by some Christians — that the two religions worship a different God. The fallacious platitude that the Jewish God is one of legalism and vengeance while the Christian one is a God of grace and love is both historically and theologically insupportable. It is the product of ignorance, not only of the Bible itself, but of the subsequent history of the two faiths, and results in a warped picture of both. I will return to this later because I am convinced that appreciating Judaism, both its history and its present manifestation, is essential to a full understanding of Christianity. It lends depth and resonance to all the ideas that are central to my faith: how I understand the nature of God, the purpose of human life, the significance of Jesus, and the meaning of faith.

I have a third purpose for writing these pages. I want to question the idea that a Jewish-Christian marriage necessarily dilutes the substance of either or both spouses' faiths. The fact is that Nina and I have come to the opposite conclusion. We have no way of knowing what might have happened in our separate faith journeys if we had never met or married. Still, I think I am probably a better Christian and she believes she may be a better Jew not in spite of but because of our marriage. We both recognize that making any marriage work is a difficult and demanding enterprise and that marrying a person of another faith does not make it any easier. But we have also come to believe that a mixed marriage can be a spiritual venture that sharpens and strengthens the faith of each partner. We think we have found some ways to help this maturation happen and to steer around the hazards that often assail marriages like ours. Both the Jew and the Christian who make this decision quickly discover — if they had not noticed before — that such a marriage is not just inter*faith*. It also entails the complicated cluster of ethnic and cultural qualities that make Jews different from Christians. But we believe these can make such marriages both more daunting and more satisfying. We hope this book can provide some hints for other couples who are either already involved in a religiously mixed marriage or may be contemplating one.[1]

Finally, I also hope that Jewish readers will profit from reading about my experience of their religion. To "see ourselves as others see us" can often help us to see ourselves in a new light. I have gained fresh insights into my own tradition by reading comments and reflections about it, and even criticisms, made by thoughtful non-Christians.[2] Sometimes what they say at first seems annoying, but it always makes me think. Discovering what there is in my own tradition that seems attractive or strange or opaque to someone who tries seriously to comprehend it from the outside often enables me to appreciate it in a new way. Today many more people are learning things about their own religions from the affectionate close observations of friends and spouses, and this has been a positive development. If, in perusing this book, Jewish readers come to apprehend something about their faith they had not recognized before, I will be gratified.

Despite our many differences, we thousands of non-Jews — men and women — who have married Jews have something important in common. But for some reason we do not talk to one another about it much. We are members of a club that never meets. Is it because talking openly about how we handle both the problems and the opportunities of such marriages is still a bit taboo? I don't know. But I do not believe marriages like ours need to be veiled in secrecy.

I write, of course, in my own voice, as the Christian husband of a Jewish wife. Nina and I have discussed all the questions I write about here at length, and the book has emerged from these conversations. But the perspective must necessarily be my own. No husband or wife in any marriage, whether mixed or not, has identical interpretations of the marriage. Also, it is vital to remember that I write not just as the non-Jewish spouse but as the man and the father. I can imagine that a book by the Christian wife of a Jewish husband would be quite different. Still, I believe that my own voice makes the book more valuable. I am not writing about a consensus already achieved but about an expedition that is still under way. Telling the story from my own point of view has allowed me to be more frank about those issues in our particular interfaith marriage, and there are some, that still remain to be sorted out.

My pilgrimage through Judaism is arranged here as a journey through the Jewish year, from one Rosh ha-Shanah — New Year's Day — to the next. Although this may puzzle some Christian readers, who might first want to know what Jews *believe*, it will come as no surprise to Jews. The first thing a Christian spouse notices about Judaism is that it is not about creed, it is about calendar. The backbone of Jewish faith is of course Torah, the written and oral law. But for most Jews the way Torah manifests itself is not with a set of beliefs. It is through a recurring series of holy days and sacred seasons. What binds Jews is not a confessional statement like the Apostles' Creed. It is the sounding of the shofar, the lighting of the menorah, the same four questions posed by the youngest child year after year at the Seder. It is the annual return of Rosh ha-Shanah, Yom Kippur, and Passover, and the weekly arrival of the Sabbath. Most Jews sense that the holidays carry an especially intense spiritual quality, and I have noticed that this calendrical core still seems to hold for those Jews who may not observe the holidays strictly or at all.

But life itself does not always unfold according to a calendar. Births, marriages, deaths, and once-in-a-lifetime events add another dimension. Therefore I have included in this Christian pilgrim's progress through the Jewish year an occasional exception — for funerals, a bar mitzvah, and trips to Israel, all hugely important to Jews. I have also added a chapter on our wedding and have described how being married to a Jewish woman, and the father of a Jewish son, has deepened my understanding of the two most important Christian seasons, Christmas and Holy Week.

One of the last great rabbis in the Polish Hasidic tradition died in 1905. A mystic and a scholar, he was known to his followers as the Sefat Emet, which means "the language of truth." He once wrote that it is during the festivals that the "inner life-force of God that exists in all creatures is revealed." Even though the Bible teaches that "the whole earth is filled with God's glory," he recognized that "in this world God remains hidden, but on the festivals, God is revealed." Commenting on this passage, Rabbi Arthur Green, a respected student of the Jewish mystical tradition, writes, "The festival is a time of inner light, a moment of special opportunity . . . such special moments are rare gifts in the spiritual quest, special opportunities that the seeker dares not allow to pass by."[3]

My hope is that some small part of this light will filter through to the reader who follows one grateful sojourner's trek through the festivals of a Jewish year.

1

A Cathedral in Time

Sabbath

> Remember the sabbath day, to keep it holy.
> Six days you shall labor and do all your work;
> but the seventh is the sabbath to the Lord your God;
> in it you shall not do any work,
> you, or your son or your daughter,
> your manservant or your maidservant,
> or your cattle, or the sojourner who is within your gates;
> for in six days the Lord made heaven and earth,
> the sea and all that is in them, and rested on the seventh day;
> therefore the Lord blessed the sabbath and hallowed it.
>
> — Exodus 20:8–11

> The Sabbath kept the Jews more than the Jews kept the Sabbath.
>
> — Ahad Ha'am (1856–1927, Russian-Jewish writer)

IT IS FRIDAY EVENING. Everyone in the family is weary, and sometimes a little testy, after a crowded week of classes, homework, phone calls made and returned, e-mail perused, vacuum cleaners taken to be repaired, leaves raked or snow shoveled, groceries purchased and unloaded, meals prepared, dishes washed, lectures prepared, papers graded, track meets run, magazines glanced through, and bills paid. The sun is just setting as we gather around the table. Nina lights the candles and intones the millennia-old prayer to the God "who has commanded us to light the Sabbath candles." I repeat the Hebrew blessing I have memorized over a porcelain kiddush cup filled with newly opened chianti. Nicholas says the blessing over the challah, the special flaky bread we buy weekly from a bakery that sets aside a loaf for us. We all take a deep breath and embrace each other and any guests who have joined us. We wish one another "Shabbat shalom!" "Have a peaceful Sabbath."

It is Sabbath, my favorite of all the Jewish holidays, and — as it happens — also the one Jewish teaching holds to be the most important of all. It is so fundamental, in fact, that even to describe it as a holiday is to say too little. Celebrated fifty-two times a year, it is described by Rabbi Abraham Joshua Heschel (1907–1972) as the "Jewish cathedral" because its centrality explains why Jews do not have cathedrals of stone and glass: they have Sabbath. This, he says, is because the Jewish faith is positioned in time much more so than in space. Judaism is calendrical, not creedal. Of course Rabbi Heschel knew that Jews have synagogues, and some of them have come to rival cathedrals in beauty. But they serve a slightly different function. They began as places to gather for study even when the Temple, where the animal sacrifice took place, was still standing. But then, when the Temple was destroyed and the Jews scattered, the synagogues assumed other purposes as well. Still, even if there were no temples and no synagogues, the Sabbath would continue to recur week after week. It requires no space, holy or otherwise, because it is made of minutes and hours.

It is also true that since the increase of Jewish immigration to Palestine in the nineteenth century, some prominent Jewish thinkers, like Rabbi Abraham Isaac Kook (1865–1935), have questioned the idea of Jews as exclusively a people of sanctified time. He and others have insisted that sanctified space is also basic to their faith. Some have even suggested that too much one-sided emphasis on time, with its implied diminution of the importance of space, can contribute to the stereotype of the Jew as an eternal wanderer.[1] This discussion is still going on. For a Christian taking part in a Sabbath meal, however, it is striking to notice that the lighting of the candles and the blessing of the wine and bread take place in the home, not in a synagogue. The home becomes the sacred place because it is where Sabbath is celebrated. And it is the wife who presides over it, not the husband. I know of no Christian ritual in which women traditionally play such an integral role. It is also fascinating for me to recall how many times in that first-century carpenter's home in Nazareth a mother named Mary blessed the candles and a son called Yeshua repeated the blessing of the bread. It may well have been the first prayer Yeshua/Jesus ever learned, and he undoubtedly said it countless times before he taught his disciples the "Our Father," the prayer for which he is more often remembered.

The marking of the Sabbath recalls the story of Creation, in which God took six days to create the world, then rested. Not all Jews today strictly observe the restrictions on travel and work that make the seventh day one of rest, enjoyment, and appreciation. But many recognize that it has a humanitarian as well as a religious meaning. Even the Almighty needs to take a break, and so should we. Sabbath suggests pace, the need for a pause in productive activity, for leaving well enough alone, at least for twenty-four hours. In Jewish law, the Sabbath rest extends to the animals and even to the fields. In our family we are not strict about avoiding all travel and work on Saturday, although we try to eschew shopping, making phone calls, and paying bills. We take leisurely walks, listen to music, converse with each other. I am glad that one is allowed, indeed encouraged, to "study" on Sabbath, since study is considered to be comparable to prayer. But I try not to overdo it. As the years have passed, I have become more and more appreciative of having a real do-nothing day. Most important, we almost never miss having the Sabbath meal together, even though this involves declining Friday dinner meetings and events.

The three prayers I mentioned above are at the heart of the celebration of the Sabbath meal. The woman of the household lights the candles, blesses God, "the sovereign of the universe," for "commanding us to kindle the Sabbath lights." She says it in Hebrew (and in our home Nina repeats it in English for guests who are unfamiliar with it). It is in many ways a prototypical Jewish prayer: it thanks God not for giving us something but for *commanding us* to do something. This suggests a striking contrast to the traditional Christian prayer often said before meals: "For what we are about to receive, O Lord, we give you thanks." Here one sees in miniature a significant difference in emphasis between Judaism and Christianity. Christians rarely if ever thank God for commandments. We thank God for his gifts. But one does not have to look into Judaism very far to notice that for Jews the commandments *are* gifts. I will come back to this important point in Chapter 5 on the holiday of Simhat Torah. Some families end the Sabbath on Saturday evening with a brief service called *havdalah* ("separation"), during which, I was fascinated to learn, there is in fact a prayer of gratitude. Also, in a very Jewish fashion, it thanks God for the distinction between the sacred and the profane. Judaism, the close observer quickly discovers, puts a considerable emphasis on distinctions.

In addition to celebrating Sabbath at home, many observant Jewish families also attend a synagogue to join in communal prayer on Saturday and sometimes on Friday evening as well. I still find it difficult, even after many years, to remember the various parts of the Sabbath service; they seem to consist of modules that are at least somewhat separable but are often strung together into one. Also, practices vary from one synagogue to another and from one season of the year to another. On Friday evening at sundown, a special short service called the *kabbalat shabbat* precedes the regular evening service. The words mean "welcoming Sabbath," and it marks the transition from the ordinary time of the weekdays by symbolizing the Sabbath as a visiting queen who is to be greeted with festivity, like royalty. Nowadays some synagogues also hold a service later in the evening, since many people find it difficult to get through the traffic by sundown on Friday afternoon. At its close, some congregations have a social hour with refreshments called the *oneg shabbat* ("joy of Sabbath").

On Saturday morning the key part of a Sabbath service is the *keriat hatorah,* the reading from the Torah (the first five books of the Bible), which Jews divide into fifty-four separate sections called *parashiyot,* one of which is read every week. Sometimes more than one is read, so that in one year the whole Torah cycle is completed. Some rabbis comment on the *parashiyot* for the week; others lead their congregations in discussing it. As one who was raised from childhood to read and discuss the Bible, this is undoubtedly the part of the Sabbath service from which I gain the most. I like it especially since — unlike what happened in my church school — even the most violent and debauched passages do not escape scrutiny and debate. Noah's drunken nakedness, Jacob's deceitful trickery and the seemingly intricate and endlessly detailed laws on sacrifice and purity laid down in Leviticus are all fair game for discussion and disputation. Not even the most impertinent question seems out of order. In these animated sessions, one soon learns something quite important about

Jewish attitudes toward the Bible. Jews take it seriously but not literally. They illustrate how important it is, not by accepting everything unquestioningly, but by demonstrating that they find it worthy of energetic engagement.

After what at times seems to me a little too much verbal and sung prayer at a Sabbath service, I welcome the *amidah*. The word means "standing," and in many synagogues it has become a period of silent personal prayer when people read quietly from their prayer books or meditate. The *maariv*, (from the Hebrew word for "evening") ends the Saturday service, not just with the setting of the sun but, as the tradition has it, when three stars are visible. I know of no Christian service that is calibrated to coincide with the appearance of stars, but I like the idea. It links a religious practice to the natural world.

There are services in the synagogue throughout the day on Saturday, but many families return only in the evening for the short *havdalah* ("separation") service, which is often also celebrated at home. It is meant to remind people that every day is not the Sabbath and that it is now time to return to the routines of the everyday world. Consequently its tone, which even someone who cannot follow Hebrew can pick up, is a blend of joy and regret. Its most dramatic symbol is the dousing of one of the candles in a cup of wine. The sizzle and the flameless wick seem to say that all good things must eventually end, that "parting is such sweet sorrow" as the royal visit of the Sabbath queen ends.

When I began to take part in Jewish religious life, both at home and in the synagogue, the first question that came to my mind was a basic one: Why do Jews pray in Hebrew, even when transliterations are often supplied or English translations follow? During my boyhood I confess that I shared with my fellow Protestants an attitude of mild derision toward Catholics, who, at that time, said their prayers in Latin. How can they possibly pray, we often asked, in a language most of them don't even understand? This was often accompanied by the implied suggestion that it was a way of keeping them ignorant so that those in charge could make the decisions for them. All this has changed, of course, in the thirty-five years since the Second Vatican Council (1962–65). Now mass is said and Catholics pray in the vernacular of the area in which they live. But my latent suspicion of people who "don't even know what they are saying when they pray" lingered, and it surfaced again when, in Judaism, I encountered people who prayed in a language that was even more inscrutable to me than Latin.

Little by little, I have come to recognize that when Jews pray they are doing some of the same things we Protestants do when we pray, but they are doing other things as well. When Jews pray, like us, they are communicating with God. But prayer also reminds them of who they are as a people. It links them to a tradition that goes back thousands of years. When praying in Hebrew, Jews immediately sense their kinship with other Jews around the world, as well as with Jews in previous centuries. Also, as I adjusted to the Jewish way of praying, I recognized that my deep suspicion of "people who pray in words they don't understand" was a distinctly Protestant bias. Russian, Ethiopian, and Armenian Orthodox Christians all pray in archaic languages. Even I myself, when I sing Mozart's Requiem or Bach's B Minor Mass, although by now I understand nearly all the words, sense the strange power of praying in a language other than the vernacular. Praying with Jews has also helped me appreciate the more liturgical and formal prayers of branches of Christianity other than mine, like the Episcopalian and the Lutheran. I no longer harbor the condescension I picked up as a child for people who "pray out of a book."

Still, there is something to be said for the spontaneous, free-form prayers I grew up with. For many Christians, the Jesus through whom we pray to God is often thought of as a friend, and we do not need to open a book and find the right page to make known our hopes and pains to a friend. It may well be that the most heartfelt prayers anyone ever utters are exclamations like "Please God, make it stop hurting" or "Thank God he wasn't on *that* plane." Still, even Jesus taught his followers a prayer that we repeat often, word for word. And when Jesus prayed with his dying breath, "My God, my God, why have you forsaken me?" it was a prayer "out of a book," the book of Psalms. In short, what I have learned is that there are many different ways of praying. I doubt that God cares very much which one we practice.

Sabbath, however, is much more than prayers. The weekly Sabbath meal is undoubtedly the element of Judaism that I have appreciated the most. Sometimes I wonder how I ever got along without it. In fact, in an age of ceaseless movement and perpetual productivity, it is the Jewish custom the whole world needs most. Many factories rumble on, night and day, for three shifts. Shopping malls bustle seven days a week. The visual images on television screens fly by faster every year as attention spans grow commensurately shorter. Time loses its gait, and whirl is king. Getting more things done speedily becomes the whole point. People junk the faster computer they bought last year and purchase a new one that is even faster. Las Vegas, Nevada, incarnates the opposite pole of the spirit of Sabbath. Its casinos, shows, and restaurants roar and glitter twenty-four hours a day, seven days a week, three hundred and sixty-five days a year. Strictly speaking, in Las Vegas it never really matters "what time it is." You can buy breakfast at four-thirty in the afternoon and devour a five-course dinner at ten o'clock in the morning.

But this hectic pace and absence of measure in the worlds of work and leisure are taking their toll. And increasing numbers of people sense it. One of the reasons for the popularity of various forms of meditation is that merely stopping and sitting still at regular intervals — whether one repeats a mantra, counts breaths, or stares at the wall — allows the brain synapses to catch up with the sensory overload. In recent years in Europe, the throngs of people who escape for periodic retreats have so crowded the old pilgrimage sites such as Lourdes and Fatima that reservations need to be made months in advance. Surveys indicate that very few of these visitors are churchgoers at home, and the vast majority do not come to seek a cure. They simply need to step back from the daily rush and the incessant reminder "You've got mail." Some take part in the liturgies at the sites, but many do not. When asked, they report that they sense a certain holiness in just getting away from it all. Of the Ten Commandments, it appears that the fourth, which tells us to do nothing once every seven days, is the one we most urgently need.

As a Christian, I see no spiritual obstacle either to following the wisdom of Sabbath or in participating fully in welcoming its arrival with prayers and bread and wine. Not just as a boy, but throughout his life, Jesus continued to observe it, warning that its rules could only be bent in cases of dire human need. Many of the rabbis of his time also taught this admonition. The earliest Christians, all Jews, undoubtedly continued to celebrate Sabbath at home but also began to congregate in one of the larger homes on Sunday to celebrate the Resurrection. This is why Sunday was called the Lord's Day, and in many languages such as French and Spanish it still is. The Russian word for Sunday is "Resurrection." Then, as Christianity became "gentilized" in the first centuries of its history, most Christians stopped observing Sabbath. But in doing so, I believe something vital was lost.

Professor Herold Weiss of St. Mary's College in Notre Dame, Indiana, has done extensive research on how early Christians, and the Jews of the same period, viewed the Sabbath.[2] His findings are fascinating. They show that among both groups there was a wide spectrum of beliefs and practices concerning the seventh day. Among Jews, for example, some believed that observing Sabbath rest was a mandate only for Jews, and became annoyed and disconcerted when gentiles observed it. Other Jews believed it was a commandment God had made as a gift to all peoples, even to animals and plants. Some Jews were enormously strict about it, a few holding that one should avoid walking across a room on Sabbath. One tiny minority insisted that one should not even move one's bowels until the first stars appeared on Saturday night. (What a relief the sight of those stars must have been!) Others held that traveling very short distances — by foot only, of course — was acceptable. Still others taught that the Sabbath command was to be taken metaphorically, not literally. It meant that we are to take time to think about spiritual things and not just the things of this world.

Given this range of first-century Jewish opinion about the Sabbath, it is not surprising to discover that, according to Weiss, Christians held a similar variety of beliefs. Most invoked the authority of Jesus to argue that although the Sabbath should be observed, it was "made for humankind, not humankind for the Sabbath" (*Mark* 2:27). This meant that deeds of mercy were not only allowed but encouraged on the seventh day, a view well in line with most of the Jewish teaching at the time. But there were also disputes on this matter among these early Christians. Some were afraid that "observing days and seasons" might lead to a relapse back into Judaism or paganism, so they discouraged it. This position was based on two convictions shared by some early Christians. The first was their suspicion that Judaism was obsessed with petty legalism, and observing Sabbath was just another example of slavish acquiescence to a rigid commandment. The second was a belief that observing calendrical holidays implicated them in honoring the astral forces, the quasi-divine spiritual "rulers of this world" revered by the pagans. Still other Christians thought that since the coming of Jesus, every day was a sort of Sabbath, so why pay special attention to only one?

Apparently more than one argument broke out within the early Christian communities over these interpretations. Poor, harried Saint Paul, racing from Corinth to Galatia to Rome, had to confront this debate, as he confronted many others. He avoided laying down hard and fast rules, and his answers were usually diplomatic. For example, to the Christians in Rome, who were apparently clashing about the Sabbath observance, he writes:

> Who are you to pass judgment on the servant of another? It is before his own master that he stands or falls. And he will be upheld, for the Master is able to make him stand. One man esteems one day as better than another, while another man esteems all days alike. Let every person be fully convinced in his own mind. He who observes the day, observes it in honor of the Lord. . . . Then, let us no more pass judgment (Romans 14:4–6, 13).

I have never felt that I had needed biblical authorization to observe the Sabbath as a Christian. But I do seem to have Saint Paul on my side (though I do not see eye to eye with the apostle on everything). For me, the most significant question is not *whether* I am free to observe the Sabbath meal. That seems quite clear. The question is rather *why* this simple weekly ritual has unexpectedly become so precious to me. This is probably not the kind of question many people would ask. But as a Christian and a theologian, for me it was unavoidable. I am not, after all, one of the first-century Jewish Christians who was accustomed to observing the Sabbath and brought it along with me, as it were, into one of the first-century Jewish Christian congregations. So why has it become such a sturdy pillar of my spiritual life?

In thinking about this question, I found help from the same Rabbi Heschel who calls Sabbath "a cathedral in time." Heschel has also taught that faith begins on a "preconceptual level," with the experience of awe or wonder or gratitude. Only later do we begin to organize and conceptualize these primal intuitions into beliefs and rituals. But, he suggests, once we have taken this second step, the initial intuitive awareness is drawn into the religious practice itself, and the two levels fuse.

This was certainly true for me and the Sabbath ritual. The candles and the bread, the blessings and the wine, none of this had been part of my life until Nina and I married. When we first began to observe it, I remember thinking it was certainly "a nice custom." It drew a welcome line between the hubbub of the week and the more relaxed pace of the weekend. I can see now that this was a minimal view. But it was only the beginning. What impressed me next was how the Hebrew words of the prayers seem to echo back over many centuries, tracing a nearly endless chain of Jewish families gathered around thousands of tables, invoking the blessing of God on the bread of the earth and the fruit of the vine. Then I noticed how our guests, including those who had rarely, if ever, taken part in a Sabbath meal, including small children, seemed captivated by the compound of joy and gravity the brief ceremony exudes. Gradually it came to the point where if, for one reason or another, we missed a Sabbath dinner, I sensed an uncomfortable absence in my life.

Within a few years of our family's marking the coming of the Sabbath each Friday, I began to read about its history and meaning. I knew something about its disputed place in the early Christian congregations, but — like most Christians — I knew practically nothing about the long history of rabbinical reflection on its meaning. I was gratified to discover that — as is true of many topics in Judaism — there is no single interpretation. The bread and wine and blessings are primal. Nearly everything else is commentary. At first I especially appreciated Rabbi Heschel's idea of the "cathedral in time." But as the years passed it was not quite enough. A cathedral, after all, is only a structure. What goes on inside is just as important, if not more so. In fact, after reading Heschel, I remembered again the first time I had ever walked into a cathedral and — to my surprise — had one of the most unforgettable religious experiences of my life.

I was seventeen, and it was my first time ever on the shores of the Old World. The merchant ship I was working on was tied up in Gdynia, Poland, the port of Gdansk (Danzig). I had taken a noisy bus to the nearby town of Oliva where, someone had told me, there was a cathedral worth visiting. It certainly was. But why had I sought it out? As the heir of Quakers and Baptists, I had not only never been in a cathedral, I harbored a smoldering suspicion of the gaudy excess and ostentation I had come to associate with them. So why was I there? Maybe because, with thirty-five hundred miles between myself and my family, I felt free to explore forbidden fruits. Some of my young shipmates were busy exploring their own versions of prohibited produce in the bars and brothels of Gdansk. But I had been intimidated by a terrifying lecture (with unnerving color slides) given to us by the ship's health officer on the running sores and scabby abscesses that would dog us until the end of our days if we so much as looked at one of the venereal-infected women in that city, so I opted for a different kind of shore leave. One shipmate, a Mennonite lad from Ohio, went with me. In retrospect I now recognize that in addition to youthful wanderlust, which is what had gotten me onto the ship in the first place, my visiting the cathedral was also a product of a certain adolescent Sturm und Drang. We are all more open to ruminations about death and passion and love and God at that age (though we rarely allow our contemporaries to know about it). I was no exception.

When we stepped into the cathedral, the organist was practicing a Bach fugue on the church's huge baroque instrument. The total effect was overwhelming. Light streamed through the cherry and ocher stained glass, the scent of incense hung in the air, the exalted music from the invisible organ seemed to soar toward another sphere. I was not only speechless, I was hardly able to move my arms or legs. My Mennonite companion had to remind me to take off my white seaman's cap. I knew almost nothing at the time about what the symbols on the windows or around the walls meant. The little church I attended as a child had clear glass windows and did not even display a cross. But I was not really thinking in the usual sense of the word. What was happening to me in the Oliva cathedral was, I am sure, a classical example of Rabbi Heschel's preconceptual level. I have spent decades of my life filling in the theological content. It happened at a cathedral in space, in a small city in northern Poland. But now, with the Sabbath celebration, a parallel process has taken place with Heschel's cathedral in time. For me, the marking of the Sabbath began with lights, the soft music of blessings, and the smell of the bread and the wine. For years now I have been filling in the conceptual details.

Particulars, of course, are never merely trivial. For example, one has to ask eventually, what does this all have to do with *me*? What happened in the Oliva cathedral involved *both* the magnificent setting *and* all that had gone into the making of a seventeen-year-old boy. As I read about the Sabbath and tried to understand both the day itself and my response to it, I found enormous help in an unexpected source.

Rabbi Isaac Luria was born in Jerusalem in 1534, the son of a Polish (Ashkenazi) father and a Sephardi mother. He spent his younger years in Egypt, where he began his study of Jewish mysticism and the Kabbalah. In 1572 he moved with his family to Safed, in what is now Israel, and spent the rest of his life studying, writing, and teaching his disciples the Jewish mystical tradition. For a variety of reasons, Luria and his ideas have not been widely discussed by most Jewish scholars until recently. Perhaps they ignored him because his speculative mysticism was something of an embarrassment, both to the orthodox rabbis who found him suspect and to the secular historians who viewed him as irrational. Since Luria was not well known among Jews, he was almost completely unknown by Christian scholars. I had never heard of him through all my years of academic training in religion at three Ivy League universities. Only with the recent rebirth of interest in Jewish mysticism, sparked in part by the influence of the great Gershom Scholem,[3] have Luria's ideas come into somewhat wider circulation. (I am sorry this happened only recently, because I would like to have learned from him earlier.) In addition, Luria's mystical reading of Judaism is becoming increasingly appealing to many young Jews who, for various reasons, are not drawn to Orthodox, Conservative, or Reform Judaism. It was reading Luria's reflections on the inner meaning of the Sabbath that brought me to a new level of appreciation for it.

Luria wrote centuries after the destruction of the Temple, in a period when the rabbis taught that the home itself should take the place of the Temple, and the Sabbath meal should take the place of the animal sacrifices. Luria and his followers added that the Sabbath meal could became the occasion when the *Shekhinah*, the exiled female side of the Godhead, returned for one night, foreshadowing not only her ultimate reunification with God but the restoration of nature and society to the harmonious condition God intends. Luria once composed this hymn, to be sung after the Sabbath meal:

To the southward I set the mystical candelabrum. I make room in the north for the table with the loaves. Let the Shekhinah be surrounded by six Sabbath loaves connected on every side with the Heavenly Sanctuary. Weakened and cast out, the impure powers, the menacing demons, are now in fetters.[4]

The Sabbath meal thus becomes a symbol and a preliminary glimpse of human life as it should be, and will be, in the design of God. It is a token of human liberation, with the evil powers in chains. It becomes an apéritif for the ultimate great banquet, the most pervasive symbol of the Messianic era in both Judaism and Christianity.[5] It is also vital to recall that, given the centuries of expulsion and exile Jews have endured, if their spiritual axis had not been centered in their homes, their chance of survival, and the survival of their faith, would have been greatly lessened.

My growing fondness for the weekly welcoming of the Sabbath has also exerted a growing, if subtle, influence on my own Christian practice. I grew up appreciating the spare but free-wheeling Baptist form of worship. I started singing the lusty hymns and gospel songs as a small child and still know scores of them by heart. I relished vigorous preaching and eventually learned to do some of it myself. The church I attended was not fundamentalist, but I learned to love the stories of the Bible and to appreciate the unique authority of scripture. In recent years, however, I have come to attach an increasing importance to the symbolic bread and wine of the Communion table and even to the scents and sounds of more liturgical Christian worship. Does this change in my own spirituality have any connection with my weekly Sabbath meal?

I am sure that in some way it does. Set aside for the moment all the scholarly discussion about how the Christian Eucharist is directly derived from older Jewish practices, including both the Sabbath and the Passover Seder. There is undoubtedly much truth in these theories. The link I have felt, however, is far more personal, and it engages me at Heschel's preconceptual level. There are, of course, enormous differences between the meanings attached to the Sabbath meal in the Jewish tradition and those Christians have attached to the Communion service over the centuries. But at the core of each ritual is an action: the breaking and blessing of bread and the pouring out of wine. Literally hundreds of Eucharistic theologies have been formulated by theologians, from the symbolism of a family meal to the reenactment of the sacrifice of Christ on the cross. These interpretations are still changing, even in the Roman Catholic Church. For example, after the Second Vatican Council, most Catholic churches moved their altars from the back wall (where the priest had officiated with his back to the congregation) closer to the nave, the better to represent a family gathering. But the core of the mass remains the same. It is the blessing and breaking of bread and the blessing and pouring out of wine. Interpretations come and go, but the central action does not change.

The actual historical connection between the Passover Seder and Communion may help explain the primal one. It is an enormously important connection but one that has often been lost among Christians. We now know that the Seder and Communion are two historical variants of the same ritual. Despite some continuing scholarly disagreement on the subject, I am convinced that when Jesus instituted what we now call the Lord's Supper (also called Holy Communion or Eucharist) with his disciples in the Upper Room in Jerusalem on the night Judas betrayed him, he was presiding over a predecessor of the present Passover Seder. This is critical to remember, because Passover was the celebration of a political and social as well as a religious liberation. A whole people who were literally — not just psychologically or spiritually — slaves in Egypt escaped, with God's help, to real historical freedom. The Passover Seder became a celebration of what we now call liberation theology centuries before the term was invented. The trouble is that in most Christian churches this central dimension of the Lord's Supper is muted or ignored. Communion is wrenched from its historical source and degraded into something far less than it should be by rendering it so ethereal that it loses all its powerful political overtones. It is made so individual that it loses its original communal meaning. It is made so spiritual that it forfeits any worldly significance. I think that, as Christians, every time we approach the Lord's Table we should be reminded that Jesus instituted this event, and told his disciples to practice it, just before he was arrested by a lynch mob and executed by the Romans for an act of insubordination to the *imperium romanum.*

There is one integral part of the Communion meal that Jews, although they can see its structural similarity to a Seder, unanimously question and reject. Christians believe that Jesus is somehow especially present in the Communion. This is not a peripheral matter. At a key point in that "last Seder," Jesus held the bread and said, "This is my body, broken for you," and then made a similar statement about the wine. It is common knowledge that for nearly two thousand years Christians have been unable to agree on exactly what these words mean. Catholics differ from Orthodox Christians, and both differ from Lutherans who, in turn, differ from most other Protestants. The disagreements have been so rancorous at times that Christians have, and sometimes still do, refuse to admit other Christians to Communion, not because they do not believe Jesus is present but because they do not agree on *how* he is present. This constitutes a continuing scandal, which angers and embarrasses me.

Still, the bread and wine of Communion, remind us of the pivotal point of Christianity: God poured out his life, insofar as an infinite God can do so, into the life of a human being, and thereby — since we are all *connected* to one another, whether we like it or not — into the lives of all human beings. The Logos of God, as the Gospel of John so bluntly puts it, "became Flesh." But what is so frequently overlooked by all churches is that the flesh into which the heart of God was poured was not just any flesh, it was — as the great theologian Karl Barth reminds us — *Jewish* flesh. This means that if we Christians are in some manner (which I think will always escape definition) linked to Jesus Christ in a special way in Communion, we are thereby united to one who lived and died a Jew. This means, in turn, that we link ourselves — in a derived and secondary way — to the whole people of Israel. I sometimes wonder if Barth's words had been repeated every time Germans, Catholic and Protestant, had taken Communion throughout the 1930s and 1940s, whether the people's attitude toward Jews might have been different.

I have never been back to that cathedral-in-space in Poland, but I often think about it. Maybe someday I will return, although I know I will probably be disappointed. Trying to reengender an old religious experience by returning to the scene is like trying to reignite an old romance by going back to that same little café. It might work, but chances are that it won't.

In the meantime, week after week, there is the cathedral in time I enter every Friday evening. Like an acolyte, Nina lights the candles. Like priests at the altar, Nicholas and I bless the wine and the bread. The melody of the prayers lifts us like the *vox humana* of an organ. What happens then is not a mass. It is Sabbath dinner.

2

Starting Over at the Right Time of Year

Rosh ha-Shanah

I call heaven and earth to witness against you this day,
That I have set before you life and death,
Blessing and curse;
Therefore, choose life,
That you and your descendants may live,
Loving the Lord your God.

— Deuteronomy 30:19, 20

I T IS SEPTEMBER. The trees are in full leaf, and here and there a splash of amber or scarlet presages the foliage feast to come. The air has a bite; the atmosphere crackles. Energy is high. Children have returned from camp suntanned and taller. Back-to-school sales are under way. It is a time of year fairly popping with new beginnings. But before they officially ring out the old and ring in the new, most people will have to wait until the end of December. And it will happen during the darkest days of winter, crammed into an already crowded "holiday season."

For those attuned to the Jewish calendar, however, which follows the lunar rather than the solar cycles, early autumn is precisely when the new year does begin. It would be nice to think that the rabbis took all these seasonal and psychological elements into consideration when they set the date, but I doubt it. Predictably, there were centuries in which Jewish authorities differed over when the new year should begin. Their argument, recounted in the Talmud, goes back to a more basic dispute about when the world itself was created. Was it in the Jewish month of Nisan, the one in which Passover falls? Or was it in Tishri, which comes in the fall? The debate was eventually settled by suggesting that, in effect, both parties were right, and some others were right too. Thus there are now, more or less officially, four different "new years" in the Jewish calendar. The first day of Nisan is used as a year marker for the length of a king's reign (although admittedly there are not many kings — let alone Jewish kings — in business nowadays). It is also the new year for months. The month of Elul is used for counting the age of animals. The fifteenth of Shuvat is the new year for trees. But Tishri marks the creation of the world and is the new year for years, so that is when the Jewish New Year's, Rosh ha-Shanah ("The Head of the Year") falls.[1]

This may sound unnecessarily confusing to those of us who are used to tacking up a new calendar, popping a bottle of champagne, singing "Auld Lang Syne," and putting the wrong date on checks during January. But I rather like the idea that for Jews, the matter of exactly when the new year begins — like so much else in their tradition — was never definitively settled. Not only does the coming of the "new year of years" in September cohere well with the way many people live their lives, but the implication that there are different kinds of new years for the flora and fauna also makes sense. It reminds us (though this may not have been the original intent) that poodles and ostriches, scrub oaks and long needle pines, may live in cycles that are different from those of human beings. Why should they all be squeezed into our human calendar? But I have learned something even more elemental from Rosh ha-Shanah, something that is at the same time both unnerving and heartening. I have learned that it is a holiday about life and death.

The truth is, I have always found something acutely unsatisfying about the way most Christians and nonreligious gentiles and nonobservant Jews commemorate the New Year. As a child I looked forward to being allowed to stay up until midnight on December 31. The next morning, while my parents slept late, I found the silly hats and noisemakers they had brought home from their merry-making the night before. In my later youth I looked forward to the dancing and singing and — to a limited extent — the drinking. But all along I felt there was something missing. It seemed to me there should be another dimension to the coming of a new year, something that was being overlooked or even avoided. As I got older, I came to recognize that what was being left out was the apprehensiveness, even trepidation, that gnaws at each of us with the realization that our time is limited, another year has passed, and a new one is beginning. If only to ourselves, we inevitably ask some difficult questions. What does the new year really hold for us? Will it be just another twelve months or could it be my last year?

New Year's Day is simply not on the Christian calendar, and as far as I know, only a few Methodists still celebrate the custom of a Watch Night service on New Year's Eve. I think this is a loss for us all. Human beings need rituals as punctuation marks. They signal changes in our lives and allow us to become more fully aware of them. Some are relatively minor changes, marked by commas and periods. Others, like new paragraphs, demarcate new but still relatively minor changes. New chapters, however, cue us that something more significant is beginning. Maybe that is why the medieval monks illuminated the first letter of each chapter in the manuscripts they copied with elaborate curlicues and gold dust. The coming of a new year is definitely a new chapter. This is why clinking glasses and cheering the descending ball in Times Square does not speak to the powerful mixed feelings New Year's Eve evokes.

Early in the twentieth century a German philosopher named Rudolf Otto published an influential book, later translated into English as *The Idea of the Holy*.[2] In it he suggests that the original impetus for all religions comes from what he called — in a phrase that has become commonplace to theologians — the *mysterium tremendum et fascinans*. The holy, he says, awakens in us both a trembling shudder at its uncanniness, and a sense of fascination with its beauty and seductiveness. For thousands of years the different religious traditions have grappled with ways to do justice to both these dimensions, and they have devised a variety of patterns. In the Bible, the anxious shudder is evoked by "the wrath of God." Those familiar with Buddhist iconography will recognize it in the so-called dreadful and grotesque deities that are especially evident in Tibetan iconography, although this dark side of that tradition is not often mentioned in the gentle version purveyed by the Dalai Lama. In Hinduism, the malicious face of the divine can be seen in the figure of Kali, with her belt of dismembered arms and her necklace of skulls.

Of course, no religion leaves it at that. Each also has its way of projecting the merciful, benevolent — even approachable and loving — side of the holy. But one reason that so many people see contemporary American versions of Judaism and Christianity as shallow is that the *fascinans* side has completely overwhelmed the *tremendum* side. A few years ago Cheryl Bridges Johns, an American theologian and religious educator, took a year off to visit churches throughout the United States in order to appraise the health of religion at the grass-roots level. What she found discouraged her. She discovered what seemed almost to be a conspiracy across denominational, and even interfaith, lines to remold God into the most pleasant and obliging deity imaginable. The Yahweh who thundered from Mount Sinai, drowned the Egyptian army, and who the prophet Amos says will bring destruction upon "who oppress the helpless and grind down the poor" has disappeared from altar and pulpit. Both churches and synagogues have tried to devise a "user-friendly" God. Indeed, some of the most successful "mega-churches" now plan their services, music, and preaching on the basis of market surveys. But this presents a problem. When the *tremendum* is short-circuited, the *fascinans* also seems to fade away. It is hard to imagine anyone shuddering in the presence of the God of American cultural religion today. But this oh-so-nice God does not seem to evoke much passionate affection either.

Still, the shudder persists, if somewhat muted. For example, Jewish religious leaders often speculate on why, even though weekly synagogue attendance is usually low in America, their buildings are full to overflowing on Rosh ha-Shanah and Yom Kippur. Indeed, it comes as a surprise to anyone with a Jewish spouse to discover that one has to get tickets in advance for the high holiday services or no seat will be available. Why the crowds? Some observers point out that Judaism actually has two calendars. The first is the annual one, which includes all the holidays. The second one is based on the individual's own life cycle, which encompasses birth (and circumcision), coming of age (bar and bat mitzvah), marriage, and death. In an individualistic society like our own, life-cycle rituals loom much larger than the prescribed annual holidays. Then why such a crowd at Rosh ha-Shanah? I think it is because, for many people, the start of a new year is not just a collective event, it is also a pivotal road mark in their own lives. But I think there is something else in the picture as well: the Rosh ha-Shanah ritual itself. It strikes exactly the right note to resonate with the mixed feelings that well up in most of us when an old year ends and a new one begins.

"Judaism," Rabbi Irving Greenberg says in *The Jewish Way*, "is a religion of life against death." Even the most uninformed gentiles often recognize this. However dimly, they know that Jews have survived more threats to their individual and corporate existence, and for more centuries, than any other people. Someone once referred to Jews as "the always dying-out race." Their disappearance has been confidently predicted time after time, most often by their enemies, but sometimes even by Jews themselves. Yet, after thousands of years filled with perils and pogroms, and even after the Nazis' attempt to murder them all, Jews are alive and well. It could even be argued that at the end of the century that treated them most harshly, most Jews are thriving today more vigorously than at any time since the halcyon days of David and Solomon. They still bury their would-be pallbearers and still stubbornly offer toasts to "life," "l'chaim." As even the most casual observer has to admit with some degree of puzzlement, they must be doing something right.

An outsider participating in Jewish religious life soon learns that the way Jews affirm life is not by denying death but by facing it down. The Rosh ha-Shanah ritual takes the form of a dramatic confrontation with death and mortality. This happens in part through a carefully staged courtroom drama in which God is the judge, and everyone who comes before his presence is being tried for his or her life. In fact, to my astonishment, according to one Jewish prayer book, even the "hosts of heaven" are called to account at this time. Nobody, human or angel, escapes this sweeping indictment. In the end, life and mercy win out over death and judgment, but the Rosh ha-Shanah liturgy is designed to elicit the same cold dread anyone would feel in a human courtroom under such formidable circumstances.

The trial actually goes on for days and ends only on Yom Kippur, a week and a half after Rosh ha-Shanah, when the verdict is finally announced. But getting to that final acquittal is not easy. Between the two come what are called *yamim noraim,* the Days of Awe. During these ten days the defendants must undergo the most intensive sort of self-scrutiny, reviewing a year's deeds and misdeeds, both major and minor. They must ask forgiveness from anyone they have wronged and — when possible — make restitution. God, the tradition says, forgives only the sins we commit against him, not those committed against other people. The objective is to move the soul to *teshuvah*, "repentance." The symbolism states that throughout the trial, God is pondering whether to inscribe our names in the Book of Life or in the Book of Death. The hope is that, having undergone such a rigorous moral inventory, the new year can begin with a clean slate.

The concept of taking a personal moral inventory has become familiar to millions of people who are not Jewish and may never have heard of Rosh ha-Shanah. It is one of the first and most basic steps one is required to take in a "twelve-step program," like Alcoholics Anonymous or Al-Anon. Scholars estimate that one out of every four adult Americans is involved in a "support group," many of which use the moral inventory approach. Christians who were raised with some exposure to the traditions of pietism and revivalism will sense something familiar about the Days of Awe. None of it should be particularly surprising, since the Christian tradition of setting aside certain days and seasons for self-examination and penitence are adaptations of earlier Jewish traditions, and the twelve-step programs evolved from the Oxford Group Movement, an evangelical Christian enterprise. The Days of Awe have shaped modern culture much more than most Jews realize.

Of course, there are differences. In Christianity it is God who is most often portrayed as the judge during penitential seasons while Jesus Christ is cast as the public defender, the source of mercy, and sometimes the innocent party who is, nonetheless, willing to accept the punishment we rightly deserve so that we may go free. In Judaism it is the different faces of God — as judge, king, and source of forgiveness — that come into play. But are these differences as deep as many people seem to believe? Most Jews once considered these dissimilarities fundamental. And so did I before I was introduced to some texts of the Kabbalah, the principal source of Jewish mysticism, at the Shalom Hartman Center in Jerusalem. There I learned that sometimes Jewish scholars and sages have *personified* the judgmental and merciful attributes of God and even portrayed them as debating with each other. From this image of God to the Christian idea of the Trinity is still a very large step — but not quite as large as I once thought. To complicate matters even more, Jesus Christ is not always cast in the role of the merciful savior. Think of Michelangelo's classic Last Judgment in the Sistine Chapel in Rome. There Christ is the cosmic judge who appears at what is called the Dies Irae, the "Day of Wrath," which has become a hymn that is sung during a Requiem Mass.

What links the Jewish Days of Awe, the Dies Irae, and, say, the Baptist revivals I attended as a youth is the mood and the atmosphere. "There is not much time," the evangelist would warn as I sat trembling in a back pew. "*This* is the moment to repent, accept God's mercy through Jesus, and come forward to make your penitence known to the world." Then the congregation would sing several verses of a hymn called "Just As I Am," which assured us that, no matter how despicable our sins (and a gifted evangelist could often make even a quite normal adolescent feel despicable indeed), we could "come forward" with the full assurance of God's pardon. In some ways it was like the Days of Awe compressed into a couple of hours, albeit often every night for a week. The sermons during the revival were replete with the stories of sinners of the worst ilk — whose trespasses were far more grievous than any I had even contemplated — hearing the Gospel, repenting, and then leading an exemplary life. I can remember people sniffling and sobbing during the revival. And why not? The dramaturgy included conscience searching, the awful threat of divine judgment, the offer of grace and forgiveness, and the pressure to decide — now. I can even remember visiting evangelists telling us that this could be our very last chance to have our names written in the Book of Life.

I was not entirely surprised, therefore, to read that on the Sabbath that falls between Rosh ha-Shanah and Yom Kippur, called Shabbat Shuvah, rabbis often used to preach eloquent and forceful sermons to try to move their people to *teshuvah* before it was too late:

> The sermon on Shabbat Shuvah was to serve as a *hit' orerut li-teshuvah*, an impassioned call for repentance. It was offered amid tears and wailing, and was so delivered as to wring dread and compassion from the most stonelike heart. . . . The prayer books for the ten days of penitence are filled with parables and simple homilies about people who were led astray by their vices, were punished for their sins, and returned to God in contrition and tears.[3]

As I read about these parallels, it occurred to me that maybe the founders of American Reform Judaism had made a mistake. When they decided to adapt their religion more closely to the existing practices of American religious life, by adding organs and using prayer books in English for example, it was the upper-middle-class denominations they had in mind. They wanted to look like Presbyterians or Unitarians, not like Baptists or Pentecostals. This may have appeared to be sensible at the time, but something was lost in the process. History has demonstrated that the more emotional and expressive side of American religion continues to be very vigorous. There are millions of American Christians who would feel more at home in an old style Sabbath *teshuvah* service, with its tears and wailings, than in a serene and cerebral Reform temple.

At the Rosh ha-Shanah service it is customary to read the biblical stories of the birth of Abraham's son, Isaac (on the first day of the holiday), and Abraham's near-sacrifice of Isaac (on the second day). The first time I attended these services, I happened to be sitting with our then-infant son asleep on my lap when the story of the near-sacrifice — which Jews usually call the binding of Isaac, the *akedah* — was read. It tells how the old man to whom God has made a promise that his descendants would become a great nation heeds the command of this same God and takes the child of his old age to Mount Moriah to sacrifice him. I had heard the story many, many times before. I knew it by heart. But here with my own son — who, like Abraham's, had been given to me late in life — comfortably nestled on my lap, the sheer horror of what God seemed to be asking of Abraham bore in on me for the first time. I could feel my palms becoming moist. "Father, here is the fire and here is the wood," Isaac says, then asks his father trustingly, "but where is the lamb?"

What did it mean? Hearing the story at a Jewish service made me see how often Christian readings of the Hebrew Bible are softened, even distorted, by projecting Christian themes back into them. In this case, of course, it means interpreting the Abraham and Isaac story as a prefiguration of the crucifixion. There may be occasions on which such an interpretation would be appropriate. It is probably impossible for Christians to hear the story without thinking of Jesus struggling up another hill carrying the means of his own sacrifice. But in most Christian worship, the interpretation comes too soon after the original story. I have come to believe that the "instant christianizing" of the Old Testament accounts often evacuates their original power and depth. It is important to listen and try to wrestle with them in their own terms instead of immediately subsuming them into Christian categories. Reflecting on this has made me suspicious of the Christian practice of pairing Old and New Testament readings in church services. This is a very old custom, often dictated by lectionaries that prescribe which passages are to be read on a given Sunday. But it often forces us to understand the Old Testament reading in the light of the New before we have even had time to ponder it.

If we try to set aside for a moment that in the Abraham and Isaac narrative a positive end is coming and let the sheer force of the awful story bear in on us, it can be unnerving in the extreme. This is especially so if we have become suspicious, as I have, of the liberal, sophisticated explanations I have read and heard in both churches and synagogues. One such pleasant explanation claims that although the Jews, of course, did not practice human sacrifice, Abraham could not help being impressed by the intense — albeit misplaced — piety of his pagan neighbors. *They* were willing to sacrifice *their* children to *their* gods. Was his devotion to his God as deep as theirs? Eventually, so this sleek modern explication goes, Abraham's concern became an idée fixe, buzzing in the poor patriarch's brain. Obsessed, mistaking this noise in his head for the voice of God, he carted young Isaac off to be sacrificed.[4] At the last minute, however, just as the handsome hero rescues Pauline from the onrushing train, God saves Isaac, and the story ends with a crescendo of strings and major chords.

This may be a nice way to recount this chilling tale to children. But I do not believe it is accurate, and I certainly do not believe that the story of the binding of Isaac is for children. It is for adults. After we have lived enough years, grappled with some no-win choices, and discarded the numerous puerile rationalizations that cheapen the story, we can begin to understand why it is one of the most powerful passages in the Bible. It is powerful not because it depicts such an extraordinary situation — which it does — but because this extraordinary situation gives us a peek into something fundamental about our own lives that we would prefer not to think about. It also gives us a glimpse of something about the nature of God that we suspect is true but would also prefer to suppress. The fact is that neither God nor life as it unfolds is always user-friendly, benevolent, and supportive. Life can be cruel, and God's ways often seem arbitrary and inscrutable, even terrifying. This is a difficult idea to get across in a culture in which nearly all the major denominations have managed to recast God into a gentle, avuncular figure, devoid of either terror or mystery. But it is hard to reconcile this soft-edged portrait with the one we find in the Bible. The Abraham and Isaac story forces us — if we listen to it — to reconsider, however briefly, whether the current cultural picture of a pliable, domesticated deity may be wildly mistaken.

Some attempts to come to grips with the inner meaning of the binding of Isaac have been thoughtful and even profound. Take, for example, Søren Kierkegaard's retelling of the story in *Fear and Trembling*.[5] Looking around him in nineteenth-century Denmark, Kierkegaard sensed that what his comfortable bourgeois neighbors called Christianity was bogus. They assumed that merely by being born into what was called a Christian country they were automatically Christian. They could pursue their petty self-serving lives, grow plump and complacent, and assume that as long as their parents had taken them in for baptism as children, that was enough. They never gave a thought to God or the meaning of life. This infuriated Kierkegaard, who fumed that all these people "call themselves Christians, are recognized as Christians by the State, are buried as Christians by the Church, are certified as Christians for eternity."[6] They were dealing, he said, in a debased currency.

Kierkegaard spent his life attacking this spurious Christendom in the name of "New Testament Christianity," which, he insisted, requires one to fight against the main currents of society, not to swim along with them. But he never wanted to organize a sectarian movement to oppose what he considered bogus Christianity. He addressed his writings solely to "the individual," which is why many writers trace twentieth-century existentialism back to him. One can see why he was drawn to the figure of Abraham, who turned his back on all conventions. Kierkegaard took the phrase "fear and trembling" from a famous saying of Saint Paul's in Philippians 2:12: "Work out your own salvation with fear and trembling" *(meta phobou kai tremou)*. The main point Kierkegaard sees in the Abraham and Isaac story is that obedience to God can require us to turn away from the cultural codes and expectations of our era. It also shows us that even though it rankles and frustrates us at times, God (and one could add life itself) gives and takes away *without giving any reason*.

This failure of God to give any reason for what he demands of Abraham remains one of the most bewildering and disconcerting elements of the story. Whenever God is depicted as acting severely in earlier biblical accounts, there is usually a reason. He punished Cain for murdering Abel. He sent the flood to chastise a world that had turned against him. But no reason at all is given in the Abraham and Isaac saga. Our understandable curiosity about God's motive, and how Abraham felt when he heard the awful command, is simply not satisfied in the biblical story. These questions are not even addressed. The idea that God was "testing" Abraham is not found in the text itself. This has allowed generations of rabbis, as well as Kierkegaard and hosts of theologians, and dozens of psychoanalysts, literary critics, and poets, to speculate. The image of Abraham and Isaac has become an inkblot test for anyone who wants to try decoding it. Kierkegaard points out that in heeding God's command, Abraham seems to cut himself off from the world in which we make most of our decisions. Abraham did not, it seems, consult with the boy's mother or any other relatives. He left behind the network of friends and family within which we usually decide something. He even abandoned the usual canons of ethical reasoning, responding to what he believed was the voice of God and God alone. Kierkegaard believed this was an example of faith transcending ethics; more important, he thought it demonstrated the fundamental conflict between the individual and the crowd. To follow the command of God, Abraham refused to submit to the ethos of the tribe or the herd.

I think there is something to Kierkegaard's reading, and it casts an old discussion between Jews and Christians in a new light. It is often said that while Jews stress a corporate identity and ethic, Christians (especially Protestants) put more emphasis on the individual. Abraham is said to have been "the first Jew," but here, at least in Kierkegaard's eyes, he looks much more Protestant than Jewish. Turning his back on family, friends, and relatives seems enormously *un*-Jewish. He does not for a moment, it seems, weigh the consequences of his action or consider, like Immanuel Kant, whether what he is about to do could be generalized into a rule for everyone. Even ignoring what at least many believe was the Jewish understanding of God at the time, he decides *tout seul*.

This reading appeals to me, but it also worries me. I immediately suspect that it makes sense because, although I disagree with Kierkegaard more often than I agree with him, he and I do share, in some respects, a common Protestant tradition. For this reason I hesitate to push his interpretation ahead of others. Yet there is something in this awful story that resonates strongly with my moral sensibility. It says to me that ultimately, not every day perhaps but in the last analysis, my final obligation is not to the national ethos, to established moral codes, or even to the teachings of my faith. It is to the "Other," and in the Abraham and Isaac story I believe God represents the claim on me of the "Other." In Kierkegaard's case the "Other" is God. In our case the "Other" is more often the human being who, at this moment, is making a claim on me. But that claim of the human other is, I believe, the way God's claim comes to us, and it trumps all the other claims.

Here the example of Dietrich Bonhoeffer, the German Lutheran pastor, comes to mind. Bonhoeffer was killed by the Gestapo in a concentration camp in 1945 for his role in the attempt to assassinate Hitler. He was a strong pacifist, an ardent admirer of Gandhi, an outspoken critic of the Nazis from the beginning. Nonetheless, he first blanched at the thought when his brother-in-law invited him to join the conspiracy to rid the world of the Führer. Killing, even killing Hitler, broke the Ten Commandments, violated the teachings of Jesus, and was completely against all his principles. But Bonhoeffer eventually came to believe that there are times when even the most sacred teachings and the highest ethical axioms have to be set aside. He believed that God comes to us in what he called "the nearest thou at hand," and in this situation, that "Other" required him to sacrifice the highest moral code he knew. So he joined the plot and consequently paid for it with his life.

Maybe this explains why the Abraham and Isaac story is about a sacrifice, or at least a near-sacrifice. We gradually discover as we grow older that to respond to the claim of *this* particular "other," I must forgo fulfilling the claims of *that* "other," maybe even of many "others." To love *her*, I cannot love *another* "her" in the same way. Choice always involves sacrifice. I cannot respond both to you and to others in the same way at the same time. Sacrifice, and precisely the sacrifice of things and persons that are extremely precious to us, is part of life. This is made grievously evident in the Abraham and Isaac story, in which the father is asked not to sacrifice his own life, which he would have done gladly, but something much more valuable to him, as any parent knows.

Still, I have my doubts. We do not live on top of Mount Moriah with a child bound at our feet and a knife in our hand every day. Most of the time our moral choices, however difficult, are not as heartbreaking. And here is where the apparent deep rift between Jewish and Christian interpretations of the moral significance of this biblical story begins to be healed. The healing came for me in the writings of the French Jewish philosopher Emmanuel Levinas. A brilliant Parisian intellectual, he was highly respected by his secular colleagues and was also a widely recognized scholar of the Talmud. Levinas brings us down from the mountain into quotidian life. He argues that we should resist the temptation to generalize the exceptional. We have canons of justice and codes of ethics and modes of moral reasoning precisely to help us sort out the conflicting demands of the various "others" that claim our attention, our love, our caring. Levinas agrees that the claim of the person whose face looks into ours at this very moment carries a certain undeniable precedence. But we should be careful, he advises, not to "spend everything on one account." It is easy to see the Talmudic mind at work behind this moral philosophy. The rabbis who composed the Talmud also knew that, although heroic and sacrificial actions are sometimes necessary, most of the decisions we need to make require balancing and weighing, and what we decide in one case may not apply to the next one.[7]

I am still stalled at the crossroads between Kierkegaard and Levinas. Maybe that is not an inappropriate place to be for one who stands in the Court of the Gentiles. I find both thinkers convincing, and I suspect that at some level they are not irreconcilable. But until some further clarity dawns on me, I will have to rely on Levinas and the Talmudic–moral reasoning approach, not only for everyday life, where it seems to make the most sense, but also for decisions that are unusually hard. Still, I recognize that there may be a time to leave behind church and state and culture, and even established ethical norms, if the self-evident claim of some "other" requires me to do so. Indeed, this is just what Jesus did on those occasions that he seemed to violate the traditional Jewish law, or at least some people's interpretations of it, in order to address the urgent need of an individual.

Rosh ha-Shanah is not unremittingly heavy. During the medieval period, a custom grew up of people gathering by a lake or river on the first day of Rosh ha-Shanah to cast their sins — symbolized by tiny pieces of bread — into the water. As the bread splashed into the stream they prayed, "O may you cast all the sins of your people Israel into a place where they will not be remembered, nor counted nor ever again minded." The ritual was called *tashlich*, which means "casting away." As Jews moved into the modern age some of their sages — especially one called the Vilna Gaon — became embarrassed by what they feared might appear to be superstitious, so in many places *tashlich* was abandoned. In more recent years, however, as people in many different traditions have again begun to appreciate the power of symbolic language, *tashlich* has made something of a comeback.

I am glad. Nina and I had been attending regular Rosh ha-Shanah services for a number of years before we heard about *tashlich* and, a few years ago, decided to revive it for ourselves. Since then it has become a regular part of our celebration of the New Year. For some reason, our marking of *tashlich* on a fall afternoon in 1998 stands out as especially memorable. At the time we were living in the residence of a faculty colleague while our home was being renovated. The colleague was also entertaining a Hindu scholar from India, his assistant, and an Episcopal priest. Taking Nicholas with us, and carrying a plastic bag of stale bread, we all made our way across Memorial Drive to the elegant little pedestrian bridge that spans the Charles River between the Harvard residential houses and the Business School. It was a splendid day. Boats with student crews churned swiftly beneath us. Ducks hovered and skidded. Nina distributed the bread and explained the meaning of the ritual. Then she read a *tashlich* prayer, and we each dropped bits of bread toward the delighted ducks. The Hindu sage and the Episcopal priest seemed enchanted as they joined in. People strolling over the bridge sometimes stopped and watched. Some inquired politely what we were doing. When I explained briefly, one said, "Great, I've got a couple of sins I'd like to feed to the ducks, too." Another simply said, "Cool!"

Advocates of what is called postmodernism sometimes claim that we have reached a stage of history in which practices that were once discarded as rank superstition can be selectively reclaimed, imbued now with a combination of their old meaning and new overtones. There is some truth in this. A few years before we started to observe *tashlich*, I attended the baptism of two young women by complete immersion in a stream next to a cornfield in Vermont. I knew that when the Baptist movement started nearly five hundred years ago, and for most of the time since, Baptists had always "gathered by the river" for their baptisms. But as they became more respectable, many Baptists wanted to avoid the jibes and mockery that were often aimed at this practice, so they discreetly moved their baptisms inside. Most now take place in a small pool behind the pulpit, which only the congregation can see. But in this little Vermont congregation, the young people who had reached the age for baptism wanted to gather by the river again. Part of it, the pastor suggested to me, was their growing appreciation for the spiritual importance of the natural environment. But another part came from their recognition that most of their high school friends, instead of making fun of them, would think it was "cool." Among Jews, a parallel reluctance to hide their faith behind closed doors is also under way. More and more young men are wearing *yarmulkas* in public. Jewish families are beginning to build Sukkot booths on their lawns for the fall harvest festival and decorate their houses with lights during Chanukah to "advertise the miracle." Buddhists, Sikhs, Muslims, and Hindus no longer lurk on the periphery of American public life but construct their mosques and pagodas across the street from synagogues and churches. All this suggests a new and welcome phase in American religious history — the public recognition, not only of religion as such, but of the diversity and particularity of specific traditions.

As Rosh ha-Shanah ebbs, everyone anticipates the unearthly blast of the shofar, the ram's horn that is sounded several times during the Days of Awe. It emits a strange sound, like nothing one hears anywhere else in modern life. It seems to cut through the buzz and static to what must be a primitive part of the brain. But why does it pierce so deeply? The answer given by Rabbi Yehudah Leib Alter of Ger, one of the last of the great Polish Hasidic teachers, makes sense to me. "The shofar blasts," he said, "are sounds without speech. Speech represents the division of sound into varied and separate movements of the mouth. But sound itself is one, united, cleaving to its source. On Rosh ha-Shanah the life force cleaves to its source, as it was before differentiation or division. And we, too, seek to attach ourselves to that inner flow of life." Commenting on this interpretation, Rabbi Arthur Green says, "The sound of the shofar takes us to that moment of outcry from deep within, to a place prior to the division of our heart's cry into the many words of prayer."[8]

But surely there is another reason that the shofar slices the air and stabs the soul. It signals, as nothing else does, the chasm between the past and the future. It splits time in two. As the old year fades and the new one begins, we realize that the old one is gone forever and that, try as we will, we can never know what lies ahead. The shofar, since it is wordless, can both scream in terror and shout for joy with the same breath. Nothing else is worthy of the beginning of a whole new year in the only life we will ever have.

3

Closing the Big Book

Yom Kippur

> "And it shall be a statute to you for ever, that in the
> seventh month, on the tenth day of the month,
> You shall afflict yourselves, and shall do no work,
> either the native or the stranger who sojourns
> among you; for on this day shall atonement be made
> for you, to cleanse you; from all your sins you
> shall be clean before the Lord."
>
> — Leviticus 16:29, 30

IN EVERY COURTROOM DRAMA, whether on the screen or in real life, the high moment comes when the jury files back to its seats and the judge solemnly asks, "Ladies and gentlemen of the jury, have you reached a verdict?" A hush falls over the crowd. In a film, the camera pans the audience, picking out faces taut with anticipation. This is not quite the mood at Temple Beth Zion when we arrive for the marathon that is Yom Kippur, the Day of Atonement. But it comes close.

This is the day on which Jews are expected to replicate death in order to emerge to a new life at sundown, when the judge at last announces the verdict. Of course here there is no jury, and the verdict is a forgone conclusion. Despite our sins, we will be spared. God's mercy is greater than our guilt, God's kindness is bigger than our petty cruelty. We are free, as they say in gangster movies, "to walk." But even though we know from the beginning how it will turn out, we cannot wholly avoid the tremors of uncertainty that assault us.

Even for an outsider, or a semi-outsider like myself, the Yom Kippur service is powerful dramaturgy. So I am trying hard, with all the others in the prisoners' box, to play my assigned role as best I can.

I have a lot of help. During most of Yom Kippur I nurse a dull headache because we are supposed to eat nothing from just before sundown the evening before (which is called Erev Yom Kippur) until after sundown on the day itself. We refrain from drinking (some people even avoid water), we do not engage in sexual activity, and we do not wear leather shoes or belts, which at one time were an expression of finery. So here I am, stifling hunger pangs, a little thirsty (although I do allow myself a glass of water now and then), wearing my only pair of suspenders and canvas running shoes. Sex is the farthest thing from my mind. A grilled cheese sandwich has more erotic appeal. Why are we doing this? Because there will be no eating or drinking or sex (or finery) in death, and Yom Kippur is about sampling some of the qualities of death so that when we are allowed to live life again, it will taste even sweeter. One rabbi suggests that there is something about the last meal one eats before the Yom Kippur fast that is reminiscent of the prisoner's final meal before the electric chair. There is some truth in the saying that there is nothing better than a firing squad in the morning to clarify the mind. For some reason (which physiologists may one day explain), fasting does produce a kind of mental clarity, despite the headache.

On Erev Yom Kippur, the evening service begins its long confessional statement with some trespasses almost anyone can identify with. It asks for forgiveness for "the sin we have committed before Thee by hardening our hearts" and goes on to mention "sins we have committed before Thee in speech" and "the sin we have committed before Thee by wronging our neighbor." I can confess these transgressions because I can think of numerous times during the year when I have done them, and it is good to get them off my chest. So far, so good.

But then comes a part of the prayer that puzzled me at first. Unlike any Christian prayer I know of, it also asks God's forgiveness for the sin we have committed "unknowingly." Immediately my mind steps back. I know that while on the cross Jesus asked God to forgive his executioners because "they know not what they do." Still, every five-year-old knows that if he can persuade his mother that he didn't mean to break his little sister's doll carriage, she cannot logically hold him responsible. The question puzzles me. Why should I be held accountable for things I have done unintentionally and without even knowing it? I am still pondering this dilemma when, a few lines later, the prayer goes on to list sins we have committed "by spurning parents and teachers"; "by denying and lying . . . by bribery . . . by scoffing . . . by slandering."

Now I am finding it hard, even with a relentless searching of my conscience, to remember when I have done these things. And when it comes to "the sin we have committed before Thee by demanding usurious interest," I begin to wonder just what it is that I am confessing. The prayer goes on to detail "being stiff-necked," "tale-bearing," in addition to "causeless hatred."[1] This section in the service is followed by assurances of God's pardon, but a few pages later another list of sins appears. Here the congregation confesses, "We have dealt treacherously, we have spoken slander, we have acted perversely . . . we have done violence, we have framed lies . . . scoffed, revolted, rebelled."

When I reached this part at my first Yom Kippur service, I was almost ready to sneak across the street for that grilled cheese sandwich and forgo any further confessing. I may be a sinner, but the sinner whom these prayers were describing was not me. Of course I did not stalk out; still, being expected to confess things I had never done bothered me. It made it almost impossible for me to enter wholeheartedly into what is, in many other respects, a moving service. It seemed that I was somehow expected to confess — more than once — not only things I was not aware of, but long lists of sins that I had never even thought of committing. It seemed unreasonable.

I only saw the logic of unintentional transgressions when a rabbi pointed out to me that during these Days of Awe, Jews do not just repent for their own sins. They repent for the sins of all the people. No wonder I felt wrongly accused. The concept of collective repentance has been, until recently, quite foreign to most of Protestant Christianity. True, in Roman Catholicism there are whole communities of monks and nuns who intercede every day for those who do not have the desire or the capacity to pray for themselves. But the Protestant tradition, with its strong emphasis on the responsibility of the individual person before God, has not ordinarily looked favorably on these practices. As Martin Luther once put it, every person has to do his own repenting and his own dying. No one else can do either one for you.

Eventually, however, contemplating the confessional prayers of Yom Kippur became one of the moments in my encounter with Judaism that most enlarged and enriched my own faith. First, with regard to confessing sins we do not know about, and did not do intentionally, in fact, of course, we do often hurt other people without intending to and sometimes without even knowing. Sometimes we learn later how something we did or said wounded someone painfully. But there may be many other times when we do such things and never hear about them, even though the sting still afflicts the other person. This is why I have come to believe that asking for forgiveness for the hurtful things we have done without even knowing them is salutary. It makes us think carefully about what we might have done in the past and remember to be more careful in the future.

But what about confessing things other people have done? Even when I realized this is a corporate confession, the concept continued to pose a problem for me, and still does. My question is quite simple: Can anyone actually repent for someone else? Wasn't Luther right? Doesn't repentance require a change of heart by the transgressor, an intention to try to do better? One of the points made by the Protestant reformers was that it was fruitless to have monks and nuns intercede for us — which was, at the time, one of the main reasons for the very existence of the monastic movement. Catholic theology held that the monastics were drawing on a "treasury of merit" stored up by people who did good deeds, transferring a kind of payment to the divine accounts of those in moral arrears. Of course at the time there were terrible abuses of this practice. Rich people could pay for endless masses to be said for the souls of their departed loved ones and — eventually — for their own. Some even thought that if they endowed enough monasteries, they could live lives of reckless violence and promiscuity while the gentle sisters and brothers faithfully intervened for them morning, noon, and night before the throne of grace. Luther, who had been an Augustinian monk in his youth, roundly condemned this whole idea. But it is sometimes not entirely clear in his writings when he is condemning a religious practice and when he is condemning its corruption and misuse. Protestants do pray for other people, for their health and well-being, even for their salvation. But they do not repent for them. Like dying, this is something they have to do for themselves.

Still, I am not fully satisfied with this. It seems to promote an extreme form of religious individualism. One can see how this kind of thinking found its way through later Lutheran pietism to Søren Kierkegaard and then to its atheistic version in Jean-Paul Sartre's existentialism. Kierkegaard asked that the inscription on his tombstone read "The Single One," and he told his fiancée, Regina Olsen, that he could not marry her because that would dilute his necessarily lonely and direct relationship with God. In one of his finest essays, the Jewish philosopher Martin Buber says of Kierkegaard, "It is through, not despite the Regina Olsens of this world that we come to God."

I believe, with Buber and against Kierkegaard, that we come to God *through* the human ties within which we have been set. We are bound together with bonds that go deeper than skin. But I also believe, with Luther, that there are some things we simply have to do for ourselves. And I am still made uncomfortable by the thought of repenting for someone else's sins or of someone else's repenting for me. Obviously, this is not just my personal plight. It points to a much larger issue in the whole area of public morality: Can a corporate entity — a nation, a tribe, a people — repent? After World War II, the German Protestant churches issued a statement of repentance for their sins of omission and commission during the Third Reich. They issued it, furthermore, not just in the name of the churches (including, presumably, members who were alive during that period but were now dead), but also in the name of the German people. It was a welcome admission. But just what did it mean? How many people from how many churches had to vote for the statement in order to make it truly representative? Does such a statement, for example, have any validity if it is passed by a closely contested vote? How can the churches speak for anyone except themselves?

Among Catholics this issue assumes a different form. According to Catholic doctrine, the pope can and does speak for the whole church. Therefore, presumably, when Pope John Paul II issued his famous apology during Lent of the Jubilee Year 2000, he was not just speaking for Karol Jozef Wojtyla. His apology, for the sins the Church had committed against women, Jews, indigenous peoples, and many others, was meant to be in the name of the nearly one billion Catholics in the world, and maybe even, in his mind at least, for all Christians.

But my nagging questions remain: Can anyone, including the pope, apologize for me? What about all those Christians who still place women in an inferior position or nurse an ugly attitude toward Jews?

These are difficult questions. We sometimes hear that America should formally apologize to Japan for dropping atomic bombs on Hiroshima and Nagasaki. Indeed, just after the end of the war, a group of American Protestant theologians and church leaders did issue a statement of repentance. But who would have the moral authority to do it today? Bill Clinton, the president of the United States in 1995, which marked the fiftieth anniversary of the bombings, was not yet born when the bombs were dropped. Many older people, especially some who were in the military in World War II, opposed any such apology, insisting that the Japanese should first apologize for Pearl Harbor. Whatever the merit of either of these ideas, they run into the same obstacle encountered by those who want America to apologize for slavery, for the murderous displacement of Native Americans, or for any of a host of obvious and grave national sins. The question is a very basic one: Who has the authority to make such a penitent apology, and for whom would that person speak?

Another question about the Yom Kippur prayer arises from my uncertainty about who is included in the corporate "we" of the Jewish prayers of repentance? Here the age-old tension between Jewish particularism and Jewish universalism enters again. Are Jews praying that all *Jews* be forgiven, including the unrepentant ones? If so, who is included in the category of Jews? At a time when the "Who is a Jew?" controversy has made the borders of the community less distinct, this is not easy to answer. But suppose it included all Jews of any category whatsoever, including secular atheists; what about the rest of us? Are Jews on Yom Kippur repenting for everyone, for all of us? This may seem like a tall order. There may be a few million unrepentant Jews in the world who need such intercession, but there are billions of non-Jews who — if such third-party prayers don't include them — are being neglected. Isn't it unfair somehow that the relatively few unrepentant people who are, nonetheless, lucky enough to have someone who repents *for* them (because they are Jewish) should have a more favorable standing before God than those who are not so fortunate? This discussion can quickly get rather silly. But the underlying riddle of the relationship between the corporate and the individual remains.

COMMON PRAYERS ❖ 46

There are two different but closely related issues here. One is whether I must repent for myself or whether the group to which I belong can repent for everyone who is part of that group. The other is whether a collectivity, be it a nation, a country, or a religious group, *can* repent and gain forgiveness either for itself or for those who are completely outside. As I reflected on these questions, thinking that maybe it was my own upbringing that made them so difficult for me, I was relieved to discover that — as in many other such matters — it was not just my upbringing. Thoughtful Jews are concerned about the same issues. On individual repentance, Rabbi Everett Gendler, albeit in a commentary on Rosh ha-Shanah, remarks, "The process of individual *teshuvah* (repentance — literally, turning around) is so demanding and requires such concentration that I don't see how we can achieve reconciliation within the groups to which we belong at the same time. Group renewal and mending should be done, but it is so easy to deflect personal *teshuvah* that we might do best not to try to find justification for it by including corporate *teshuvah* in Rosh ha-Shanah."[2]

He goes on to suggest that maybe it would be better "to adopt a more frequent process of personal *teshuvah* all year round [or] on each Sabbath." The issue this rabbi is wrestling with is a troubling one: What is the connection between the spiritual responsibilities of the individual and those of the community?

This may well be an area in which Jews and Christians can help each other. Christians do practice personal *teshuvah* on a weekly basis but have a weak sense of corporate responsibility. According to Rabbi Gendler, Jews may have the opposite problem. In any case, what I have learned from my unending struggle with the idea of *teshuvah* is this: at its heart is the radical idea that people can change. Both Judaism and Christianity, in opposition to the many forms of determinism that dominate our culture today, insist that human beings are created with the freedom to examine their lives and — with the help of God and of fellow human beings — mend their ways and alter their courses. We are not totally determined by our genes or our early toilet training, though both of these, and many more factors, supply the material we must work with. Our destiny is to be born in one century and not another, with a particular skin color, brain capacity, and gender. But what we do with all these is up to us. In the courtroom of Yom Kippur, none of the excuses offered in the courts of this world by creative defense counsels are acceptable. The judge knows we are free and that we can change, if we decide to do so.

I have another issue with Yom Kippur. If we can confess other people's shortcomings, can we also profit from their virtues? Here, it had always seemed to me, we reach a precarious divide between Jews and Christians. Most Christians, although they may be suspicious of vicarious confession, do believe in vicarious atonement: the idea that someone's virtue or suffering can benefit someone else. Catholics teach that one can draw on the "treasury of merit" stored up for everyone by the righteousness of the saints and that one can benefit from the atoning death of Jesus Christ. Protestants, representing a more individual faith, generally reject the intercession of saints, but they believe that Christ's blameless life and undeserved death provide the primary source of their reconciliation to God.

For decades I was under the impression that a major theological difference between Jews and Christians ran along this fault line. Jews, I had read and heard (including from many Jews) simply do not believe in vicarious atonement, whereas Christians obviously do. Further, I had been led to believe, while Christians rely on God's grace for receiving mercy and forgiveness, Jews must demonstrate acts of compassion that outweigh their deeds of selfishness. But now this has become yet another point on which I have had to jettison my old ideas. During the traditional Yom Kippur service, it was once the custom, and still is in many congregations, to retell the story of the so-called Ten Rabbinic Martyrs. These rabbis were killed by the Roman authorities for refusing to obey the prohibitions against Jewish religious practices after the legions had suppressed the revolt led by the Jewish rebel Simeon Bar Kochba in the second century c.e. Why is this saga told again? Here is what one of the most eminent American Orthodox rabbis, Irving Greenberg, says on the subject: "In a way, the ten Rabbis, like Isaac, were invoked for the sake of vicarious atonement; the merit of their devotion and martyrdom should win forgiveness for their descendants, the living people of Israel."[3] Today, he adds, the martyrs of the Holocaust are sometimes invoked in the same way. This makes sense. In a tradition like Judaism, which emphasizes the corporate nature of human life, including its reach back into history, why should one not benefit today from the lives of the righteous who have gone before? We profit from those long gone in many other respects. We cherish the music they composed, savor the books they wrote, marvel at the pictures they painted, and use the scientific discoveries they made. Why should we not benefit from them on the spiritual level? It must also be said that we still chafe under many of their follies, still mourn the dead of their many wars, and are just beginning to clean up the putrid mess they have made of our rivers. But that is another story.

"Yes but," one Jewish answer has been. "But why do Christians focus so much on Jesus, on one man's merits and martyr's death?" It is a fair question. My own response is inspired by the French artist Georges Rouault's vivid portrayals of the crucifixion in his *Misérère* series. Rouault's conviction, derived from Pascal, was that "Christ will be in agony until the end of the world." Consequently, he systematically pairs the traditional Stations of the Cross with depictions of the suffering of ordinary people. As Christ is led to his place of torture and death, we see at every stage a prisoner being led to the gallows, a lonely woman in a barren suburb, or a poor old man dying alone in a tenement. Christ does continue to suffer, the *Misérère* series says, with all who suffer unjustly in the world. When Christians say he suffered and died for us, we mean that, in some sense, the kind of people Rouault pictures suffer and die for us as well, and whether they are, or were, Christians makes no difference. From this perspective, there is no reason why the Ten Rabbinic Martyrs of the Yom Kippur service should not be included. Might the day come when Jews can remember that Jesus of Nazareth was also a rabbi who was martyred by the Romans?

My understanding of the atoning vicarious death of Christ is not shared by every Christian. Some Christians insist that Christ and Christ alone died for us. But if Jesus Christ was a human being, as all Christians believe, then his suffering cannot be completely severed from all human suffering. "No man is an island," as John Donne reminds us, and this includes Jesus. Catholic spirituality over the years has rightly recognized this in the devotion it has encouraged to the sorrows of Mary, the mother of Jesus. The suffering of one person inevitably causes the suffering of others. This insight has become increasingly valuable to me, and it plays an important part in Christian mysticism as well as in feminist and liberation theologies. We are all in this together.

There is another point of convergence between Jews and Christians on the vexed question of grace and good works. At the end of the Yom Kippur service, having prayed for mercy and forgiveness, Jews finally throw themselves totally on the mercy of the court. As Rabbi Greenberg puts it, "This atonement is by divine grace; it is above and beyond the individual's own effort or merit." I was astonished when I first read this sentence. Martin Luther once ignited a whole Reformation with his preaching of *sole gratia* (by grace alone). When the hour of decision, forgiving, or sentencing finally comes, do Jews cling to the same hope? Again, Rabbi Greenberg: "Many Jews assume that only Christianity focuses on grace and on the merits of another's sacrifice for their behavior, but in biblical times, Temple worship had strong sacramental overtones. . . . Modern Jews would do well to recover the sense of grace that brings us forgiveness even when we do not earn it for ourselves."[4]

This is another instance in which the core convictions of Jews and Christians have been distorted by centuries of polemic. Christians have frequently been told that we believe in justification by grace (or in the case of Catholics, by grace and works), while Jews believe they are justified by adhering to the precepts of the Law. Jews have often been taught the same thing, so for millions of ordinary Jews and Christians, this alleged difference has become a hallmark contrast, even a flat contradiction, and has often been presented as an either-or proposition. The truth, however, is quite different.

Maybe the wooden term "justification," with its cold, judicial overtones, has misled everyone. The underlying question is a simple one: How do God and human beings enter into a fruitful relationship with each other? Do we somehow earn the privilege of receiving God's compassion? Or does God love and forgive us freely, regardless of our merits? Or is there some mixture of the two?

In recent years Catholic theologians, drawing closer to what has been considered the "Protestant" position, have insisted that in the final analysis, no one enters God's presence except by God's grace. And Jews, freed now from the chafing need always to stress their differences from the Christian majorities around them, have begun, as Rabbi Greenberg demonstrates, to reclaim their own traditional teaching on the divine grace that brings forgiveness "even when we do not earn it for ourselves." This whole development is a healthy one. It suggests that the teachings of these traditions on the relationship between God's grace and human works of justice and compassion simply do not differ as much as we have been told in the past.

Jewish teaching does not hold that God's favor is gained merely by accumulating good deeds. And the New Testament emphasizes that "faith without works is dead." A recent translation of the Epistle of James, where this famous quotation is found, clarifies the matter considerably:

> But someone may say: "One chooses faith, another action." To which I reply: "Show me this faith you speak of with no actions to prove it, while I by my actions will prove to you my faith." You have faith and believe that there is one God. Excellent! Even demons have faith like that, and it makes them tremble. Do you have to be told, you fool, that faith divorced from action is futile? (James 2:18–20)

On many other matters touched on in this book there are important distinctions between Jewish and Christian beliefs and many critical differences in emphasis. But there is no point whatever in perpetuating the exaggerations of those differences that have plagued us for so long. What we can do is to explain how and why they arose and then discuss how much weight they should have now.

Historically, for example, there have been genuine differences between Jewish and Christian thinkers about the meaning of "sin," but also some common ground. Outsiders, and many Jews as well, can get the impression that in Judaism "sins" are specific acts, such as the list of misdeeds confessed at Yom Kippur. But the rabbinical tradition suggests something more complicated. The rabbis drew a distinction between what they called the *yetser ha-tov*, which is the inner inclination to do good, and the *yetser ha-ra*, the inclination to do evil. Sometimes Jewish stories depict these two urges as arguing inside our heads, pushing us in one direction or the other.[5] The tradition suggests that God, candid self-examination, and the firm exercise of the will help the good urges to prevail.[6]

Jews have never attached much credence to what Christian theology calls original sin, which plays an important role in Christianity. They understandably wonder how we can all be implicated by Adam's fatal bite into the forbidden fruit. But these disagreements are often obscured by biblical literalism and ignorance on both sides.[7] People once believed Adam was a real historical figure, so it is little wonder that our being cursed for his disobedience caused such confusion. But Adam and Eve mean "mankind" and "life." They are the metaphorical representatives of all humankind. The story in Genesis is not about primeval ancestors but about us.

But what does it say about us? Here there are some differences. Christians have said that the story of the Fall is about how we invariably try to deny our finitude and escape our mortality ("to be as gods") and end up making things worse. We find ourselves expelled from Eden and barred from returning by an angel with a fiery sword, a favorite theme in Christian art. Christian theologians have therefore thought of sin more as a kind of congenital disability, with specific failings as its symptoms. But it is also a disability we somehow have a role in perpetuating, like a fly gets itself ever more entangled in a web the more it tries to get out.

In recent years, some thoughtful Christians have asked whether even the term "sin" is still useful when the word is used as a lure to market sexy perfume and rich chocolate. But I do not think we can give up the word so easily. Indeed, several sophisticated modern Christian writers, like Søren Kierkegaard, Paul Tillich, and Reinhold Niebuhr, all defend its validity, interpreting original sin as a metaphor for our flawed and precarious human condition. Each, in his own way, saw sin not as the opposite of virtue but as the opposite of faith and as an expression of the distressing mixture of freedom and fate that keeps prompting us to do things that in our better moments we know are wrong. Kierkegaard, contemplating human existence psychologically, noticed the sense of vertigo and anxiety that arises when we become aware of our finitude and how expert we are at deceiving ourselves about it. Tillich, more philosophically inclined, saw original sin as a result of "man's existential predicament," our haunting sense of "estrangement" from ourselves, from each other, and from the mysterious source of our being. It is no wonder that he welcomed existential philosophy and literature as allies of Christian theology. In a more ethical vein, Niebuhr thought of original sin as our tendency to make our own perspectives absolute, to transform our sense of the good into the good for everyone. For each of these influential thinkers, the story of Adam and Eve is not about something that happened in a garden long ago but a powerful symbol of the human situation we confront every day. Whether or not we call it original sin, it remains a stubborn fact of the human condition.

The differing conceptions of sin found in Judaism and Christianity generate somewhat different ideas of God's forgiveness. Since for Christians sin is more a condition than an act, more an inner flaw than an infraction, God's grace must penetrate to the core of our being. We must be inwardly transformed. The Jewish tradition teaches that if we are appropriately penitent, God will forgive the transgression we have committed against him, but that even God cannot or will not forgive the misdeed we perpetrate against our fellow human beings. For these we must seek their forgiveness. I think Christians have much to learn from the Jewish idea of seeking the forgiveness of those we have mistreated. Too often Christians believe that once they have confessed to God, they do not need to reconcile themselves to the other party. But this makes it too easy. Jesus himself told his followers that if, on the way to the temple to offer a sacrifice, they remember something that has undermined their relationship with a neighbor, they should first go and make peace with the neighbor and only then go and offer the sacrifice. Jesus was never more rabbinical than at this moment.

But I also find something powerfully attractive in the Christian understanding of sin as a tragic flaw, as it is interpreted by the thinkers I have mentioned. They are grappling, as we all do, with something about us that goes even deeper than questions about ethics and morality ("sins"), as important as those questions are. They are engaging a mystery that traces back to the classical Greek recognition of the inescapably tragic dimension in life and to the universal human intuition that, although we know ourselves to be free in some sense, we also wrestle constantly with forces within us and around us that make living a moral life hazardous and enigmatic. Indeed, two secular Jews, Sigmund Freud and Karl Marx, have enabled us to see these inner and outer forces more clearly than the more naive generation before them did. As Herman Melville puts it in describing Ishmael's coming to terms with his new friend Queequeg's odd pagan ideas, "Heaven have mercy on us all — Presbyterians and pagans alike — for we are all somehow dreadfully cracked about the head, and sadly in need of mending."

Like a Shakespeare play, Yom Kippur also has its antic interval. During the afternoon service, the congregation listens to a reading of the biblical book of Jonah. I look forward to this part of the service. First of all, the confessing is now over, and like most people present, I think I have had enough. Also, I love the story of Jonah, the recalcitrant Jewish prophet who is sent to call the pagan peoples of Nineveh to repentance. He takes a ship in the opposite direction to escape God's command, is thrown overboard during a storm, is swallowed by "a great fish," and regurgitated at the very place he was trying to avoid. Understandably in a bad mood, still Jonah reluctantly preaches to the people of Nineveh and — much to his chagrin — they do repent and find God's favor.

It is a charming story with all the elements of high camp. Its sheer tall-tale absurdity and blatant caricaturing appeal to the contemporary consciousness. In his pathetic ineptitude, Jonah is a kind of Mr. Magoo or one of the clueless characters Woody Allen plays in his early films. Still, its very farcical quality drives home the lesson of Jonah, painlessly but unmistakably. First of all, it is radically opposed to narrow ethnic particularism. It says that gentiles, even from a nation the Jews hated at the time, are fully capable of living righteously and basking in God's blessedness. This is a nice touch when one hears it, as I do with the ears of a gentile. It is also about the paradoxical tension between human freedom and divine providence. Wiggle as you may, it warns, you will not ultimately escape your destiny, even if it requires being ingested by a carnivorous sea creature. Destiny is not fate. Destiny is the framework within which we exercise our freedom and without which freedom would be meaningless. I was born a white male in America in the twentieth century, with a certain body type and brain capacity. That is my destiny. I cannot change it. What I do with it is my freedom.

Yom Kippur is high drama, and it can be physically and emotionally draining. The first time I attended a Yom Kippur service, I was astonished at one point to see the rabbi and some of the people in the congregation prostrate themselves toward the Torah, some touching their foreheads to the floor. I had been led to believe that Jews never kneel or bow, but here they were, resembling Muslims at prayer or Christians venerating the cross on Good Friday. But the more I understand the meaning of Yom Kippur, the more I understand why they fall on their knees. It is a day of primal terror and soaring release. The human questions it so boldly addresses — guilt, death, repentance, forgiveness, destiny, and freedom — are hardly minor considerations. They are so enormous that they knock the wind out of us and drop us, if only temporarily, to the floor.

Rabbi Gendler suggests that it is worthwhile to prepare for Yom

Kippur, not only by rereading Jonah, but by reading some of the great world literature derived from it. He especially recommends Father Mapple's famous sermon from Melville's *Moby-Dick*. (He mischievously calls the author "Reb Hayim Melville.")[8] I dutifully followed his advice and was glad I did. Father Mapple, an old whaling man himself, preaches the sermon based on Jonah from a pulpit shaped like a bowsprit in a chapel in New Bedford which is laid out in the shape of a ship. After he has climbed into the pulpit up a nautical rope ladder, he tells his congregation that he holds Jonah out to them not as an exemplar of character but as a model of repentance. This is indeed an appropriate theme for the Days of Awe and Yom Kippur, when *teshuvah* is what is called for.

But after I read the sermon scene in *Moby-Dick*, I turned to the masterly last paragraphs of the book, my favorites in all of American literature. This is the point at which the vengeful white whale has staved in and sunk the *Pequod*. Ishmael, the only survivor, is floating on the ocean spray, awaiting what he is sure will be his demise as well. As he watches the ship slip under the waves, the arm of the pagan harpooner, Tashtego, emerges from the surface with a hammer clutched in his brown fingers, nailing the flag to the mast. Suddenly a sky-hawk darts down "from its natural home among the stars" and pecks at the flag.

> [T]his bird now chanced to intercept its broad fluttering wing between the hammer and the wood, and simultaneously feeling that ethereal thrill, the submerged savage beneath, in his death-gasp, kept his hammer frozen there; so the bird of heaven, with archangelic shrieks, and his imperial beak thrust upwards, and his whole captive form folded in the flag of Ahab, went down with his ship, which, like Satan, would not sink to hell till she had dragged a living part of heaven with her.[9]

Then, just as suddenly, the casket that the ship's carpenter had crafted for Queequeg on the ill-fated voyage bursts out of the deep and floats over to Ishmael, providing him with an unexpected life raft to cling to until, eventually, he is picked up by a passing schooner. Here, in Melville's literary genius, hell and heaven are locked in mortal combat, and death comes to the rescue of life. The coffin, lovingly carved and decorated by the pagan, saves the life of the wavering Christian.

I wish Rabbi Gendler had recommended this passage too. It is just as suitable for Yom Kippur and for the Jonah story (where the repentance of a pagan people saves God's prophet), and it is all about life and death and destiny. Furthermore, it includes repentance, a new beginning, and resurrection, thus linking the Jewish and the Christian themes superbly. Melville, it is said, had a lifelong "quarrel with God." He could not fully believe in the stern deity of his New England Calvinist forebears. But he could not completely reject that God either. Jonah was a little like that. I believe many of us in the twenty-first century are too. If Yom Kippur is about the timeless themes that are stated so well in Jonah and *Moby-Dick,* then it is well worth the fasting and the headache.

4

The Strength of Fragility

Sukkot

> You shall keep the feast of harvest, of the first fruits of your labor,
> Of what you sow in the field. You shall keep the feast of ingathering
> at the end of the year, when you gather in from the field the fruit of
> your labor.
>
> — Exodus 23:16

ERE WE ARE — Nina and Nicholas and I — crouched under a jerry-built shanty in our scrawny front yard, munching on sandwiches and drinking lemonade with Allen and Darryl from across the street and their two boys. Sometimes neighbors stroll by, look with interest, and wave. We invite them to stop in for a glass of lemonade. Some do, and we reassure them that this ramshackle shed will not be a permanent addition to the neighborhood. We realize the structure would not pass even the most indifferent zoning standards. Not to worry: it will be torn down in a few days.

It is Sukkot, the annual Jewish harvest festival, and one of the customs is to construct a temporary hut and live in it (more or less) during the holiday in keeping with the biblical injunction, found in Leviticus 23:42, 43, "You shall live in huts seven days; all citizens of Israel shall live in huts in order that future generations may know that I made the Israelite people live in huts when I brought them out of the land of Egypt." So, for centuries, the custom is to tack together a small, fragile hut or booth, called a *sukkah,* somewhere near the house. It should be obviously temporary, perhaps to recall the flimsy overnight shelters harvesters rested and slept in while gathering the crops. The walls are decorated with fruits and vegetables, but the roof — usually made of leaves and branches — must allow the sun to be seen by day and the moon and stars by night. Groups of families sometimes build one together, especially in cities where yard space is at a premium, and then eat some meals and entertain friends there. Children love the whole *sukkah* scenario. It's like a religiously sanctioned tree house. For adults it affords yet another typically Jewish opportunity for eating, drinking, and schmoozing.

Sukkot arrives a week after Yom Kippur, in late September or early October. It is a harvest festival that the Israelites boldly incorporated into their religious practice from the agricultural peoples they encountered when they arrived in Canaan. One of the Sukkot customs is to gather what are called "the four species" of fruit tree branches, palm branches, and other leafy things and use them as part of the synagogue worship during the holiday. This aspect of Sukkot bears a clear resemblance to comparable holidays in other religions. Historians of religion have pointed out how many of these holidays focus on a female deity, a "corn mother" for example, whose image was honored in order to assure the fertility of the soil for the next season. The Greek goddess Demeter was a corn mother, as was the Roman goddess Ceres, from whom our word for "cereal" derives. This makes Sukkot a good example of how religions *can* creatively borrow from one another and a persuasive argument against purists who warn that any example of such "syncretism" is always corrupting.

The meaning of Sukkot has been explained in different ways over the years. Is it just a harvest festival, a sort of Jewish Thanksgiving? Or, as the passage from Leviticus suggests, is it intended to remind the Jews of their precarious years in the wilderness? Who knows for sure. And why should a holiday have only one explanation anyway. This ambiguity is part of what makes this holiday so fascinating.[1]

It was my old friend Rabbi Arthur Waskow, however, who pointed out a spiritual significance of Sukkot that seems to underlie both its traditional meanings, namely, the obvious *fragility* of the *sukkah*, the temporary shelter. He remembered that when he was a young man, the papers reported that some people were frantically building bomb shelters, actually discussing whether it would be legal to bar neighbors from one's bunker with a gun. In such an atmosphere, he said, the *sukkah* was a vivid reminder that we can never construct a secure safeguard against all the threats of life and must ultimately rely on God. Even though no one is digging shelters today, the *sukkah* is still an invaluable reminder of the fragility of all life. But it also reminds us that even within this fragile shanty, and exposed to all the vicissitudes of life, we can still eat and drink and enjoy friends and family.

The explanation appealed to me because, since most of us now live in cities, we sometimes have a hard time appreciating harvest festivals. But cancer, plane crashes, and the inevitable onset of senility all remind us that as human beings we are frail and highly vulnerable. And we know that even within a gated community, and with the best health insurance policies and retirement plans, disaster can strike at any moment. We mostly manage to repress that awareness, but it is spiritually important to bring it to mind occasionally. Tibetan monks are required to spend a week sleeping in a cemetery. On Ash Wednesday, Christians are reminded that "we are dust." Traditionally, Sukkot is supposed to be a "season of joy" *(zeman simhateinu)*. But even during such a happy time, it seems natural that intimations of finitude and vulnerability frequently come to mind.

Historians of Judaism report that Sukkot was once a major holiday, as important as Passover and Yom Kippur. At one point it was even called *ha-chag* ("the festival"). But that is hardly the case today, perhaps because as Jews became more urban, harvest festivals did not touch them so directly. It is true that some Jewish thinkers have tried recently, with some success, to position it as an ecological occasion, a time to remind ourselves of our dependence on the crops and the cycle of the seasons. It seems to me, however, that the holiday has an even deeper ecological significance, and it has to do with the very flimsiness the *sukkah* symbolizes. It is not only we as human beings who are fragile, it is the earth itself, and its fragility has become more and more evident in recent years. Resources are running out. Species are dying. The atmosphere is poisoned. The ozone layer is punctured. In this respect, human beings, animals, plants, and the great globe itself are in an identical situation. We all live together in the same teetering shack.

In recent years both Jewish and Christian theologians have been trying to rethink their traditions in light of our environmental moment of truth. So far some progress has been made, but not much. The reformulation must go much deeper. We need to rethink the relationship of humankind to the animals, the plants and soil, what is now sometimes called otherkind. When one studies these attempts, it becomes clear that Christian theology has a lot to learn from Judaism in this matter. It is true that Jesus taught his disciples to pray for the Kingdom of God to come *on earth*. Still, the New Testament has a certain tendency to look beyond and above the earth to the fulfillment of history in a world beyond history. This is due in part to the apocalyptic religious milieu in which it was written, because the apocalyptic mentality often denigrates this world in favor of some other one. Christianity needs Judaism to keep it anchored in the soil of this world. But Jewish thinkers also have work to do. The truth is that as the environmental plight deepens, both traditions are caught in the grip of a common theological morass. Both need to disentangle the web of religious and cultural premises that have contributed to pushing us ever closer to planetary and species disaster.

The first issue that both Judaism and Christianity must now think through concerns the relationship of the human species to the plants and animals, and the minerals, with whom and with which we share the earth. The historian Lynn White, Jr., in his famous essay "The Historical Roots of Our Ecological Crisis," first published in 1967, charged Christianity (and indirectly Judaism) with what he termed "a huge burden of guilt" for creating and perpetuating a cluster of religious beliefs that place God outside nature, exalt man over the animals and plants, and teach that creation and everything in it exist primarily to serve the needs of man.[2] In such a worldview, White pointed out, there appears to be no religious restraint on digging up, paving over, and despoiling the earth or on devouring resources as fast as human beings feel they need them. It is a devastating criticism, and not an easy one to answer. Indeed, one of the most beautiful passages in the Bible, Psalm 8, cherished by both Jews and Christians, seems to confirm White's indictment. It begins:

O Lord, our Lord,
How excellent is thy name in all the earth!
Thou whose glory above the heavens is chanted
By the mouths of babes and infants.

It then goes on to pose the very question that concerned White and that worries ecologists today: What is the right relationship between humankind and otherkind?

> When I look at the heavens, the work of thy fingers,
> The moon and the stars which thou hast established;
> What is man that thou art mindful of him
> And the son of man that thou dost care for him?

Few people have looked up into a starry night and not wondered about this, even if they never heard the psalm and do not phrase their awe and bafflement as a question to God. We humans seem so puny. What significance can we possibly have in this vast terrain of stars and space?

The psalmist's answer has comforted many generations of Jews and Christians. But it concerns ecologists like White, and it troubles a growing host of Jews and Christians today.

> Yet thou hast made him little less than God,
> And dost crown him with glory and honor.
> Thou hast given him dominion over the works of thy hands;
> thou hast put all things under his feet,
> all sheep and oxen,
> and also the beasts of the field,
> the birds of the air, and the fish of the sea,
> Whatever passes through the paths of the sea.

Here the psalmist not only places man at the pinnacle of God's creation but defines the human relationship to the creatures as one of what the military now calls command and control ("dominion"). I appreciate the exalted position in which this psalm places human life. It could serve as an elemental text for human rights. But in its depiction of the relationship between human beings and animals, there are other possibilities. Man might have been placed in a special position, then encouraged to love and live amid his fellow creatures. Instead, he is not only enthroned far above the animals, whether wild or domesticated, he is also expected to rule over them, like a king over his subjects. No commonwealth of creatures here: this is monarchy in its most severe form.

From its earliest years, Christian theology absorbed this man-on-top pattern and succeeded mainly in making it worse. Origen (185?–254?), who is often considered the first Christian theologian, saw the whole cosmos as an immense hierarchy, a "great chain of being." At its summit is God, who is pure and perfect spirit. Below God are the angelic beings, who are also spirit but not always totally pure. Under them comes man, a spirit trapped in a material body. Below him are the animals and plants, who have bodies but no spirits. Farther down are the rocks and minerals. It is a tidy picture, but it drives the wedge between human and other forms of life even deeper than the psalmist does. Saint Augustine (354–430), the single most influential theologian in Christian history, builds on Origen and puts special emphasis on the sharp dichotomy between soul and body, which for him formed the frontier of a battle to the death. The body, prodded by passions, fights an endless war of attrition against the soul. His thought became the dominant influence throughout medieval Christianity and was not seriously challenged, at least not on this point, by the Protestant reformers. Only here and there in the course of those centuries was the basic model questioned, and not until the twentieth century was it fundamentally challenged — mainly by liberation theologians and feminists. Still, though battered and buffeted, it remains the dominant view among many Christian theologians even today.

However, the vertical stepladder view of the human relationship to God and the other creatures that we saw in Psalm 8 is not the only one in the Bible. Only a few pages later, in Psalm 104, for example, a wholly different picture is painted. Here, in sharp distinction, humankind is placed *among* the other creatures without a scepter in its hand. This psalm portrays a God who has fashioned trees so that the storks have a place to build their nests, high mountains so the wild goats can clamber, and rocks for the badgers to hide behind (17, 18). Man is, so far, nowhere in sight. The psalm then continues its nonanthropocentric vision as follows:

> Thou makest the darkness, and it is Night
> when all the beasts of the forest crawl forth.
> The young lions roar for their prey,
> Seeking their food from God.
> When the sun rises, they get them away

And lie down in their dens.
Man goes forth to his work
And to his labor until the evening (20–23).

"These all look to thee," the psalm goes on to say, meaning both man and the animals, and when God hides his face, both man and beast suffer equally. Finally, when God takes away their breath, they all die "and return to the dust." Here we have a far more egalitarian, nonhierarchical portrait of humankind and otherkind. Not only are all the creatures equal, but none is more equal than the others.

The same tension between markedly variant answers to the persistent human question posed by Psalm 8 can be found in the two widely differing accounts of creation preserved in the Book of Genesis. In the first, recorded in Genesis 1, God creates humankind (and only humankind), male and female, "in his own image," and then says to them, "Be fruitful and multiply, and fill the earth and subdue it; and have dominion over the fish of the sea and over the birds of the air and over every living thing that moves upon the face of the earth" (1:27, 28).

The Hebrew Bible scholar Theodore Hiebert has pointed out that the words for "dominion" and "subdue" used here are not gentle ones. The word *rada* ("have dominion") means "to exercise power," and it is often used elsewhere in the Bible to describe how the kings of Israel are to treat enemies they have defeated in battle. Indeed, as Hiebert reports, "[I]t occurs in descriptions of military conquest, where it is paired with such verbs as 'destroy' (Numbers 24:19) and 'strike down' (Isaiah 14:6)." If anything, the word *kabas* ("subdue") is even more violent. It is also associated with military conquest and to "depict the destruction and occupation of conquered territory (Numbers 32:22, 29). In Jeremiah, the same word is used to describe the enslavement of foreign peoples (which God forbids), and in Esther it is used for rape.[3]

None of this is good news, and if Lynn White had been aware of these texts when he wrote his historic essay, his indictment could have been even more stinging. But, once again, this is not the only account of creation or of humankind's relationship to the rest of the earthly community we have in the Bible. In the second chapter of Genesis, a somewhat different story appears. Here God creates human beings from the same topsoil (*'adama*) from which he fashions the animals. Both the humans and the animals receive the breath of God, which gives them life, and all of them alike are called "living beings" *(nepes hayya)*. Unfortunately, this kinship of human beings and animals has been obscured by a long tradition of interpretation which either calls the animals "living creatures" and the humans "living souls" (in the King James Version) or "living creature" for the animals and "living being" for the human. This, even though they all translate from the same Hebrew word.[4] It is truly remarkable how, after centuries of assuming that man is not only above but must conquer, subdue, and rule the rest of creation, even trained linguistic scholars cannot set aside these prejudices long enough to tell the rest of us, who must rely on their expertise, what the text actually says.

It would be a mistake to discard the first creation story and keep only the second. Both are part of our tradition, and the first one undergirds the conviction that all people are created by God, and are therefore children of God, even before God begins making any covenants. But in the light of our impending ecological debacle, today's thoughtful reader of these texts must ask at least two questions. First, how could two quite different stories of creation, with such radically divergent views of a question that has become so central to us, coexist for so long in the same religious tradition? And second, why did the first view I described — typified by the man-over-beast motif of Psalm 8 and the first creation narrative — become the dominant interpretation, and why has it maintained that position for so long?

In answering these questions, there is no way of avoiding an analysis of where and how these radically different perspectives — at least as portrayed in Genesis — came into existence and became part of the Bible. It has long been agreed by most scholars that the first story, called the priestly account (though based on earlier myths), received its final form during what is known as the Persian period of Israelite history. In this period the Israelites, under the sponsorship of the Persian king Cyrus, returned from Babylonian captivity. The Jewish priests were closely aligned with the monarchy and assumed an important role in both political and religious leadership. The priestly account bears the clear mark of the superior status of the priestly class in the Hebrew society of the time. It casts "man" in the same powerful and prestigious position over animals and nature that the priests exercised over the people. In doing so, it adds sacral legitimation to the priestly rank and the priestly office. It is an account told by the people on top, and it therefore paints a top-down picture.

The second version is called the Yahwist account because of the name it uses for God, Yahweh, usually translated as "Lord" in English. According to Hiebert, this version is told, not from a priestly perspective, but from that of a farmer, and reflects the kind of life peasants lived in the eastern Mediterranean world in that era. Here God has created human beings not in the priestly image but in that of the average Israelite. He and she are farmers who know they have to depend on the earth and on their fellow creatures rather than exalt themselves over them. Hiebert puts the contrast in very stark terms as inverse images of each other. The priestly writer, he says,

> views the human, created alone in God's image, as distinct from other forms of life, while the Yahwist views the human, made like the animals from the arable soil, as related to other forms of life. The priestly writer views the human as master of the earth, while the Yahwist views the human as its servant. For the priestly writer, the human vocation is one of dominion and supervision. For the Yahwist, the human vocation is one of dependence and service.[5]

Hiebert's painstaking linguistic work may help us answer both of the questions I posed. First, we have two versions of the human-animal-nature nexus because the editors who assembled the collection we now call the Bible were reluctant to come down squarely on one side or the other. But second, the reason that the priestly domination story has reigned for so long is that the interpretation of the Bible itself has almost always been in elite hands, and this version makes elites more secure and comfortable in their own power. It has only been in recent years, as non-elite interpreters such as women, poor people, and minority groups have challenged these prevailing interpretations, that the alternative one has become more visible. At the same time, our ecological plight has now made the question of the relationship of humans to the rest of creation a far more urgent one, and we obviously need new answers.

This suggests that both Jews and Christians need to reconfigure some well-established patterns of thought if both humankind and otherkind, and the earth that sustains both, are to survive the many-faceted crunch some scientists now predict for about 2040. In order to survive, we, the human element of the team, will have to make some fundamental changes in our thinking and living before it is too late. Such basic ideas as what we mean by sin and salvation, and our images of God, need to be reformulated. For example, for many centuries, especially among Christians, the story of Adam and Eve and the Fall has been interpreted in terms of human disobedience. Eve, followed by Adam, did what God forbade them to do and were punished by mortality ("You shall surely die") and expulsion from the Garden of Eden. But this interpretation obviously carries with it both the attitude of the Hebrew writers who told the story and — more important — of the Christian priests and theologians who, for centuries, tried to use the Bible to instill unquestioning obedience into the lower classes (not always with complete success, it should be added, since the Bible is also replete with stories of rebellion and insubordination). A more careful reading reveals that Adam and Eve are not meant to refer to some ancient couple clothed in fig leaves but to us. And their "sin" is not primarily disobedience but their vain attempt to escape vulnerability and mortality: "And the serpent said . . . You will not die. For God knows that when you eat of the fruits, your eyes will be open and you shall be like God" (Genesis 3:4). Understood in this light, the whole of human history can be seen as the futile attempt, led in the main by warrior-kings, priest-kings, and their current descendants in the corridors of power, to escape from the inevitable vulnerability and finitude of the human condition. In doing so, they have created not only stone pyramids in their unavailing endeavor but social and religious pyramids, in which they installed themselves at the top and consigned most of humankind and otherkind to the lower tiers. Women and slaves were at the bottom, and the earth itself was under them.

But just as dominated and outcast peoples have often tried to revolt from this pyramidal social architecture, in recent decades it seems that the earth itself has entered into the revolt. The measurable warming of the oceans, unprecedented and destructive weather patterns, and a new generation of environmentally generated diseases all remind us how urgent these issues have become. The religious patterns that have shored up the pyramids in a futile attempt to secure invulnerability and immortality for those at the top are wobbling. We learn every day, not just during Sukkot and on Ash Wednesday, that there is no escaping who we are: feeble creatures on a fragile planet, sharing our frail lives not only with the other creatures and plants but with the earth itself, which is also small and mortal. But the good news (the season of rejoicing) aspect of Sukkot is that, despite the ramshackle vulnerability of our situation, we can sing and laugh and share lemonade and sandwiches with one another. We need not permit the awareness of our exposed human condition to make us dejected and morose. It is the very transience of human life (and of all life) that is the greatest cause for joy.

That the recognition of evanescence is essential to beauty bore in on me most forcefully when I was visiting Japan just when the cherry blossoms appeared. As most people know, these delicate buds last only a few short days, then they fade and are gone until the following year. Weather and horticultural experts in Japan watch carefully and inform the populace when the eagerly anticipated day will come. At that time, everything stops. Offices empty. Stores close. People pack lunches and bottles of *saki* and gather in parks and fields. They sing, drink, and eat. Often they also cry. It is precisely the impermanence of the delicate blossoms that gives them their special meaning. For the Japanese, they are a powerful symbol of life itself.

Among Christian theologians, Rosemary Radford Ruether and Ivonne Gebara[6] have drawn attention to the immense task of reconfiguring Christian theology and practice that lies before us. It is not surprising that women theologians came to this insight before anyone else. Women have been the special target of the pyramid builders because they stand as a constant and awkward reminder of the earthbound and finite character of all life. We are all born of women, and in most traditional societies women care for the dying and prepare the dead for cremation or burial. The strategy of the priest-rulers was to demote women to a lower status. They were often identified with the body and the passions while men were equated with mind and spirit. And of course mind must rule over body, and spirit must control passions. The paradigm both established male domination over women and nature and envisioned the eventual escape of the mind or soul to a realm of pure spiritual essences untroubled by the cloying messiness of earth, bodies, and sexuality.

Gebara's intuition of the scope of the needed reconfiguration is acute and far-reaching. It also has enormous ramifications for the relationship between Judaism and Christianity. She questions what she calls the messianic myth itself as little more than the image of the warrior god seen, as it were, from the perspective of the victim. It expresses the desperate hope that the powerful dominator and great subduer will come back to save those who are now dominated and subdued. It is based on fantasy and hope and tinged with a desire for revenge. The day will come, it declares, when one of insuperable power, like the "black ship" in Brecht's song "Pirate Jenny," will "pull into the harbor" to rescue those who are now suffering and wreak retribution on their tormentors. When the fantasy becomes a hope, something like a messiah is first longed for, then expected and anticipated.

This brings us to the long-standing disagreement between Jews and Christians about whether Jesus was "the" or even "a" messiah. Jews rightly point out that the messiah their ancestors expected was supposed to end suffering, war, and tyranny. But since these evils continue to scar the world, Jesus was obviously not the Expected One. He was a false, or at best a failed, messiah, and the true one is still to come. Christians often respond by saying that Jesus was a different kind of messiah, one who came in weakness and defeat. Then, however, they often add that one day he will "come again" and deliver the goods as they were originally expected, including rescue and revenge.

Gebara rejects both interpretations. She claims that Jesus refused to perpetuate the warrior-messiah myth, that he called, instead, for those in power to accept a new and reciprocal relationship to their fellow creatures. This was not a message that rulers who had drunk deeply of the cup of "dominate and subdue" could accept. So they rejected him. Up to this point many Christians would agree with Gebara. But then she says that after his death, his followers — who had already betrayed and abandoned him in his lifetime — continued their behavior. They too ignored his message and transformed him into yet another warrior-messiah who would one day come again and enact the very scenario he had spurned. But Gebara challenges the idea of a triumphal "second coming." Neither a false nor a failed messiah, Jesus, she believes, called the whole "messianic myth" into question.

If Gebara is right, both Jews and Christians could look once again at our different long-standing ideas of a messiah. This in turn could move us all toward the reconstruction of the religious idiom that our ecological blind alley requires. If God is not somewhere far off in a spiritual realm, waiting for things to get bad enough before intervening, then it does not really matter if we are talking about a first or second (or third or tenth) "coming." We are concerned rather with a Holy Presence that will not save us from either our fragility or our vulnerability or deliver us from our finitude or our mortality. These are all simply part of the human condition, and we try to escape from them at our peril. Rather this Holy Presence, whose heart is revealed to us by the prophets and Jesus, and by many others, already dwells in our midst as Emmanuel ("God with us"), beckoning us toward a planetary existence marked by mutuality rather than domination. Once the "lordship" of men over women, one race over another, and humans over otherkind and the earth is broken, we can become, as Ruether eloquently puts it, "a community of shared joys and sorrows as earth creatures, former Pharisees and prostitutes, the lame and the blind, women and men on the edges of the dominant system breaking bread together."[7]

But this analysis also forces us to ask a question that is singularly appropriate for Sukkot. In view of the crisis that our species and all others now face in the fragile little *sukkah* we call the earth, have Jews and Christians been arguing about the wrong question? Could we shelve, or redefine, the vexed question of who was, or was not, or might one day be, the messiah? There are already hints that we may be able to. Scholars in both traditions remind us that the idea of a messianic era, an age of *shalom*, historically preceded the idea of a *shalom*-bringer in Jewish thought. Some rabbis have suggested that the entire Jewish people have a nonviolent messianic mission to accomplish. Others suggest that the "coming" will occur when the work of "repairing" the world, what Jews call *tikkun*, brings all human beings together into a just community of *shalom*. One Hasidic rebbe even told his disciples, in one of my favorite interpretations, that the messiah will come only when we no longer need him. Christian thinkers for centuries have also questioned the literal meaning of the Second Coming. It plays no role in the Gospel of John, in which Jesus, at his death, transmits his Spirit to his disciples. Consequently, the Spirit that was in Jesus continues to be present. Christian mystics have often translated the symbol of the Second Coming as a reminder that although the Holy is present with us here and now, the cosmic process is still incomplete. Something else needs to happen to complete the drama.

Both Jews and Christians have resources that allow all of us to move on to another level of our old conversation. We are now ready to ask ourselves a question that is equally basic and equally urgent for both traditions. Hunkered down as we are in this flimsy little shack, sipping lemonade as the stars blink through the slats, we have become painfully aware of how badly things are going for the wounded earth we sit on and the fractured sky we glimpse above. Do we really hope or expect that someday Someone will swoop down and save us from it all? Or must we listen to a Voice that says, "What are you waiting for? Just as in the harvest of old, I have created the conditions that have allowed your seeds to sprout and your grain to ripen, I have already done my part, and will continue to do it. But as for the harvesting itself, that is up to you." Neglected as it sometimes now is, Sukkot — given the ecological deadline we face — should become a much more important holiday. Maybe it should even become "*the festival*" again.

5

Gamboling with God

Simhat Torah

Let the Torah never be for you an antiquated decree, but rather like a decree freshly issued, no more than two or three days old. . . . But Ben Azzai said: Not even as old as a decree issued two or three days ago, but as a decree issued this very day.

— *Peskita* of Rab Kahana, piska 12:12[1]

I T IS A COOL New England autumn evening. Black-and-yellow-striped police barriers have closed off traffic on Tremont Street in Cambridge. No wonder. In front of the old Tremont Street shul, a Conservative synagogue just off the avenue that connects Harvard with MIT, the road is jammed with two hundred people, young and old, whirling and jumping and holding hands in serpentine circles to the beat of blaring Klezmer music. It is the holiday when Jews act most like Pentecostals. But look again. Scattered here and there, some of the prancers are hugging large, rolled-up scrolls encased in silk covers. On this night Jews dance with the Torah — sometimes into the wee hours — in near-euphoria to thank God for the gift of the Law.

The Hebrew words "simhat torah" mean "the rejoicing of the Torah." The holiday comes just after the completion of the eight days of Sukkot and marks the end of the annual reading of the Torah (the first five books of the Bible). The service on Simhat Torah begins inside the synagogue with the reading of the last chapters of Deuteronomy, the last of the five books of Moses, thus completing the cycle.

To celebrate the event, a procession with the scrolls snakes up and down the aisles, becomes more and more energized, and then, in many synagogues, spills out into the street.

Simhat Torah is one of the Jewish holidays I relish the most, and not just because I enjoy street parties and Klezmer music. It is a holiday in which I catch a glimpse of something utterly fundamental to Judaism and realize how many of my stereotypes about "legalistic" Judaism have to be discarded. Simhat Torah also offers a splendid example of how my growing understanding of Judaism has helped enhance my appreciation for important elements of my own faith.

It takes a while to dawn on Christians that for Jews the Law is not a burden, a hindrance, or an obstacle to living a fully human and vitally spiritual life. The Law (Torah) is a condition of being human. It is a generous gift which God bestows on his people simply out of love. But there is little wonder that many Christians have difficulty with this concept. It is true that Jesus says he has not come to change even one "jot or tittle" of the Law; yet he also frequently says, "You have heard it said of old . . . , but I say unto you. . . ." The Gospels often portray him debating with the scribes and pharisees, the scholars who interpreted the Law in his day, but Christians are often unaware that these were not debates about the validity of the Law itself. They were arguments, often spirited ones, on how the Law was to be applied. Much Christian Sunday school material still wrongly suggests that while Judaism is a severe religion of the Law, Christianity is the religion of love, but this is an uninformed and erroneous comparison. So here I am, whirling in a circle with my wife and son, and what appear to be hundreds of other people, to celebrate God's gift of the Law.

I have not just been swept up in the heady exhilaration of the trombones, clarinets, and gyrating bodies. It is true that at first I took part in this holiday mainly out of curiosity and familial loyalty. But now I have come to the conclusion that most Christian theology has unnecessarily given the Law a bad name (not helped, perhaps, by the low estate to which lawyers have slipped in today's popular jokes). A more accurate grasp of the enormous but subtle significance of the Law in Judaism is the first and indispensable step Christians must take to end some of the suspicion and hostility that have divided the two communities. The Torah is utterly pivotal to traditional rabbinic Judaism, and it also plays a beguiling role in the mystical and esoteric tradition of Kabbalistic Judaism, in which God is envisioned consulting the Torah before creating the world. I am convinced that the false opposition that has often been set up by Christian theology between Law on the one hand and Gospel on the other is still one of the principal hindrances to dialogue and reconciliation. I only wish that those Christians who still picture Judaism as the image of a bent and burdened figure crushed into a slump by the excessive weight of the Law could spend one evening at a Simhat Torah street whirl. These buoyant dancers are anything but bowed down. They seem to be soaring.

One source of much Christian understanding is that we have rarely, if ever, heard that the Torah "speaks in two voices." Every informed Jew knows that there is not only the written Torah. There is also, and of equal importance, the oral Torah, the accumulated history of centuries of rabbinical interpretation and application of the written Torah. The Torah is not just a scroll. It is not just the tablets that, according to the biblical account, God gave to Moses on Mount Sinai. The Torah is a lively, continuing conversation, still going on at this moment.[2] When a Christian comes to understand this (and not many do), it is hard not to think of an obvious analogy. The Torah is not only like Christ, the physical presence of God among the people; it is also a bit like what Christians say about the Holy Spirit. It is God's spiritual presence in the midst of his people today, teaching, sustaining, and inspiring.

I think I am a little closer today to understanding the significance of Torah to Jews than I once was. But my head was not originally turned by reading books and articles. It happened in an unexpected and memorable episode that took place at the B'nai Jeshurun synagogue just a few years after Nina and I were married. B'nai Jeshurun is a conservative congregation on the Upper West Side of New York City, not far from where Nina grew up. At that time a new rabbi assumed the leadership of the synagogue who, by chance, I already happened to know, Marshall Meyer. I had met him many years earlier in Buenos Aires, where he had spent much of his career serving a Jewish congregation and leading a seminary. When the military regime came to power in Argentina, he quickly became one of its most fearless and outspoken opponents. Jacob Timerman later dedicated his moving testimony, *Prisoner Without a Name, Cell Without a Number*, to Meyer, "a rabbi who brought comfort to Jewish, Christian and atheist prisoners in Argentine jails."[3] When Marshall came to New York, he and I renewed our acquaintance and quickly became fast friends. A few years later, I arranged for him to continue his research and do some teaching with me at Harvard. But it was long before that, during the first year of his service at B'nai Jeshurun, that my most formative encounter with Torah took place.

Whenever we visited Nina's family, we made it our custom to attend a Friday evening or Saturday morning service at B'nai Jeshurun. It was always enlivening. A congregation that had been declining fast was, under Marshall's leadership, growing by leaps and bounds. The music, drawn in part from Rabbi Meyer's Latin American years and in part from many other sources, infused both the Hebrew and the English prayers with melodic magic.

Marshall made many changes. Instead of giving a sermon, he instituted the practice of a congregation-wide open discussion of the Torah passage of the week. After it was read and Marshall made a brief commentary, ushers roamed the aisles with portable microphones while anyone who had anything to say about the text was invited to speak up. Many people did, and every time we were there, an animated discussion brought even the most obscure passage to life. People puzzled over what it could possibly mean, chewed on it, agreed with it, and disagreed with it. They often spoke about how a text did or did not intersect their lives as active New Yorkers. Marshall handled what might have become pandemonium with diplomacy and tact. Whatever else those discussions proved, they demonstrated that Torah is anything but a fossil, a code of outmoded regulations rolled up in a fancy scroll. This was the living Torah at its liveliest.

But, interestingly, my moment of truth did not come during the discussion. At every service, the Torah scroll is reverently removed from its place in the ark at the front of the synagogue and carried in procession up and down the aisles. The worshipers reach out and touch it with their prayer books or the corners of their prayer shawls. I was always impressed by this display of reverence for the scroll and what it stands for. Then, one Saturday morning, just before the procession began, Marshall beckoned me to come forward to where he was standing. When the Torah was removed from the ark, without saying a word he held it out to me and indicated that I was to bear it around the synagogue. I was nearly overwhelmed, not just with surprise but with a powerful sense of affection for him, for the congregation, and for this precious scroll I was cradling. As people reached out to touch it with their prayer shawls and books, I could sense their heartfelt attachment to it and to the millennia of history and tradition it symbolized. In the first century C.E., the Roman governor Apostomus publicly burned the Torah in Jerusalem to signal its extinction as the Jews were driven into exile. During the medieval period, Christians often insisted that only they could give authoritative interpretations of the scriptures, and they periodically seized Torah scrolls from Jews and burned them. The Nazis regularly desecrated Torah scrolls, sometimes pouring filth and refuse on them.

Still, here I was, a gentile and a Christian, granted the privilege of carrying this sacred scroll while the Jews in B'nai Jeshurun caressed it. It is a moment I will never forget, and when I eventually returned to my seat, I knew that my attitude toward Torah could never be the same again. As Abraham Joshua Heschel says, I had an experience of awe and wonder, and it was now inextricably fused with the scroll of the Torah. I later learned that I was not the first non-Jew to have this privilege. It happens rarely, but on occasion, that a special guest or visitor can be asked by the leaders of the synagogue to carry the Torah in procession. For a short time afterward I was annoyed at Marshall for not at least warning me that it was going to happen. But I have since changed my mind about that. First of all, Marshall Meyer was a famously impulsive person whose impulses were almost always right. This one — at least for me — was certainly right. Also, if I had been warned (or even invited), I might have steeled myself and could even have slipped into a pose. I might have acted out the "honored guest carries Torah" scenario. But because of Marshall's impetuosity (or was it calculation?), I had no time for that, which made the experience even fresher and more compelling.

However, I soon came to realize that even an indelible encounter with a Torah scroll was not enough to change my intellectual understanding of the Torah itself; so I began to read both the Jewish editions, with their commentaries on it, and articles written by Jews about the meaning of the Torah in Jewish life. I found many useful sources. The most informative, however, was a chapter entitled "The Joy of Torah" in a book by Rabbi David Hartman. I had met Rabbi Hartman during one of my visits to Jerusalem, where he heads a study and research center (the Shalom Hartman Institute) named for his father, which is dedicated to trying to develop the classical Orthodox Jewish tradition and its relationship to religious pluralism and contemporary life. Hartman's ideas are important for the current Jewish-Christian conversation because, as Christians finally become a little more familiar with Jewish thought, some respond more favorably to the Judaism of Martin Buber and the more effervescent, mystical Hasidic tradition of the Baal Shem Tov. For some Christians, these Jewish masters seem to lack the "legalism" they expect in Judaism. This was certainly true of me in my earlier years, and I have met many Christians, including scholars, who have never read any Jewish thinker but Martin Buber.

David Hartman's writings demonstrate what they have been missing. An Orthodox rabbi, he shows how a spiritual life based on studying and trying to follow *halakah,* the law that is derived from the study of the Torah, can also be joyful. Furthermore, he is a daring thinker. He holds that God himself is learning from his experience with human beings. Although Adam and Eve may have been created to be perfect and placed in a paradise, it quickly became evident that God had been a bit unrealistic in imagining that they would stay that way. It was clear that they would need some help, lots of help in fact, given their inclination to self-centeredness and their hankering to "become as god," which they immediately displayed. True, it was God's first inclination to wipe the slate clean, go back to the drawing board, and start over, possibly with a new design. He came close to doing so in the story of Noah and the great deluge. But then God, having learned something from his experience, decided on another tactic. God gave humanity the Torah, which might be thought of as a gift of love for an imperfect — all too human — people.[4]

The gift of Torah suggests that God is becoming a realist, no longer expecting perfection, but seeing us human beings as we are, a mixture of good and evil inclinations and impulses with both attractive and distinctly unattractive features. The great experiment of creating a truly free being who would return God's love and would love his and her fellow creatures was not a complete failure. But it was not turning out as well as God had apparently anticipated. The Torah is an expression of love, not of romantic indulgence or sentimental self-delusion. It is the kind of love that sometimes eventually ripens between parents and children, and between spouses when they become aware of each other's faults and limitations, but do not stop loving. Rather, their love deepens into a more mature kind, one that takes the reality — rather than the idealized image — of the loved one into consideration. Living with the Law, therefore, for Hartman, is "inherently related to the joy of feeling accepted and confirmed by God. Not only are realism and responsibility not antithetical to love and joy, they are their very grounds."[5]

Nothing in Rabbi Hartman's chapter on the joy of Torah suggests that he is searching for correlations to Christianity. But I could not help noticing some, especially in his discussion of the relationship of the divine to the human. It has often been said, by Christians and Jews alike, that Jews recoil from what appears to be a mixture of the human and the divine in the Christian understanding of Jesus. He was, according to classical Christian teaching, both fully man and fully God. But is this really such an impossible thought? Hartman, discussing what he calls "the experience of the love of God" that is characteristic of the "halakic way of life," inspired and based on Torah, says that here "the distinction between what is the Word of God and what is humanly derived loses all significance."[6] This claim is at least reminiscent, if not almost identical, to what Christians say about Jesus. It is not that part of him is divine and part human. In him these two seemingly incommensurable elements meet in such a way that making the distinction "loses all significance." Later, when describing Torah, Hartman says, "The Word that mediates divine love becomes integrated with the human response."[7] I see here a clear parallel to at least one classical Christian explanation of how Jesus could be thought of as "divine," namely, that he became the complete human receptor of God's love, the one who, more than any other person we know, was so totally open to God's love that he became its bearer and its vehicle.

Even when Hartman discusses what he describes as the legal minutiae of the endless rabbinical arguments about the meaning of the Law for everyday life, he reveals — perhaps unintentionally — further parallels. Why is the Torah full of so many discussions of what we do when someone's ox gores someone else's, or when a fungus growth appears on the wall of a house, or where one may safely defecate? These seemingly humdrum affairs are all discussed by the rabbis in the Talmud and elsewhere. But why are they in the sacred books? Because, Hartman says, they all have to do with "a God who is involved in the world of ordinary human beings." This is exactly what Christians say about Jesus. Even the tempestuous discussions that have sometimes raged between Christians and Jews fade several decibels for me when Hartman cites a certain Rab Kahana. It seems that this legendary rabbi wanted to assure his students that although God appears at different times in history and in different roles, it is indeed one and the same God. Speaking for God, Rab Kahana says, "Come to no false conclusions because you see Me in many guises, for I am He who was with you at Sinai: I am the Lord thy God."[8]

Jews and Christians could ponder for a long time how much this statement of Rab Kahana about the different "guises" in which God appears resembles Christian language about the Trinity. Personally, I do not think the two are all that far apart. When Rab Kahana's Jewish pupils began to wonder whether all these different manifestations of God — as Creator, Redeemer, Lawgiver, Teacher of Wisdom — could be of the same God, he reassured them that they were. The idea of the Trinity arose from a similar puzzlement for the early Christians over their experience of the different faces of God. The Trinity is described as "one God in three persons," understandably causing Jews (and many Christians) to wonder whether monotheism was being endangered. But Paul Tillich explains that this is not really the case. The Greek *persona*, first used by the early Christian theologian Tertullian (c. 160–c. 230) to describe the different faces of God, does not mean the same as "person" does now. Today the word stands for a human being who can reason and decide. "Such a concept of person," Tillich says, was not applied to the three ways God had been experienced, the three *hypostases* in God. He continues: "*Persona*, like the Greek word *prosopon*, is the mask of the actor through which a special character is acted out. Thus we have three faces, three countenances, three characteristic expressions of the divine self-explication."[9]

In light of this clarification, it is not so difficult to imagine how the early Christians hit on the idea of the Trinity. They believed God had created the world, called Israel, given the Ten Commandments on Sinai, and spoken through the prophets. But they also believed they had met the same God in the person of the rabbi from Nazareth, and they still felt his Spirit to be alive in their midst even after his death by torture under the Romans. Was this really the same God? Their answer was phrased in the metaphorical language of theater masks, through which one actor could play different roles. But it could just as easily have been expressed in the words of Rab Kahana: "Come to no false conclusions because you see me in many guises . . . I am the Lord thy God."

Discovering these parallels has convinced me that the Trinitarian language nearly all Christians use to describe God need not pose an insurmountable barrier between Christians and Jews. Rab Kahana with his "guises" and Tertullian with his *personae*, had they ever met, would have had many issues to disagree about, but that the one God has many "faces" would have been acceptable to both.

But what about the alleged opposition between Law and Gospel? How big an obstacle is that? Usually the responsibility for inventing the opposition is laid at the feet of Saint Paul, and there are indeed parts of some of his writings that could be read to support such an opposition. In recent years, however, scholars who investigate Saint Paul have suggested a more fruitful way to understand him. The newer approach — although it does not resolve all the difficulties — at least throws into question some of the harsh opposition between Law and Grace which characterized the old one. This important shift in Pauline studies was largely begun by E. P. Sanders twenty years ago and has won wide acceptance since then.[10] It suggests that throughout the whole of Saint Paul's adult life — both before and after his experience on the Damascus Road — his driving motivation was twofold. First, he wanted to convince gentiles to become a part of the Commonwealth of Israel and therefore to escape the inevitable approaching judgment of God, which he believed would not be long in coming. Second, he wanted to convince Jews that the time for gentiles to be welcomed into the household of Israel, long foreseen by the Hebrew prophets, had now come. There is indeed some evidence that Paul (who in his earlier years called himself Saul) had this dream even before his famous mystical confrontation with Christ. This encounter has usually been referred to as the "conversion" of Saint Paul. But that is hardly the right word for it. It was more a "calling" than a "conversion." Paul never stopped thinking of himself as a Jew, a Hebrew, and a pharisee; he continued to take fierce pride in this heritage. But like earlier Hebrew prophets, he now believed God had sent him on a specific prophetic mission, like Jeremiah's or Jonah's. What had changed in his mind was the means by which this ingathering of the gentiles should proceed. Before his Damascus road vision, the only way he could see its happening was by the gentiles undergoing a ritual purification bath and circumcision and endeavoring to study and observe the Law. Now, however, God — by enlarging the covenant through Jesus — had made it possible for gentiles to become a part of Israel without a "circumcision of the flesh." What was now required was a "circumcision of the heart." He still expected Jews to be circumcised, and gentiles were expected to observe the moral laws of the Torah but not its ritual requirements, such as keeping kosher. Through Jesus, gentiles could begin worshiping and serving the God of Israel without any prerequisites. In other words, it was not — as I sometimes heard in my seminary training — justification by faith versus the Law that was the central impulse of Paul's theology. This is a partial reading of Saint Paul, which Luther, who had his own peculiar agenda, passed on to almost all subsequent Protestant theology. But it turns out to be misleading. Rather than faith versus law, the pivotal point for Saint Paul was the new relationship God had made possible between the people of Israel and "the nations" (gentiles).

Terence L. Donaldson, in *Paul and the Gentiles — Remapping the Apostle's World*, helps explain why the misreading of Saint Paul became so widespread. He says we have tended to generalize from specific segments in his writings. But, he adds, we should not be misled by the way Paul responds to particular situations in the early churches, at Corinth or Galatia or Philippi, where one or another of his basic teachings was being questioned.[11] In such situations, obviously anyone emphasizes a corrective element. But in these epistles Paul was putting out brushfires, not composing a coherently organized theology. Only in Romans does he try to be systematic. Therefore, what Donaldson calls Paul's convictional world must be seen as a kind of substratum under what consists mainly of ad hoc writings. This substratum begins with God the creator of all humanity, then includes the calling of Israel and the gift of Torah, and goes on to the special role of Jesus Christ and to Paul's belief that he himself had been called by God to carry God's message to the gentiles.

But Paul's underlying motive remains the same. He knows the earlier prophets had promised a time when "the nations" would be gathered into the people of God. He believes this time has come, and he desperately wants these gentile nations to take advantage of it and to become a part of the family of Abraham. He is not calling on Jews to abandon the Law. For those who are children of Abraham "according to the flesh," the Torah continues to be authoritative. It is simply no longer the only gateway for the outsiders to enter the family circle. This is why he is so adament that gentiles have absolutely nothing to boast about. God has made this adoption possible solely because he loves the gentiles as well as the Jews, not to reward them for something they have done. In short, until the final culmination of history, which Paul believed — at least in some of his many changing moods — is not far off, Jews would continue to be Jews, and gentiles would become a part of the Covenant community through a different entrance. In short, Law is for the Jews, and Gospel is for the gentiles. God has called both into one family.

I have no illusion that the blissful young people — and some not so young — who are gamboling with God on a warm autumn night on Tremont Street know, or even care, about the intricacies of either God's many guises or the mysteries of Law and Gospel. Why should they? And as I look over the crowd I can recognize some of my non-Jewish students skipping in the circles as well. They have no doubt been invited to this frolic by their Jewish friends. They are obviously having what the younger ones would call an "awesome" evening, and if anyone ever tries to tell them that for the Jews, Torah/Law is nothing but burden, bother, and bad news, they will know that it just isn't so.

6

December Madness

Chanukah

Who can retell the things that befell us,
Who can count them?
In every age a hero or sage
Came to our aid.

— Traditional Chanukah song

I heard the bells on Christmas day
Their old familiar carols play,
And wild and sweet the words repeat,
Of "Peace on Earth, good will to men."

— Henry Wadsworth Longfellow, 1864

MENTAL HEALTH PROFESSIONALS say they always steel themselves for a sharp increase in their caseloads in mid-December. Depressed people get even more morose, and manic patients go over the top. Violent crimes surge. And, if one heeds the dire warnings directed at Jewish-Christian families, or even at Jewish families with gentile friends and neighbors, 'tis the season to be wary. Predictably, in early December of 1999 the *New York Times* dutifully alerted its devotees that "the December holidays have long been a source of angst for many dual-faith couples, and the tug is particularly acute for Christians and Jews, whose seasonal celebrations collide head-on."[1] Jewish publications begin weeks in advance to prepare their readers for the "December madness" or, more mildly phrased, the "December dilemma." In the minds of many skeptics, the lethal iceberg on which even the most secure Jewish-Christian marriage is fated to founder will surely loom out of the cold water sometime in early December. That is when the Yuletide delirium sets in, and — according to the received wisdom — it is sure to puncture the connubial hull at its most vulnerable point. I understand why the warnings are posted. But I do not believe such a crash is inevitable. In fact, if our Jewish-Christian family's experience means anything, December need not be charged with angst. Ours is not, but I admit that getting there took some doing. We start by making it very clear, to ourselves and to our friends, that Chanukah ("the Season of Lights") and Christmas ("the Feast of the Nativity") celebrate different things. When we remember that, I believe everyone in the family can appreciate both, albeit in quite different ways.

I first became aware of Chanukah decades ago when I saw the film version of *The Diary of Anne Frank* and watched, engrossed, as little Anne desperately tried to cheer up the despondent Jewish family she was hiding with in Holland by giving them each a tiny gift and leading them in a Chanukah song.

> Chanukah, oh Chanukah, come light the menorah,
> Let's have a party and we'll all dance the hora.
> Gather round the table, we'll give you a treat
> Dreidels to play with, and latkes to eat.

I had no idea at the time what Chanukah was about, only that it seemed, if only temporarily, to perk up the spirits of Jews who found themselves in a dangerous and wretched situation. Consequently I started out in our mixed marriage with a positive, if extremely vague, impression of the holiday. Later, however, when I learned something about its meaning, Chanukah became — at least for a while — the Jewish holiday I had the most trouble with.

The story told at Chanukah is a perfect example of the joke about a generic Jewish holiday. "What does it mean?" the child asks about virtually any holiday. The parent's answer is always the same: "They tried to kill us. We won. Let's eat." Chanukah, which means "dedication," has at times been called the Festival of Lights, the Feast of Consecration, and the Feast of the Maccabees. It was instituted in 165 B.C.E. by Judas Maccabeus and his brothers to consecrate the newly purified altar in the Temple in Jerusalem. It had been defiled by Antiochus Epiphanes three years earlier when, in an effort to coerce the Jews to embrace the Hellenistic culture and religion, he demanded that they offer sacrifices to the Greek deities. One day, it is said, some of the enforcers of this policy came to the Jewish village of Modi'in, set up an altar, and demanded that the Jews sacrifice a pig. However, when an elderly Jewish priest named Mattathias saw that one of the Jews was actually about to go through with this sacrilege, he became so furious that he killed him. Then he and his five sons fled to the mountains, where they began to fight what we would now call a guerrilla war against Antiochus and his Jewish allies. Although outnumbered, the Maccabees and their followers, led later by Mattathias's son Judas, managed to capture Jerusalem. When they reached the Temple, there was only one small vessel of oil to light the menorah, but it burned miraculously for eight days.

Chanukah commemorates this rededication of the Temple and the victory of the Maccabees that made it possible. Each night an additional candle is lit on the *menorah*. The holiday's most familiar symbol is this menorah, which, along with the six-pointed Star of David, is also the symbol for Judaism as such. Chanukah now lasts for eight days, and on each evening one additional candle is lit until, on the last night, all eight are blazing. But even before any candles are lit, the following traditional prayers are said: "Praised are you, Lord our God, Ruler of the universe, who has sanctified our lives through your commandments, commanding us to kindle the Chanukah lights. Praised are you, Lord our God, Ruler of the universe, Who performed miracles for our ancestors in those days, in this season."[2]

By the time I heard this prayer I had already heard the Sabbath prayers many times and had become accustomed to Jews thanking God for commandments, something Christians almost never do. But I was surprised by how much emphasis is placed on the miraculous nature of God's help. In fact, after the candles are lit, another prayer, the *ha-neirot hallalu* is recited. It begins: "We kindle these lights to commemorate the miracles, wonders, triumphs and victories which You performed through your holy priests for our ancestors in those days, in this season."[3] I noticed right away how this prayer celebrates "miracles, wonders, triumphs and victories." For a people who have indeed experienced some victories but perhaps more than their share of defeats and humiliations through the centuries, maybe this should not be surprising.

Chanukah is a superb holiday for children. On each of the eight nights each child customarily receives a present (sometimes in the form of candy money or "Chanukah *gelt*"). Children also enjoy hearing the story of the gallant Maccabees, eating potato pancakes (*latkes*), singing spirited songs, and playing games with little tops called dreidels. This may have been one of the first "educational games" in history. Each side of the dreidel is etched with a Hebrew letter, *nun, gimel, hē,* or *shin,* and the child must learn to recognize them. Together the letters form an acronym for *Neis gadol hayah sham,* "A great miracle happened there." It is interesting, and illustrates how Jewish customs change, that in Israel the letter *shin* is replaced with *peh* for the Hebrew word *poh,* meaning the miracle happened "here." To heighten the excitement, children are encouraged to stake a few coins, perhaps from their Chanukah *gelt,* on each spin. You win or lose according to which letter comes up. There was a time when the rabbis had some doubts about this custom. Was it leading the little ones into wasted lives as gamblers? Would they go on to roulette or blackjack, grow up to be croupiers? But cooler rabbinical heads eventually prevailed, and playing dreidels is now allowed, indeed encouraged.[4]

The saga of Chanukah is a gripping one, and the celebration is delightful. I can see why it cheered up Anne Frank's family. So why did I have trouble appreciating it? First, I noticed that Chanukah is also somewhat controversial among Jews. A distinctly minor holiday on the Jewish calendar, it has recently been promoted far above its traditional importance, mainly because it falls in late November or early December and can therefore more easily be mingled with Advent and Christmas into a generic "holiday season." Like many other serious Jews and Christians, I am troubled by this soggy blending of two quite distinct holidays. I am also bothered by the blurring of discrete aspects of Christianity and Judaism, which do have many common features, though this is not one of them. I sympathize with the rabbi who once told me that year after year he is invited to speak to the children in the neighborhood public school about Chanukah, although he has told the teacher repeatedly he would prefer to come in at Passover. Presumably, however, from the teacher's point of view, that talk would not mesh well with the homogenized "holiday season." Indeed it would not. And this is the whole point of Chanukah. Its underlying significance is that Judaism is a particular tradition and does not mingle well with a majority cultural religion. The events of Chanukah remind Jews every year that some of their ancestors fought to the death rather than meld their spiritual practices into the prevailing Hellenistic culture of Palestine in the second century B.C.E. It is ironical in the extreme that precisely this holiday — the one that hails Jewish resistance to assimilation — is the one that today faces the biggest risk of being lost through cultural amalgamation.

Paradoxically, the other troubling aspect about Chanukah for me arises precisely out of what it does memorialize. The real story is a little different from the storybook version I have just recounted. Here a little historical background is required. In the fourth century B.C.E., the youthful but ruthless Alexander the Great led his Greek armies in the conquest of much of Asia before, it is said, he sat down and wept because there was no more world to conquer. (This legend, alas, is probably not true.) After his death, his vast empire was divided into areas ruled over by his generals. One of his ablest commanders, Seleucus, took over Asia Minor and Syria, which then included what is now Israel. Like Alexander, Seleucus was an enthusiastic advocate of Greek ideas and ideals, a cultural package that we call hellenism. It included the building of gymnasiums, which combined physical with mental training, and Greek customs, clothing, and religious practices. Some Jews, especially from the upper classes, greeted the Hellenist wave with enthusiasm. Some of them even changed their names to ones sounding more Greek, and a few even underwent an operation that attempted to reverse their circumcision. Their attitude is not difficult to understand. Hellenism for them represented the "modern," enlightened, cosmopolitan world culture. No doubt, they also calculated that they would gain a commercial advantage by pulling their nation out of what they considered a backwater and into the mainstream of world civilization. Furthermore, Greek religion was anything but inflexible. It is doubtful that the Greeks ever wanted the Jews to abandon their own religion, only to add the gods of the Olympic pantheon.

But many other Jews — it is hard to say how many — would have none of it. They insisted they should worship only the God of their forefathers and no other gods. Pantheons may be acceptable for Greeks, but not for Jews. Therefore they were especially enraged by their fellow Jews who were assimilating. The Maccabean revolt grew out of this nasty internal split. On one side were the cosmopolitans, intent on incorporating what they saw as the advanced Hellenistic ideas. On the other side were those — also, of course, Jews — who were determined to resist them. The quarrel reached its boiling point when Antiochus, who succeeded Alexander the Great as the ruler of Syria and — like Alexander — was a devoted Hellenist, entered this domestic fray. He had already been quietly backing one Jewish faction (the "Hellenizers" or cosmopolitans) against the other. But now, perhaps responding to their urgent request, he intervened and sent troops to support them. A bloody war broke out in which the Maccabee family led the resisting Jews to what proved to be a short-term victory. They did indeed capture Jerusalem and reconsecrate the Temple. But within a remarkably short time, they became just as Hellenized and just as cosmopolitan as the people they had fought.

This is what really happened, and it is a chronicle with many lessons to teach us — among other things, about the ambiguity of power. But that is not how the story is generally told today. Instead, we mostly hear the storybook version of Chanukah. It depicts the Jews, led by the fearless Maccabee family, defending their religion against a foreign tyrant, winning — with God's help — against overwhelming odds, and reestablishing a purified Judaism. It is an inspiring story, but what is left out is that the battle was as much one between different Jewish parties as it was against the outside oppressor. We almost never hear that when the Maccabees finally captured Jerusalem and the Temple, they killed not only the Syrians but their Jewish collaborators as well. Nor do we hear that within a few generations, the grandchildren of the brave Maccabees were assimilating as fast as their ancestors' enemies had.

Jews who are aware of their history know about this ambiguous but valuable chapter, and it is not always covered up at Chanukah. I once heard a rabbi tell a largely reform and liberal group of Jews something like this: "Since we are now the ones who are making accommodations to American culture, we would have been the 'bad guys' in this historic battle. We would have been on the opposite side from the heroic Maccabees, and might well have had our throats slit along with the other 'polluters' of the Temple. You and I would all be seen as the betrayers, along with virtually all American Jews except perhaps for the Hasids in Brooklyn." But this kind of brutal honesty does not normally reign at Chanukah.

The more I learned about the real history of Chanukah and its subsequent mythological reshaping, the more uncomfortable I became with it, especially since young children — including my own child — naturally love it. Who can resist a yarn about good guys rebelling against oppressors? It is like Davy Crockett at the Alamo, except in this case the good guys won. And what child does not want to pocket a present every night for eight nights running? But I also found it hard to forget Anne Frank when I heard the catchy Chanukah song that says, "In every age a hero or sage came to our aid." No hero came to her aid, no sage. No one. Maybe it was my enduring Protestant suspicion of mere legend, but the fact that Chanukah celebrated the victory of one side, in what was in reality a civil war among Jews, troubled me. Is it any wonder that it became a holiday I was glad to see pass?

But as Chanukah approached each year I began to notice that I was being harder on it than I am on Christmas, which is also embellished with layers of mythological overlay. For years I have been able to set aside my realization that the stories in the gospels about choirs of angels, awestruck shepherds, and wise men from the East were legendary enhancements and to celebrate the underlying meaning of the holiday. Why shouldn't I grant Chanukah the same privilege? Besides, I like stories of brave dissenters myself, and the songs of Chanukah are upbeat, so I participated in it, albeit sometimes with my fingers symbolically crossed behind my back.

One day in early December, some years ago, all this changed. I confessed my discomfort about Chanukah to my friend Rabbi Marshall Meyer. Marshall told me he also had reservations about the holiday himself, but he found it a useful time to reflect on just how much any religion can accommodate to any culture. His remark rescued Chanukah for me, because the issue is one that has fascinated me for years. Not only do theologians ask this question in every age, ordinary religious people ask it in different ways day after day. No religion ever exists in a vacuum. All of them are constantly surrounded by pressures from the culture to incorporate, accommodate, assimilate. How much adjustment should be made? Religions that make no accommodation disappear, or they hang on at the margins like the Hasids of Brooklyn or the Amish in Pennsylvania (and even they make some adjustments). But religions that make too many accommodations end up disappearing into the woodwork. There is no permanent answer to this dilemma, and religions have to ask it again and again in every generation.

This helped. Now I look forward to Chanukah — the presents, the songs, and all the rest — while I seize the occasion to recognize once again how precarious any religious tradition is. All religions are caught today in the swirling currents, not now of Hellenism, but of mass media and consumer culture. I have come to savor the flickering menorah lights. They seem so tiny. They remind me of what a miracle it is that any religious tradition survives when they are all endangered species, threatened not only from without but — more subtly, and ultimately perhaps more destructively — by erosion from within.

Rabbi Meyer's explanation also prompted me to think more carefully about the remarkable ways in which vital religious traditions manage to combine continuity and change. This capacity is reflected in the changing history of their sacred writings and their holidays. During different periods, different parts of the scriptures seem to come to the fore while at other times they recede into the background, only to be retrieved again when the times require it. In Judaism, the Torah occupies center stage. The other parts of the scripture play supporting roles. But sometimes prophets like Jeremiah and Isaiah are studied just as carefully. For many Jews, the mystical Kabbalah and the Hasidic traditions faded from attention during the last century, but now, with the rebirth of interest in the element of experience in all traditions, they are being recovered and read again with enthusiasm. Similarly, there are moments in Christian history when this or that portion of the Bible, like the gospels, or the Epistles of Paul or the technicolor book of Revelation, command more attention. There are times when various sages and saints stage a comeback. Many Christians grew up hearing little about the desert fathers, the ascetics who began living in great simplicity in the Egyptian desert in the third century C.E. But now, with the increased interest in the spiritual wisdom of all the traditions, bookstores carry collections of their sayings in paperback. We also heard nothing of the German mystical nun Hildegard of Bingen (1098–1179). But with the recent dramatic rebirth of women's spirituality, her songs are available on CDs.[5]

Holidays likewise also have their ups and downs, and Chanukah is a particularly good example. Still considered a minor holiday by the rabbis, it is now more important to many Jewish families than Sukkot or Tisha B'Av. But what Jews have highlighted at Chanukah has also changed over the years. During the medieval period, when they often faced persecution for their faith, the sages emphasized its martyr stories. The moral was that it is better to die than to deny your faith. In Israel, the nationalistic aspects of the stories have received more emphasis: Jews valiantly standing up against mighty enemies to safeguard their independence. Maybe it was inevitable that in America, and with a holiday that occurs so close to Christmas, the gift-giving part of Chanukah should now become so central. Holidays and religious rituals are like that. Once they become established, people continuously infuse them with new meanings — sometimes on top of the old ones, sometimes supplanting them. Jewish teachers have suggested that the reason their prayer books are crammed with so many rituals, some of which are rarely used, is that you never know when they might come in handy. Times change, and a ritual that seemed quaintly obsolete last year may suddenly find a new valence, bringing both old and new meanings to the present situation.

The shifting shape and constantly evolving significance of holidays and rituals, in Judaism and in other faiths as well, remind us once again of the dynamic blending of continuity and change demonstrated by all living religions. Religions that never change die, but religions that adapt too quickly and thoroughly to new conditions die too as soon as those conditions change. Religions point to something eternal, but they are in part products of their times and places, so they point imperfectly. The mystics of all traditions do us a great service by reminding us that the divine infinitely transcends the words and symbols we use to describe it. A religious belief or doctrine or ritual is true only insofar as it points beyond itself. We need these pointers, but when we confuse them with the reality they are pointing to we fall into a kind of idolatry, confusing the finite with the infinite. These are the kinds of things that come to mind when we think about the meaning of the "real Chanukah," the one that is more for adults than for children. True, today's rabbis may still consider it a minor holiday. But it raises some very basic questions and should not be considered one bulb on the string of "holiday season" lights.

Chanukah is surely not the Jewish equivalent of Christmas. That, however, obviously leaves us with the question of what Christmas can mean for a mixed Jewish-Christian family and how it can be marked without merging it into the general December dilemma. The answer to this question begins, but does not end, in reminding ourselves of the inner significance of the Christmas story, which differs so dramatically from the tournament of frantic shopping and wrapping it has become. Christmas marks, after all, the birth of a Jewish child to a Jewish mother. The child first saw the light of day in a stable in a society ruled by the Roman legions with coarse brutality, and he took his first steps as a refugee in Egypt. The details of the birth stories are not trivial. They suggest that when God chose to become present in human flesh in this new way, it was not just Jewish flesh but the flesh of a displaced person.

The child grew up and, as every respectable biblical scholar now agrees, became a Torah-observing man, indeed a teacher of the Law, whose disciples called him rabbi. As one of my Jewish colleagues used to remark facetiously, "Look, for me Christmas is just one more Jewish birthday." He was, I think, half right. But for Christians it is also something more. We believe it marks the day when the intimate involvement of God in human life and history — something Jews had affirmed for centuries — took a new and decisive step, one of immense importance for Christians. Most Jews, of course, do not see it this way. But in my opinion, the way Christian theology has tried to explain this decisive step has often made the disagreement deeper than it needs to be.

Let us take, for example, the word Christian theologians have frequently used to describe this decisive new step: incarnation. The intention of the word is clear: it means the presence of God *en carne*, in human flesh. But the word can also be deceptive if it is not clearly defined. It might seem to imply that there was a time when God was not involved in the flesh, but that sometime around the beginning of the first century C.E. God suddenly became so involved. But this is misleading. "Incarnation" should not mean there have not been other manifestations of God's mysterious presence in human form, sharing our sorrows and our hopes. Nor does it mean there can never be any future embodiments of this divine-human entwinement. The Roman Catholic theologian John C. Merkle puts it very eloquently: "By its doctrine of the Incarnation, the church does not — or should not — intend to absolutize a particular manifestation of God, but to keep alive that the memory of that divine manifestation on which Christianity is based."[6] There have been other statements by Catholic authorities that differ with this interpretation. But I think Merkle is right, and I am glad he acknowledges, if only between dashes, that Christianity has too often made the claim he says it "should not" make. If we as Christians ever expect our Jewish friends and relatives to join in our celebration of Christmas, just as they invite us to participate in the celebration of Passover, for example, then there is one thing we must be clear about. We must realize that we have often made just the exclusive and absolute claim that Merkle rightly insists we should not make.

The best insight Christians ever picked up from Jews — though it is an insight frequently forgotten or neglected — is that it is wrong to turn something relative into an absolute. Only God is absolute. Therefore not even an incarnation of God is absolute. God, Christianity teaches, is present in the very marrow of human life, "closer than hands and feet." But God also transcends all divine manifestations. This is something that Jesus, as a teacher of Torah, surely believed. It makes a cruel mockery of his birth to celebrate it by denying the foundation stone of his own faith. It would be absurd for Christians who claim to have faith in Jesus to express it by a denial of the faith of Jesus. Is there anything Christians can do to rescue the Feast of the Nativity from its present degraded state as a retailer's bacchanalia, a source of pain to many Jewish families, and a cause of awkward controversy in mixed marriages? And is there anything spiritually sensitive Jews who recognize this problem can do to help?

The answer to both questions is yes. First, Christians must explain what we are celebrating and what we are not. We should firmly reject the idea that Christmas is some sort of generic holiday. We must gently insist that what we celebrate on the quite accidental date of December 25 is a birth which, when it occurred, appeared so insignificant that no public record of it has ever come to light. We celebrate the birthday of Jesus of Nazareth on a day selected by the early

Christians, while they were still suffering persecution, because it was already a pagan holiday marking the winter solstice, and the public hubbub would mask their own celebration. It has always seemed a bit odd to me, therefore, that Christians have complained about the pagan elements that emerge in mid-December. The pagans, after all, were there first.

Christmas was not widely celebrated until the fourth century, but it is now by far the most popular Christian holiday. On this day we "sing in exultation" that the same God who, through his gift of the Torah, called the Jewish people to a special role in history, has now given himself. And he has reached out and included us — "the nations," "the gentiles" — into his covenant of justice and hope. We can toast this "blessed event," whose meaning is that "to us a child is born" without for a moment denying that the same compassionate God can speak to other peoples in whatever way he chooses. For us, therefore, Christmas is a Christian festival, even though for others it may be a shopping spree or a brief season of general goodwill. I do not join those self-righteous Christians who every year roundly (and unavailingly) condemn the modern despoiling of "our holiday." The pagans, as I have said, had their mid-December fête before the Christians moved in. Why be a sanctimonious Scrooge who tries to spoil their fun? But, for Christians, I also strongly favor "putting Christ back into Christmas." And I believe that, paradoxically, the more Christians clarify the significance the day has *for us*, the more Jews can appreciate it without feeling unwillingly "included" in something they have no interest being included in.

But what do we actually do about December 25? There is no reason that Christians should not welcome their Jewish friends and relatives to the carols-and-candlelight liturgies that illuminate Christmas Eve or to the feast and exchange of gifts on the following day. Just as we invite friends to celebrate a birth, a wedding, or an anniversary in our family — even though it is our family's and not theirs — it is natural to welcome friends to this birthday party. There is a difference, of course. We need to assure our Jewish friends that what we are celebrating is the birth of the one through whom we believe God has done for us at Bethlehem what he had already done for them at Sinai. This may, of course, evoke some queries and even some sharp disagreement. But having enjoyed a number of exciting arguments at Passover Seders, I see no reason why the Christmas feast cannot also be the occasion for the same kind of questioning and open discussions that go on over the *matzot*. I am sure the rabbi whose birth we are toasting would savor the give-and-take.

Since Chanukah and Christmas are different holidays, I do not favor blending their respective symbols. Therefore I do not think that those cute, all-purpose holiday cards help. One, for example, shows two Santas greeting each other. One doffs his cap and says, "Merry Christmas," and the other takes off his cap, revealing a *yarmulka*, and says, "Shalom."[7] This may be droll and may appeal to busy shoppers who don't know what card to send to the growing number of mixed-marriage families. But it waters down the differences and, in a country where Christianity is so much larger, inevitably works to the detriment of the Jewish holiday. It is Wal-Mart and Hallmark trying to dilute Jewish particularism with jocularity just as the legions of Antiochus tried to do it with sword and fire. But the result could be the same.

Once I thought I had hit on a solution to the December dilemma. It was for everyone to enjoy a modern winter solstice holiday. Everyone, regardless of religion, must be glad to see the days beginning to grow longer and the nights shorter (though only in the Northern Hemisphere, of course). Why not, I thought, simply call a truce in the annual battle while we all revel in a seasonal turning point people probably celebrated before either Judaism or Christianity appeared. I have come to see, however, that this solution is unrealistic. Festivals and holidays, wherever they are celebrated, exhibit a marked tendency to blur into one another. The holidays we now recognize as Jewish and the ones we think of as Christian all contain elements they have picked up from their neighbors along the route. There is no way a holiday can be kept entirely pure except in the most exclusive ghetto, and few people want to pay that price. So to try to substitute the solstice for what we now have just wouldn't succeed.

Holidays invariably borrow symbols, which brings up the unavoidable question that needs to be treated before any discussion of Chanukah and Christmas ends. I once considered it a trivial, even silly one, but I no longer do. It is the "*genus picea* issue" (the word means "spruce"), the vexed matter of Christmas trees. At first I was puzzled when I heard Jewish friends and relatives argue over this question as though it were the final litmus test of genuine Jewish-ness or of whether a gentile spouse really respected the Jewish part-ner. I know one couple in which the Jewish husband watches his wife — a convert to Judaism from Catholicism — like a hawk from Thanksgiving Day on to see if he can detect any hints of apostasy. Was that "Jingle Bells" she was just humming under her breath? Will she decorate the table with greens? Might she be secretly wishing she could wrestle some nondeciduous bush into the living room?

I now realize, however, that there are some things which — though they may appear trivial — should not be taken lightly. For many Jews Christmas trees have become a symbol of something much deeper — the slippery slope toward assimilation and the eventual loss of Jewish identity. I confess that before I realized this, when I talked with Jews who worried about greenery, I took a certain perverse glee in telling them that in the small, very Protestant town I was raised in, there were also people who were stalwartly opposed to Christmas trees. They were fundamentalist Christians. They doggedly refused to have the trees in their houses and claimed that those of us who did were not real Christians at all but had obviously lapsed into paganism. As a child, I was irked by their condescending suggestion that they were better Christians than we were. Later I came to realize that their posi-tion was not so ridiculous. Christmas trees are (or at least once were) pagan.

The religious significance of pine trees, holly, mistletoe, and ever-green shrubs has been traced back to pre-Christian Teutonic days, when they provided the dwelling places of woodland sprites and spirits. It is also easy to see why the shivering denizens of northern Europe saw them as symbols of life. All through the dreary winter, when all the other trees were dark and lifeless, the evergreen seemed to blossom. Legend credits Martin Luther with being the first to drag a tree in from the forest and deck it with candles to recall the star of Bethlehem. But that is another legend in a season brimming over with them. Actually, historians claim that Christmas trees were al-ready a custom in Germany in the late Middle Ages. In any case, the idea certainly originated in northern Europe, where pagan cus-toms had never really disappeared. Still, for a long time it was viewed with determined suspicion by the more puritanical streams of Prot-estantism. The pilgrims who settled in New England opposed not only Christmas trees but any observance of Christmas whatsoever and dutifully trudged off to work on December 25. They scoffed at Christmas as a popish rite, an attempt, as it were, to get the mass back into Christmas. But gradually the Puritans lost. Indeed, I was surprised to learn some time ago that one of the first Christmas trees reported in American history appeared in 1835 in the Cambridge living room of Professor Charles Follen (who lived only a few blocks from where I now live). A professor of German, Follen had learned of the custom during a trip abroad. The idea burgeoned rapidly, and by midcentury it was becoming widespread. Clearly one did not have to be much of a churchgoer to partake in the custom. Soon the aroma of romantic nostalgia for the mythical "good old days," a sentiment that came to classic expression a century later in Irving Berlin's "White Christmas," was already beginning to suffuse the Christmas tree. By 1891, President Benjamin Harrison told reporters that he and his wife intended to have an "old-fashioned Christmas tree" in the White House.[8]

It is amazing how quickly a relatively new ritual can appear to have been there all along. Now, in the vast majority of Christian homes and churches, and in many places around the world, the star-topped evergreen tree is a nearly inextricable part of the celebration of Christmas. It is not the only thing with a pagan history that has been brought into Christian practice — or Jewish practice either, for that matter. But the question for Jews is not the pagan roots of spruce trees, it is the Christian branches. It is the Christian meanings that, like tinsel and glass orbs, have been attached to the tree. It is the fusing of the trees with manger scenes and stars of Bethlehem that goes on in many people's minds even if they are not displayed together. The consequence is sad. In a season supposed to signify peace on earth and goodwill, the tree that symbolizes the season is often a cause of community rancor and family acrimony. Does displaying Christmas trees on public property constitute a threat to the separation of church and state? Are Jewish families betraying their heritage to have one in their homes, if only to avoid being the single dark house on what in some towns is an otherwise garishly lit row of lawns and bushes? Are the trees merely a part of the seasonal atmosphere?

Maybe one reason the argument over Christmas trees becomes so inflamed is that, as such, they do not mean one thing at all. They have had many meanings over the centuries. Just as they were originally pagan and were baptized into Christian custom, in more recent years they have begun to take on (for some people) a secular, commercial, or generically seasonal significance. For millions of shoppers and revelers they represent neither pagan nor Christian spirituality but an icon of the bland blend of vague religiosity and mercenary hype we call "the holiday season." No wonder people get confused and testy about a green flora that, in its natural state, consists merely of roots, bark, and needles.

But what about the public square? I am against banning all religious symbols from public places. That would say something inaccurate and misleading about our history as Americans and about who we are today. We are not a secular nation; we are religiously pluralistic. But in such a society there has to be a careful evenhandedness. If religious communities want to display their symbols in public, they should be allowed to do so — within reasonable limits and provided no group is discriminated against. Recently, in many cities, Jewish organizations have been permitted to place large menorahs on public land during Chanukah. Every year a Jewish group places a huge one on a prominent street in the Downtown Crossing section of Boston. I see no reason that they should not, or why Muslims and Hindus and Buddhists should not be allowed the same privilege during their holidays. I favor this policy not, however, as some courts have ruled, because such symbols are cultural and not religious. This attitude is condescending, and under such an interpretation, religious groups should ask themselves if they really wish to allow their precious symbols to be treated with such legal disdain. I resent the people, many of them Christians, who defend the display of religious symbols on public property because — they say — "they no longer have a religious meaning." No doubt for many people this is true. But it is the nature of symbols that they never have an inherent meaning. Symbols mean what people make them mean, and the same symbol can mean different things for different people. For some people, Christmas trees have obviously lost their religious meaning. But for many others they have not. For most Christians and most Jews, it would be silly to pretend that a manger scene or a menorah has no religious meaning. And the reason they should be allowed to display them in public is not that we are a nonreligious nation, but because we are a religiously mixed people, and we need to be reminded of it periodically. Displaying our own and appreciating each other's symbols remind us of who we are.

What about the well-intentioned Jewish families who justify having a Christmas tree because they see the holiday as merely a cultural one? As a Christian, I wish they would not. Doing so only further cheapens a holiday that serious Christians are desperately, and perhaps futilely, trying to retrieve. Consequently, I was pleased to see the Jewish magazine *Tikkun* remind its readers that Christians need the help of religiously serious Jews as we try to rescue Christmas from its Babylonian captivity by the credit card cartel. I do realize, however, that while *Tikkun*'s advice may be practical for most Jewish families, it may be asking too much of those who live as a tiny minority in a relatively small, overwhelmingly Christian community. The one or two Jewish families in Garrison Keillor's mythical small town, "Lake Wobegon," Minnesota, with its population of Scandinavian Lutherans and Catholics, might decide that they would pay too high a price for seeming to ignore the seasonal sentiment. I appreciate their perspective, and I know that Jews have rarely expected martyrdom from one another except in very rare circumstances. I can even understand why a certain Susan Greenberg of Chatham, New Jersey, a Jew in a mixed marriage and the mother of two children, reports that having some Chanukah ornaments on the Christmas tree makes having the tree "easier for me to stomach, and it does not make me feel so alienated and excluded from Christmas when my kids are enjoying it." This is an understandable and, I would say, allowable exception. Still, I think that in principle *Tikkun* has it right, and I hope the day will come when even the sturdy parishioners of "Our Lady of Perpetual Responsibility" in Lake Wobegon will applaud the fact that a few houses in town do not place manger scenes in their windows but, a few days earlier, display those brave little flickering candles.

What about the increasing number of families like ours, however, in which one partner is Jewish and the other is Christian? Every such family has to make its own decision about this. We always have a Christmas tree, but not because it has "only cultural significance." Just the opposite. We have it because it is part of my tradition, just as we light the menorah during Chanukah because that is part of my wife's (and now our son's) tradition. This is an important point. Jews celebrate many of their holidays — like Sabbath and Passover — at home. But Christmas is one of the very few holidays that Christians celebrate at home. We have the tree in our living room, with a star on top and the manger scene at the bottom. But we do not have it because it is a generic icon. We have it because without it, the celebration of the birth of Jesus would seem incomplete to me, and because my wife and I try to respect each other's traditions and to participate in each other's practices as far as our consciences will allow. Not to celebrate Christmas at home, with the traditional songs and readings and feast, would deprive the Christian partner of the one day of the year in which that faith is customarily marked at home. It would be the equivalent of the Christian partner insisting there should be no Passover Seder.

But what about the children? the skeptics ask. Won't they get terribly confused? There is no reason for this to create disorientation among children. Our son, for example, realizes that Christmas is his father's holiday, but he also knows it is a holiday in which he and his mother participate, just as I share the Sabbath, Passover, and the others. But preparing children to live out their faith in a religiously multifaceted world is not just a task for mixed-marriage families. As the twenty-first century begins to unfold, all children should be prepared to live in a society where the different world religions are no longer across the ocean but across the street. Learning to appreciate the foods and festivals of "the others" not only inoculates children against bigotry, it also helps them appreciate the distinctiveness of their own tradition.

Our orchestration works well. Nicholas especially relishes it, because he receives a present for eight nights during Chanukah and another pile of gifts on Christmas morning. My wife enjoys it, because it conforms to her Jewish expectation of having a house full of friends and family, whether the holiday we are celebrating is hers or mine. Besides, we both believe that wives and husbands, whatever their faith, should learn to find joy in the satisfaction their spouses derive from their spiritual practices. Most important, however, Christmas provides one of the few strictly religious occasions when the children of my former marriage — now all grown — arrive with their companions or spouses and their children to celebrate the birthday of Jesus Christ. We sing the traditional carols, roast chestnuts over the fire, drink eggnog, and eat mincemeat pies. We exchange gifts under the star-topped tree, which is decorated with the ornaments they remember from their childhood and has a manger scene beside it. In other words, we pass on a tradition none of them wants to lose, one that their children will pass on when I am gone.

But there is a problem. When I try to tell friends what our mixed-marriage family does and why we do it, they sometimes shake their heads. "We can understand it," the Jewish partner often says, "but how can we explain it to my parents?"

The question is serious, but there is an answer. Jewish parents, understandably worried that the tree and the crèche mark the first step on the downward slide of Judaism, need to be reassured. Practicing religious hospitality and affirming religious pluralism are not the same as drifting into relativism and secularism. Today, half the young Jews in this country marry non-Jews (thirty years ago, it was less than 10 percent) and about one third of the 3.2 million American households with Jewish adults have an interfaith marriage. This means that all of us, including Christians, need to find ways, not only to ensure the continuity of the Jewish faith, but to reassure the older generation that we can do it. Of course it can be confusing to Jewish parents to visit their intermarried children and find the grandson, who was just a bar mitzvah boy last year, stringing the lights on a *genus picea* tree. But it also provides the occasion for reassuring them.

The present generation of Jews and Christians has an opportunity their parents did not have. Jews today, at least in America, do not have to make the cruel choice between retreating to a self-imposed ghetto or losing their identity completely in a secular post-Christian society. December need not be either a season of dilemma or a season of madness. It now affords us the opportunity to nourish a new kind of religious Jew and a new kind of religious Christian, for each of whom treasuring the uniqueness and worth of the other is not optional but indispensable. Maybe, if Jews and Christians work at it together, we might be able to save December from being trampled to death by mobs of hysterical shoppers. Who knows, the whole month, if not exactly jolly, might at least not be filled with angst and collisions. It might even provide us with an opportunity to toast our diversity without falling into generic blandness.

7

Funny Masks and Texts of Terror

Purim

The mask is magic. Character is not innate: a man's
character is his demon, his tutelar spirit;
received in a dream. His character is his destiny,
which is to act out his dream.

— Geza Roheim

They slaughtered seventy-five thousand
of those who hated them, but took no plunder.
That was on the thirteenth day of the month of Adar;
On the fourteenth day they rested,
and made it a day of feasting and joy.

— Esther 9:16, 17

WHAT'S THIS? The rabbi is wearing a cowboy hat, bandanna, and chaps, and he is packing an ugly sixshooter (a fake one, I presume) in his leather holster. Somehow I am not surprised. Last year at this time he was decked out as a strutting renaissance courtier in a cylindrical purple fur hat, a pink and burgundy robe over black tights, fawngray cloth boots, and a swirly cape. He sported a necklace of rhinestones set in something that looked like (but probably wasn't) gold around his neck, hidden in front by his black beard.[1] Around me in the crowded synagogue, like last year, I see ballet dancers in tutus, at least three hooded sheiks, four witches with towering black peaked hats, children in white coats with stethoscopes around their necks, a dozen clowns stuffed with pillows and wearing shiny red false noses, four dragons, three crocodiles, and other assorted monsters. Furthermore, as we entered the synagogue, Rabbi Moshe Waldoks signaled to me to join him in a small room behind the *bimah* where he displayed a bottle of slivovitz, one of dark rum, and another of vodka. Then he handed me a small cup and gave me my druthers. I chose the vodka while he tossed down the slivovitz. Then I returned to Nina, who wore the uniform of a Russian soldier, with battle medals, and Nicholas, wearing a T-shirt with the picture of a sneering hirsute figure in a red circle crossed out by a red line. It is Haman, the villain of the evening's burlesque. I am resplendent in a pink shirt, long purple blouse, flamboyant polka-dotted tie, and a gray Alpine cap covered with my collection of political campaign buttons dating back to Wendell Willkie and Thomas E. Dewey (my parents were active Republicans). People are talking loudly, and children are racing up and down the aisles making a racket with clappers. The whole synagogue is churning in a happy state of pandemonium.

It is Purim, the most antic and surely the noisiest of the Jewish holidays. Also, for me, one of the most ambiguous ones. The holiday commemorates the beautiful Jewish woman Esther (originally named Hadassah, from which the Jewish women's organization gets its name), and how she saves her people from destruction. When Jews gather for Purim, they read the entire biblical book of Esther. People assemble dressed not only as Esther or one of the other characters in her story but, in recent times, as almost anything. As the tale is read, whenever the name of the villain, Haman, is pronounced, everyone boos, stamps their feet, or splits the air with a noisemaker. Clearly, children especially love this holiday. But so do their parents. On this particular Purim a distinguished-looking man, a recent immigrant from Russia, who wears a plain black robe and a flat, round black hat, is reading the text.

The plot of Esther, with its generous portions of sex, violence, and intrigue, is made to order for a Hollywood blockbuster. The great Persian king Ahasuerus, it is told, was enjoying a bounteous feast with all his officers and courtiers. After what appears to have been considerable quaffing from "golden goblets, each of a different design," the king hit on one of those bad ideas kings sometimes get when the wine has been flowing freely. He decided to show off his ravishing wife, Vashti, who was at the same moment entertaining her women friends in another part of the palace. Vashti declined, which greatly annoyed the king, who summoned his advisers to help him decide how to deal with such wifely insubordination. The advisers recommended a radical solution. Banish Vashti from her throne, then hold the Persian equivalent of the Miss America pageant to pick her successor. The king enthusiastically agreed, and comely Esther won the contest hands down.

Esther, it seems, was an orphan, the adopted daughter of a Jew named Mordecai. At first she merely became a part of the king's sizable harem. But such were her charms that the king liked her better than any of his other women, plied her with special cosmetics and foods, and finally placed a diadem on her head. She was now Queen Esther. But at the urging of Mordecai, she did not tell the king, or anyone else, that she was Jewish. Then the plot thickens.

Having learned that two of the king's eunuchs are scheming to overthrow him, Mordecai tells Esther about the conspiracy, and she reports it to the king. The matter is investigated and the two culprits summarily hanged. Shortly thereafter the king appoints a new chief minister, Haman, and orders everyone who enters his court to prostrate themselves before him. Mordecai, however, will not bow, and — when pressed for why — tells his questioners that he is a Jew — the implication being that this should explain his conduct. It was nothing personal, so to speak, but his religion forbade him from prostrating himself before anyone. This appeal to conscientious objection, however, so infuriates Haman that he becomes determined, not only to get rid of Mordecai, but to purge the empire of his whole troublesome people.

I have always found this part of the story intriguing. Maybe it is because my ancestors, the ones who immigrated to Pennsylvania from England, were Quakers, who often got themselves into difficulty for refusing to remove their hats in the presence of nobles and kings. Consequently I have always felt some kinship with Mordecai and with the long history of Jewish refusal to display unseemly obeisance to worldly authority. I have also wondered at times whether Mordecai thought that the religious basis for his refusal to bow might somehow have been accepted as legitimate. After all, the Persians did try to respect the religious customs of the peoples they conquered; and later, the Romans did not draft Jews into their legions because they would not fight on the Sabbath, thus strapping their commanders with a serious tactical disadvantage. But Mordecai got no such consideration. One might also wonder what Mordecai and Esther and the rest of the Jews were doing in Persia after they had been freed from their captivity in Babylon by the Persian king Cyrus and allowed to return to Palestine. The answer is that apparently many of the Jews, after seventy years in what was not so hard a captivity, opted to stay rather than return to the uncertainties of the old country. Theologically, the rabbis have seen this as an assurance that God continued to favor and protect his chosen people wherever they were.

What happened after Haman decided to make the kingdom "*Judenrein*" — cleansed of Jews — suggests that there was a good deal of incipient sentiment against them in Persia waiting to be mobilized. Haman went to the king and gave him the following description, so reminiscent of what their enemies have said about the Jews in country after country and age after age ever since.

> Dispersed in scattered groups among the peoples throughout the provinces of your realm, there is a certain people whose laws are different from those of every other people. They do not observe the king's laws and it does not befit your majesty to tolerate them. If it please your majesty, let an order be drawn up for their destruction; and I shall hand over to your majesty's officials the sum of ten thousand talents of silver, to be deposited in the royal treasury (Esther 3:8, 9).

Haman appeared to be taking no chances. He appealed not only to the king's doubts about the security of his rule — caused in part by the recently uncovered plot against him — but sweetened the deal with a sizable bribe. The king refused the bribe, but ordered Haman to "deal with the people as you think best." Haman drew up a royal order to "destroy, slay, and exterminate all Jews, young and old, women and children, in one day, the thirteenth day of the twelfth month, the month of Adar." Mordecai brought this directive to the attention of Esther, who hesitated at first. Even as the king's wife, she was forbidden to seek him out unless he called for her. But Mordecai warned her that if she thought she would escape the genocide just because she lived in the palace, she was sadly mistaken. So she went to the king, but instead of confronting him right away she invited him and Haman to come to her quarters for dinner. They both enjoyed themselves, but as Haman was returning he happened to see Mordecai, who, as usual, did not grant him the deference of bowing. Haman, infuriated, had a huge gallows built in front of his house and planned to have the king order Mordecai to be hanged on it.

Now the plot reversal is sprung, and to dramatize the twist, the elderly Russian gentleman who has been reading the narrative takes a break, and an attractive woman in a gray miniskirt and boots takes his place. She leans against the desk in a relaxed posture and continues the story with voice changes for the various characters. She throws in some other tricks as well. When she comes to "Haman" she pauses, teasingly, before she says it. Once she feigned a sneeze and repeated the *H* several times. Everyone, including the solemn, elderly Muscovite, seemed to enjoy it. But it occurred to me that this was just what many Orthodox Jews feared was bound to happen if women were allowed to mix with men in the synagogue: boots and miniskirts on the *bimah*. Still, after all, is this not the tale of a beautiful Jewish woman whose charm swept a king off his feet? Why shouldn't a modern Esther read the story?

Now the old Jew from Moscow is reading again. When Haman approached him, the king — who had been wondering how to reward Mordecai for saving his throne from the usurpers — asked him how he could honor someone who greatly merited it. Haman, thinking the king meant him, described the honors in lavish terms — only to find that they were intended for Mordecai. In the meantime, Esther had prepared yet another banquet that so pleased the king that — like the king in a hundred other fables — he promised to grant her any wish. She told the king she was Jewish and requested that the lives of her people be spared, then went on to tell him that Haman had been the author of this devilish machination. Already enraged, the king also learned that Haman was planning to hang Mordecai. He ordered that Haman be hanged instead on the same gallows — hoist, as it were, by his own petard. The noisemakers whir.

Here the story could end happily, and with the bad guy getting his just desserts. But it does not. Nina stirs uneasily next to me. "Now comes the part I don't like," she says. I understand. Now the king gives Mordecai the same blanket permission to deal with the enemies of the Jews that he had given the luckless Haman (*rattle, whir, bang*) to get rid of the Jews. And Mordecai does. The text, with a cruel sense of irony, uses exactly the same words to describe the writ and the procedures for promulgating it. Only now the people to be exterminated are the enemies of the Jews, wherever they are.

> By these dispatches the king granted permission to the Jews in each and every city to assemble in self-defense, and to destroy, slay and exterminate every man, woman and child, of any people or province which might attack them, and to treat their goods as spoil, throughout the provinces of king Ahasuerus, in one day, the thirteenth day of Adar, the twelfth month (Esther 8:11, 12).

According to the text, the Jews "slaughtered seventy-five thousand of those who hated them, but they took no plunder"(Esther 9:16). Also, to finish things off properly, Queen Esther asks the king to have the ten sons of the late lamented Haman also hanged on the same gallows, so they also swing. To call her a femme fatale is an exercise in understatement.

Purim was obviously going to require another family discussion. Fortunately, we were prepared for it. A few weeks before we donned our costumes and whirled our noisemakers amid the witches and sheiks, a teacher in Nicholas's school received a telephone call from a parent who expressed her concern that the sixth grade was planning to perform Dial "M" for Murder. The parent was alarmed that staging a play about a murder might upset the children. I wondered what that parent would have thought of their doing Romeo and Juliet or Hamlet? Or what about Hansel and Gretel or The Wizard of Oz (remember that the witches in both are murdered at the end)? What is more pertinent here, what might she have thought of the ending of the Purim story, with tens of thousands of bodies rotting in the Persian sun and the ten sons of Haman dangling from the gallows? Would she object to their reading The Iliad, the classic epic of jealousy, violence, and revenge? Or the Mahabharata, the Hindu epic poem, with its story after story of the ruthless clan conflicts between the Kauravas and the Pandavas? Even the Sinhalese Buddhist chronicles are crammed with accounts of bloody religious wars. In truth, virtually all our great literature, religious and secular, seethes with violence. It seems hypocritical of me as a Christian to object to the ending of the Purim story (which is undoubtedly fiction anyway) when it was the leaders of my own religion who launched the Crusades and the Inquisition, burned the Salem witches, and whose Gospel accounts blame the crucifixion of Jesus on "the Jews," inspiring so many pogroms and so much anti-Semitism. There is probably a difference in how such texts are to be read depending on whether those who originally composed them were tyrants shoring up their power or — as in the Esther story — oppressed peoples dreaming of revenge. Among Christians, one often finds a large measure of disingenuousness on the question of religiously inspired violence. After all, wasn't the founder of our religion the victim, not the perpetrator, of religiously inspired imperial violence? Didn't he teach us to love our enemies and turn the other cheek? Weren't the Inquisition and the witch burnings really violations of his teaching and his example, not fidelity to them? It is someone else's religion, not ours, that inspires jihads and the burnings of widows on funeral pyres.

The truth, as usual, is more complicated and more uncomfortable. Yes, Jesus, in an oft-quoted utterance, said, "Put your sword back in its place; for all who take the sword will perish by the sword" (Matthew 26:52). Just as he was saying this, the posse came to seize him in the Garden of Gethsemane, and his disciple Peter swung his blade and lopped off the ear of one of the gendarmes. Was Jesus enunciating a general principle of nonviolence? Or was he simply advising this particular hothead not to waste good steel in useless resistance against overwhelming odds? Besides, this is not all Jesus had to say about swords. In an earlier chapter, the same Gospel writer has him saying, "I have not come to bring peace, but a sword." Another Gospel writer, Luke, describes the scene in which Jesus, anticipating his crucifixion, sends his disciples out to spread his message:

> He said to them, "When I sent you out barefoot without purse or pack, were you ever short of anything?" "No," they answered. "It is different now," he said, "whoever has a purse had better take it with him, and his pack too; and if he has no sword, let him sell his cloak and buy one" (Luke 22:35, 36).

This is curious advice from an alleged teacher of nonviolence. It is also a text on which I never remember hearing a single sermon in my youth among the Baptists and Quakers of southeastern Pennsylvania. I still have a hard time with these verses, especially since I admire the modern exemplars of nonviolence such as Gandhi and Martin

Luther King, Jr., both of whom cite Jesus as their model. This has forced me to ask myself a hard question: Why have so many Christians worked so hard to make Jesus into a prototype of nonviolence when the evidence is at best very mixed? Is it because at some level we realize how violent our religion has been and we desperately need a corrective? In church we hear about the Jesus who courageously "spoke truth to power" without resorting to force. Then, as we grow up, we hear about the carnage the crusaders created in the streets of Jerusalem, the slaughter of the Native Americans, the enslavement of Africans, all performed in the name of Christ or to guard Christian civilization. Even though Jesus was the casualty of a colonial empire, Christians have happily mined the "elect nation" and "promised land" rhetoric of the Hebrew scriptures and used them to plunder the homelands of the Iroquois and the Bantu. Our hands are at least as bloody as anyone else's, and much of the blood was drawn from the veins of the victims of our sacrifices on the altars of our faith.

Christianity is sometimes identified in textbooks as the "religion of love," and in one sense that is true. But its history is strewn with the severed heads and burned cities of religiously sanctified violence. Some of our faith's most attractive figures were shining embodiments of compassion and gentleness. Others have few rivals in their capacity for brutality and cruelty. Sometimes the contradiction comes very close to home and is almost too much to bear. A few years ago I attended a memorial service at the Arlington Street Church in Boston for two women who had worked for a women's health clinic in nearby Brookline and had just been shot to death at their desks. The man, who quickly admitted his action, was an anti-abortion activist named John Salvi who later told the judge that his lifelong ambition had been to become a Catholic priest. On the same day the shooting took place, Philip Berrigan, who had spent most of his life as a Catholic priest, was arrested yet again for leading a protest at an American nuclear weapons facility. Even in the depth of my distress and confusion about these incidents, I could not help imagining what might happen if these two men were placed in the same cell block.

As a Christian, I know that my tradition shares the dilemma of what to do about religiously sanctioned violence with many other traditions. We are not exempt, but we are not alone either. It seems there have always been people who were willing not only to die for their faith but to kill for it as well. This disagreeable fact presents us all with a challenge we need to work on together. As we do, it might be helpful to make a distinction between real violence and what might be called "ritual violence," as it is enacted, for example, in the Esther story. But we cannot stop there. We must also ask ourselves, What is the relationship between the two? Does symbolic violence cause real violence, or does it substitute for or displace it? This is certainly not just a Jewish issue. All religions have their "texts of terror." How can we understand them?

One of the most respected thinkers about this question, René Girard, devoted what has now become a classic study to this theme. In *Violence and the Sacred*, he suggests that ritual violence is essential to human civilization because it enables people to displace and sublimate real violence. Instead of killing their enemies or their neighbors, people can slaughter bulls or cows or offer up other objects of sacrifice. "Violence," Girard writes, in his most famous sentence, "is the heart and secret soul of the sacred." He concedes, of course, that this displacement does not always work, that ritual violence sometimes gushes out into the real world. But, he argues, given the immense potential for violence that seems to be built into human nature and in view of the many tensions that can provoke it, draining it off into a harmless expression — rather than vainly trying to repress it — is by far the best course. The violent impulse can be "tricked," as it were, and heaped onto a symbolic rather than a real enemy.[2]

Without ever having read Girard, Nina expressed the core of his theory when we talked about Purim. "Well," she said, "you can't just pick and choose what you like and don't like about a religion, and there are some ugly things there along with the good things. Besides," she added, "maybe it's better to get the bad stuff out with footstamping and noisemakers rather than doing the real thing."

Virtually every religious tradition perpetuates tales of violence in its sacred texts and traditions. Judaism is no exception. It is simply one example of something quite common and terribly unnerving. If anything, Jews are to be credited for positioning Esther in a holiday of mirth and make-believe — one of the best methods I know of coping with a gory text. When I have discussed this matter with Jews, some have assured me that, of course, no one takes the words in Esther seriously. It is plainly fiction, they say, and is read as a story of re-demption, not revenge.

I wish I could be so sure. There is unfortunately some evidence that this is not always the case. In recent years religious Jews, along with believers in virtually every other tradition, have perpetrated some sickening acts of violence in what someone apparently believed was a direct application of such texts. When, in 1994, Captain Baruch Goldstein of the Israeli Defense Force murdered twenty-nine Mus-lims while they were praying in the Ibrahimaye Mosque (which is also the ancestral cave of Machpelah) in Hebron, he did it on Purim. It is hard to believe that the story of Esther and Haman, and the de-struction by the Jews of all those who were thought to be their ene-mies, was very far from his mind. In March 2000, before Purim, Rabbi Ovadiah Yosef, the spiritual adviser to the Shas political party in Israel, gave a powerful sermon heard by hundreds in his syna-gogue and by tens of thousands watching on television. In it he ac-cused Yossi Sarid, then Israeli minister of education, in the following words: "Yossi Sarid," he said, "is Haman. . . . May his name and mem-ory be blotted out. . . . He is Satan. . . . God will destroy him as He de-stroyed Amalek." At least one Israeli journalist considered this a clear case of incitement of murder under Israeli law. He compared it to the *fatwa* issued by the Ayatollah Khomeini against Salman Rushdie after the publication of Rushdie's *Satanic Verses*. He wrote that a poll con-ducted just after the sermon indicated that 5 percent of the rabbi's followers believed that his rabbinic *fatwa* should actually be carried out, and that adds up "to roughly 25,000 potential assassins." This is an especially sensitive issue in Israel since the assassination of Prime Minister Yitzhak Rabin, and pressure was immediately brought to bear on the attorney general to seek a criminal indictment.[3] It was never issued. But the hard question remains: If at times what Girard calls the "tricking of violence" does not work as it should, how and why does that happen? Why, in some situations, do the interpreta-tions that soften, sublimate, and spiritualize these brutal narratives not work?

Masks and violence: Is there any connection? Do bandits wear bandannas and terrorists ski masks just to hide their identity? Or do they assume another identity because as their everyday selves, they would not rob and murder? Examining the history of masks in religion yields some fascinating information. Some anthropologists trace them to primitive warfare, in which tribal peoples stained horrible faces on their shields to terrify their enemies. This practice persisted up to World War II, when American pilots painted shark's heads on the noses of their P-40 pursuit planes. But the connection is still obscure.

A. David Napier, in his book on the psychology of masks, tells about one that he finds especially representative. It was found in eastern Java and dates from 1239 C.E. On its front it depicts the benign, somewhat indolent Hindu god Ganesha, with his elephant head and bloated potbelly. Nothing to be afraid of. But on the back is a mask with "huge bulbous eyes," fierce teeth, and a long lolling tongue. Its claws are raised in a menacing manner. Napier reports, "[A]nd below its bared fangs there is, voraciously, no lower jaw. The demonic appearance of the mask is arresting and terrifying."[4] One could also add that this Javanese example starkly illustrates a disquieting truth about most religions and most cultures: they bind people together with symbols that are both positive and negative. Most national cultures, in their holidays, patriotic songs, and memories — some of them genuine, some concocted — recall the humiliating defeats and glorious triumphs of the past. The world is strewn with markers and memorials of the terrible things "they" did to us and how "we" finally defeated them, often with the sanction and help of God, or at least of the Zeitgeist. The American and the French national anthems recall gory battles with "bombs bursting in air" and enemies who want to "devour our wives and children." And they are hardly alone in this respect. The irony is that they continue to be sung long after those particular enemies have become allies and most people have forgotten what the battles were about.

There is no way every culture and every faith tradition can purge its songs and stories of all violent elements. This too would falsify history. But I do not believe these abhorrent elements should be ignored or trivialized either. I hope Purim continues to be an antic holiday that sends people into the backs of their closets to dig out silly hats, false mustaches, and swishy capes. But I also hope it might evolve into a time of reflection as well. Just because our holidays come back year after year, both Christians and Jews have the opportunity to seize on the occasions to think carefully once again about the damage done to all parties concerned by nursing grudges, scratching the scars of wounds that have begun to heal, and gloating over past victories. Let the name of Haman *(rattle, bang!)* stand, not just for the mortal enemy of one people, but also for the spirit of violence and hatred we all sometimes find within ourselves as well.

8

A Night Different from All Others

Passover

> In every generation, each person should feel as though
> She or he were redeemed from Egypt, as it is said:
> "You shall tell your children on that day saying,
> 'It is because of what the Lord did for me
> When I went free out of Egypt.'
> For the Holy One redeemed not only our ancestors;
> He redeemed us with them."
>
> — *Haggadah for Pesach*

Ma *nish-ta-na ha lai-la ha-zeh, mee-kol ha-lei-lot?*" "Why is this night different from all other nights?" asks the youngest child at the table in one of the oldest continuing rituals of any religious tradition. It is the Seder, the festive meal that is the centerpiece of *pesach* (Passover), when Jews tell the story of God's liberation of the Israelites from their bondage in Egypt. Nicholas has just asked this big question in the impressive Hebrew he learned for his bar mitzvah. Now what will follow is like no ritual I know of in the Christian tradition: part ceremony, part banquet, part television panel show, part Platonic symposium, and, at least at our house, part seminar on religion, politics, history, and ethics.

Passover is not just a meal but an eight-day celebration. It begins on the fifteenth day of the Jewish month of Nisan, which arrives at the end of March or in early or mid-April. Because Jesus was in Jerusalem to celebrate Passover when he was arrested and executed, Holy

Week and Easter Sunday usually come at the same time. Sometimes they occur in the same week. Were it not for a change made centuries ago in the western Christian calendar, they would always occur in the same week. I wish the change had never been made, because the juxtaposition of the two holidays during the same days would serve as an annual reminder of the historical and religious link between the two traditions.

Passover is one of the Jewish holidays I enter into wholeheartedly. I think most Christians can, and many Jewish families have recognized this by inviting non-Jews to share in the Seder. Passover is a celebration of freedom. At its core is the saga of God's delivery of the Israelites from their captivity in Egypt, so it is also sometimes called *zeman heiruteinu* ("the season of our liberation"). But for many people the story is about the God whose purpose is to liberate all captive and oppressed peoples, which is why the story of Moses and the exodus has played such a prominent part in the faith of black Americans.[1] The purpose of Passover, and especially that of the Seder, is to tell this powerful old story yet again, and to tell it so well that everyone who hears it feels as if he or she were actually there when the original liberation took place. This is not too hard to do, since the account itself is so dramatic and so many people are already familiar with its plot. It tells of the Israelites in Egypt toiling under cruel taskmasters but nonetheless multiplying, of the fearful pharaoh's brutal decision to kill all the male Jewish babies, and of God's summons to Moses from the burning bush to order the pharaoh to "let my people go." It goes on to rehearse the confrontation between this reluctant prophet and the powerful monarch, who refuses God's command. We then hear about the ten plagues God sends to try to persuade the pharaoh: the hail, the locusts, the boils, and all the rest, culminating in the deaths of all the Egyptian firstborn. But just before the angel of death swoops through the land, God warns the Israelites to smear the blood of a lamb over their doorposts so the angel will pass over them (hence "Passover"). At last the pharaoh relents and the Israelites leave. Then the pharaoh changes his mind and sends his cavalry to recapture the slaves. Again God intervenes, splitting the Red Sea so the Israelites can cross over without getting their feet wet, then causing the mighty waters to rush back and drown the pursuing Egyptian host. It is a captivating yarn, and I admit that, like many people in my age bracket, I can never hear it without the throngs of perspiring men, women, and children and the overloaded camels and donkeys paraded across the screen in Cecil B. De Mille's epic film *The Ten Commandments* coming to mind.

I am not particularly troubled by the knowledge, now well documented by archaeologists, that the exodus did not actually happen in history in quite the way the Bible (or De Mille) describes it. There are mounds of evidence about the history of Egypt, including letters, pottery, court records, and tomb inscriptions, which show that Egypt was indeed a refuge for the people of Canaan when famines struck during the early centuries described in the legends of Joseph and the patriarchs. Some of these refugees also apparently did well, as Joseph did, while others became bonded servants. But, with all this evidence, there is none that even hints at the massive departure of a large body of slaves at any time at all, to say nothing of around 1440 B.C.E., when the Bible's internal dating would place the exodus. Even though archaeologists can now find vestiges of tiny campsites in the Sinai desert from thousands of years ago, there is not a single trace from the forty years the Bible says the Israelites wandered there. In short, there is no evidence whatever, and little likelihood, that the grand events in the story took place as described.

Then what is this story, and what value does it have for us? The exodus account that we have now, the one from the Bible that is used at Passover, was written during the reign of King Josiah of Israel in the seventh century B.C.E., six hundred years after the events it depicts would have taken place. It is an artful creation, more like a historical novel than history, and it was crafted for a particular purpose. At the time of its writing, Egypt, after a long period of decline, was reasserting its power in Canaan. Feeling threatened, King Josiah wanted an inspiring chronicle that would draw on old folk memories, mix in current references and places, and unify his people against the very current threat posed by the Egyptian chariots and legions. Israel Finkelstein and Neil Asher Silberman explain this eloquently in their excellent book, *The Bible Unearthed:*

> The great saga of a new beginning and a second chance must have resonated in the consciousness of the seventh century's readers, reminding them of their own difficulties and giving them hope for the future. . . . The saga of Israel's Exodus from Egypt is neither historical

truth or literary fiction. It is a powerful expression of memory and
hope, born in a world in the midst of change.[2]

In other words, the story we tell and hear at Passover is just that, a
story. It is neither sheer fact nor mere fiction. But just as it freely
mixed together events and legends from different eras, it has since
then accumulated many further layers of meaning as it has been told
countless times by Jews and other peoples. Trying to reduce this
grand narrative to a news story from thirty-five hundred years ago is
to do it a grave injustice. It is bigger and more authoritative than
that. It may well be that Christians, who often tend to have a more
literal view of the Bible than Jews do, can therefore become more upset by the lack of fact in the Exodus account. Yeshayahu Liebowitz, an
Orthodox Jewish scholar and an Israeli, for example, puts the whole
issue in the right perspective when he says that what makes the Bible,
including this story, authoritative is not some claim to factuality but
a long Jewish tradition, guided by generations of rabbis, which has
declared it to be authoritative. In this light, the Bible is seen not as a
source of literal information but as a source of normative spiritual
life. This gives the myths and legends and poetry and laws it contains
an authority that does not have to wait anxiously for the results of
the next archaeological expedition. I wish more Christians could
read the Bible this way. If we could, it might end for good the so-
called warfare between science and religion and render the long battle of attrition between "liberals" and "fundamentalists" obsolete.[3]

For this year's Seder, and the retelling of this old story, we are gathered around our dining room table with the traditional foods piled
on a large glazed Passover platter. Other customary dishes are
grouped around it. On the platter itself is the roasted shank bone of a
lamb (given out free this week at our supermarket). It calls to mind
those days long ago when Jews actually sacrificed a lamb to recall the
one that was killed in Egypt so that its blood could be splattered over
their doorposts. Next to the lamb shank nestles a bowl of *maror,* or
"bitter herbs," to evoke the acrid taste of humiliation and captivity.
Beside the bowl an orange glistens in this strange company, a relative
newcomer to the Seder platter. It seems that some years ago an oppo-
nent of women rabbis remarked that having a woman on the *bimah*
was as incongruous as having an orange on the Seder plate. Hearing

this, Susannah Heschel, a Jewish feminist scholar and the daughter of the late rabbi Abraham Joshua Heschel, suggested that the orange be added to the plate. It now seems to have won a permanent place in many households (and today there are many women rabbis).

On separate dishes around the central platter's collage of old and new edibles cluster the other elements. Here is an egg, the symbol of life. Here are the *karpas*, the spring greens (in our house parsley), to remind us of springtime and renewal but dipped in salt water to recall the tears of enslavement. Next is the *charoset*, the finely chopped apples, nuts, and wine that represent the mortar the Jews used to make the bricks for the pharaoh's pyramids — those crumbling monuments to man's efforts to outlast death — and pretentious public buildings. There is also the plate of *matzot*, the unleavened cracker-like bread we will be eating tonight and for eight days in place of any baked goods that require yeast. According to the story, when the Jews left Egypt, there was no time to wait for the bread to rise. *Matzah*, it is sometimes said, is a recurrent warning against procrastination: when the moment comes, go for it.

I am all too familiar with these strange foods by now because, at Nina's gentle but firm urging, all three of us have spent the afternoon preparing them. I have peeled and shredded the misshapen horse-radish. Nicholas has mixed the *charoset*, sampling it frequently with his forefinger. At first I went about my assignments out of a sense of duty. I was "helping out" with what was, after all, an ambitious provisioning for ourselves and our guests. But as the afternoon wore on, I realized I was doing more than mere preparation. It was an integral part of the event itself. Why, Nicholas wanted to know, licking the savory *charoset* from his finger for the tenth time, did something that was supposed to represent toil and captivity taste so good? I actually began to enjoy the feel of the kitchen knife in my hand and the little piles of peels accumulating on yesterday's newspaper at my feet. Some years before, I had been the guest at a Japanese tea ceremony, and I remembered how impatient I was at first with the long and intricate preparations until another guest, the Japanese friend who had brought me, explained that the process itself was the essence. The actual drinking of the tea is little more than the last measure of the cantata.

The preparation for the Seder had started the day before, when all the *chametz*, the various kinds of food that are not allowed during

Passover, have to be sought out from the refrigerator and the corners of the kitchen closets and discarded. The list of prohibited items is long, including bread, cakes, cookies, muffins, and crackers. Beer and whiskey are also *chametz*. Some Ashkenazic rabbis have added peas, corn, rice, lentils, and mustard. (Late-night snacking during the eight days of Passover is a serious culinary challenge.) Of course, not everyone agrees on exactly what ought to be proscribed. Still, the scavenging for *chametz* has often been a serious business. Engravings of Passovers in years gone by show the women of the house scrutinizing the corners with candles and feathers. No crumb should be left undetected.

As a Christian, I had been familiar with the custom of "giving something up for Lent." I even do it myself, albeit sporadically. But my first impression of this dogged scrounging for the last stray chocolate chip cookie crumb seemed a bit overdone, and it took me a few years to get it. There is a practice in Christianity, perfected by the Jesuits, of searching one's conscience, looking in all the corners of the mind for the destructive thoughts, useless ideas, and self-deluding habits that we would normally rather overlook. Rightly understood, the pursuit of the *chametz* is like that. Like many other features of Judaism, it does not rely on mental effort alone but incorporates food and the body. Still, for me at least, it requires a sustained effort to remember that I am not just pursuing stray specks of last week's raisin toast. While looking for the crumbs, I am sweeping out the junk from my own soul. I am not sure all Jews grasp this deeper significance.

Chametz, however, is not junk. During the rest of the year blueberry muffins from Starbucks and Kellogg's Corn Flakes and Jack Daniel's are not forbidden. Judaism is not an ascetic religion. The foraging for *chametz* reminds me that this search-and-destroy mission is not about what is good and bad but what is — at certain times and seasons in life — appropriate and inappropriate. This is a critical spiritual and ethical insight. *Chametz* is not like pork chops or bacon, which are not considered kosher and which Jews who keep kosher are always supposed to avoid. It consists of food you can gladly eat all the other days of the year. "For everything there is a season," writes Koheleth (known in the Christian translations of the Old Testament as Ecclesiastes), "and a time for every matter under heaven." The candle-and-feathers routine (we actually use a flashlight and dustpan) can of course become merely that — a routine. It can degenerate into exactly the kind of anal-compulsive neurosis Sigmund Freud saw in all religious ritual. But I wonder if that grandson of rabbis ever mused that what he was putting his patients through on that famous couch in the Sackgasse — poking into those dark recesses of the subconscious — might be a secular descendant of the uncovering of the *chametz?* I can't believe it never occurred to him.

Once the *chametz* is dispatched, preparation for the Seder can begin. There is, of course, a guidebook to this unique ritual. It is called a Haggadah, which simply means "telling." But unlike the prayers and formulas for every other ritual I know, there is no standard version of the Haggadah. The essential framework is the same, but there have been hundreds of different variants. I have seen kibbutz Haggadot, a feminist adaptation, and a Freedom Haggadah, which appeared during the American civil rights movement. I have even heard of something called the Moscow Communist Haggadah, which was published in 1927. The foodstuffs used are dictated by custom (but changes are apparently permitted, as the presence of the orange suggests). Some songs are almost always sung, but even these vary from century to century, from region to region, and from family to family. Wine is always drunk, and *matzah* and the ritual foods are always eaten, but the rest of the meal itself can vary from high French cuisine to Thai takeout. The only indispensable content is the older generation telling the younger generation once again of the exodus from Egypt, trying to tell it so that everyone somehow feels he or she is present at the original event.

Not only do the various Haggadot vary widely, the manner in which they are used varies even more so. Before he died, Nina's genial uncle Emmanuel, a physician in New York, presided over the event like a benevolent sixth-grade teacher, explaining each parsley sprig and horseradish slice as well as each stage of the ceremony in his own whimsical style. The rolled eyeballs of his grown children and their spouses, then in their forties, hinted that they had heard these homey illustrations many times before. His performance might not have pleased the great Jewish philosopher Maimonides, who once said that the Seder ought to be done differently every time so that the children will notice and ask: Why is this night different? In this respect, the Seder stands at the opposite end of the spectrum from the Catholic mass, in which not even a syllable can be changed without the permission of a pope. The Seder is not a late Beethoven string quartet, which even the most accomplished musician tries to play as written. It is more like the chord structure of a jazz standard, which requires riffs and innovations and which every serious musician tries to play differently, not only from the way others play it but from his or her own last performance.

The Seder and the story that goes with it are not only feasts for the taste buds and the memory. They are also a treasure trove for some-one with an interest in the history of religions. It echoes creation myths that predate the one in Genesis, and which tell of gods who create the earth by defeating the great cosmic sea dragon (alluded to in the Bible as Tiamat). The prophet Isaiah later recalled this primal scene when he conveyed God's promise to the exiled Jews in Babylon that the same God who once split the seas asunder would once again come to their rescue (Isaiah 5:19–21). The fusing of the exodus from Egypt with both the original creation and the deliverance from Baby-lonian captivity — and also with the eventual coming on earth of God's reign of *shalom* — makes the story recounted at the Seder one of the most potent ever told anywhere. No wonder it has lasted so long and gone far beyond the confines of a single religious tradition.

Back to our dining room table. The opening bars having been sounded, and with everyone's stomach beginning to ask "Why the long delay?" the riffs and runs of our own Seder are about to begin. One standard chord concerns the traditional "four children" and how to cope with their various ways of responding to the Seder. The children are the wise one, the wicked (or rebellious) one, the simple one, and the one who does not know how to ask. But just as any imaginative actor can enliven a stock character, so the four children can be interpreted in four thousand different ways. The Haggadah we are using this year, a new one from the Shalom Hartman Institute in Jerusalem, portrays the four children — among many other illus-trations — as the Marx brothers. In this slapstick variant, Chico is the wicked child; Groucho, surprisingly, is the wise one; Zeppo is the simple one; and Harpo is the one who doesn't know how to ask (or in this case cannot ask because he cannot talk and his celebrated honking horn will not quite do). Another picture, dating from 1949, shows the four children as adults. One is sitting with a puzzled look on his face; one is blissfully perusing the racing form; one is menac-ing the tablets of the Law with an ax; one is quietly studying Torah.

My favorite picture comes from the Rabbinical Association of America. Entitled "Four Aspects in Each of Us," it shows four colored cut-out figures in which parts of each one appear in each of the others. Although our Haggadah dutifully presents all these interpretations, it seems to favor the last one. It quotes Yaariv Ben Ahahoron, an Israeli author, who says he recoils from the stereotyping that some views of the four children seem to suggest. He prefers, he says, to view them as a set of diverse "strategies for addressing four different facets of each and every child." Thus, combining the wise with the rebellious ("wicked") qualities can produce a revolutionary *chalutz,* a pioneer, who challenges the status quo and the inherited meanings of the feast. The suggestion is that each of the children has a legitimate place in the family and in Judaism itself.

I am grateful for this generous interpretation of the four children when, during the animated discussion that goes on during the Seder, Nicholas asks why, if God was so powerful he could roll back the Red Sea, he could not just liberate the Jews without sending all those awful plagues, especially the death of the firstborn. "He sounds like some kind of a sadist," he says, surprising some of our guests that he knows the word. There is a brief, embarrassed silence, but then — buoyed by the Haggadah's implicit encouragement of a little rebellion, I assure him that it is an excellent question.

It is, of course. The rabbis have struggled with it for generations. An energetic argument ensues. Some of the guests — resorting to a typical liberal trope — say this must reflect a primitive idea of God, which the progress of civilization has now happily left behind. Others say it is just a story, so we shouldn't take it so seriously. The Haggadah itself, however, has its own opinion on this eternal puzzler. God's ultimate purpose, it argues, was not just the physical liberation of slaves but "the spiritual liberation of Pharaoh from his illusions of total power." The Egyptian empire was, after all, one of the most powerful and most enduring in history. All empires seem to be subject to illusions of omnipotence and endless life; it takes a lot to shake pride and complacency on that grand scale. But as history demonstrates, empires are not immortal. They rise, they reign, they fall. Still, it often takes a series of painful setbacks to disabuse an empire of its pretensions to permanence. Nicholas, unwittingly playing the role of the rebellious child, has prompted a memorable discussion.

The traditional Seder also contains a warning to the participants about the danger of crowing over the defeat of the proud Egyptians. As the plagues are solemnly ticked off, one by one — blood, frogs, lice, gnats, hail, murrain, boils, locusts, darkness, the death of the firstborn (these vary slightly in the different accounts) — each diner spills a drop of wine on the plate. As the small red pool accumulates, we acknowledge that our joy at being liberated is incomplete because it came at the expense of the suffering and death of others. Indeed, in a famous commentary, Rabbi Yochanan forcibly reminds his readers that God was not happy at the downfall of even the most wicked. "When the angels tried to sing songs of praise to God at the Red Sea," he writes, "God silenced them: 'My handiwork, my human creatures, are drowning in the sea and you want to sing a song of praise?'"

This endearing quotation, which is included in most Haggadot, is an invaluable reminder that in God's eyes all human beings are equally valuable. But I also remember that, if the angels were forbidden to celebrate the destruction of the Egyptian cavalry, the Israelites, mere human beings as they were, could not help doing so. One of the oldest fragments in the Bible, now incorporated in chapter 15 of the Book of Exodus, is the so-called Song of Miriam and occurs just after the Egyptians have met their watery fate.

> Sing to the Lord, for he has triumphed gloriously,
> The horse and his rider, he has thrown into the sea (1).

This raises a question for me, but after turning it over in my mind, I decide to save it for another Seder. Why does God warn the angels not to exalt over the destruction of their enemies but seems to allow the human beings to go ahead and flaunt their enjoyment at seeing their captors drowned? Is the angelic restraint too much to expect from mere mortals? Did the rabbis add the divine scolding only years later, when their consciences began to bother them? Or is there some other (or many other) answer(s)?

I'm not sure why I did not raise the question when it first occurred to me. Maybe it was because it was already getting late, and Seder discussions have a way of prolonging themselves unduly. But of course, some of it was due to a residual "goyische" reluctance to appear too critical, to become a maladroit guest at my own table. In retrospect, I wish I had raised it. Maybe next year I will. The continued vitality of the Seder over so many centuries testifies to its capacity to absorb any and all questions. Not to raise one that is on your mind comes close to violating, or at least not trusting, the durability of a ceremony that is sturdy because it is flexible, and it has handled much tougher questions than that one.

Listening in on all the discussion at a lively Seder might well make a guest wonder whether the old cliché of Jews as an unusually argumentative, even haggling, people has a grain of truth. But the convivial spirit in which the participants enter the discussion belies the stereotype. Also, to one who knows a little about Jewish history, the back-and-forth around the Seder table illustrates something very fundamental about the whole tradition, namely, that it is open to continuous and incremental revision. In fact, the Talmud, which is the authoritative religious and ethical source for Jews, is a vast compilation of the commentaries, interpretations, and elaborations that the rabbis have made through many centuries on the original scriptures. True, in reading some parts of the Talmud, one can get the impression that what is going on sounds at times like splitting hairs. But to follow the arguments is to learn an indispensable lesson about law and ethics: that no two cases, however similar they may first appear, are exactly alike.

Our own experience tells us this is true. We can claim that we do not like to make fine distinctions, but when we are accused of something or when we have an anguishing choice to make, we do not want our case to be subsumed under some general principle. We know it is in some ways unique, if only because circumstances change and each person is a unique individual. Jewish religious thought, from the most esoteric debates recorded in the Talmud, to the most recent exchange at a Seder, to the latest rabbinical commentary, is an ongoing, open-ended process, striving always to think through current, often unprecedented, issues in the light of a very old tradition.

Naturally, it is hardly possible for a Christian to sit through a Seder, watch the breaking of the *matzah* and the pouring of the wine, and not be reminded of Christ's last supper with his disciples in the upper room in Jerusalem. Was it a Seder the Galilean rabbi was celebrating? It certainly looks that way, though scholars are not certain. Was it thought appropriate in those days to raise difficult questions and to welcome new interpretations? If so, the words Jesus uttered, now repeated at the Christian rite of Holy Communion, might be a kind of Haggadah.[4] If it is, it is one that has unfortunately become terribly frozen over the centuries. It has turned both solemn and, too often, static. It is hard to imagine participants in a Communion service cross-examining the ceremony while it is in progress or voicing their doubts about the validity or morality of the stories. I do not advocate the abolition of the austere, simple, almost bleak commemorations of "the Lord's Supper" that I knew as a child, nor the ornate, high liturgical masses I prefer on special occasions, like Christmas Eve. But whenever I attend a Seder, it does seem to me that we Christians have lost the zesty conversation and reinterpretation that were there when Jesus participated in it.

Some Christian congregations have tried to hold a kind of Christian Seder in an effort to understand the Jewish roots of their faith better and to improve relations with Jewish neighbors. But this effort, albeit usually well intentioned, gives many Jews the heebie-jeebies. Christians have so many ceremonies of their own, runs the complaint, why do they have to take over one of ours? It does little good to remind Jews (and some Christians) that for the first three generations most Christians were Jews and probably celebrated Seders at Passover. In fact, some scholars argue that whole sections in the Gospels probably emerged from discussions among those early Jewish Christians as they celebrated their holidays about how to understand the disgraceful death of the man they believed was their Messiah.

Still, even Jewish scholars who understand this history quite well often remain skeptical and uncomfortable about Christian Seders. Their uneasiness is understandable. In some measure I share it. Even though the original "Last Supper" may well have been a "Last Seder," or the forerunner of what would now be recognized as a Seder, there is something insensitive about leaping over the two millennia that have elapsed since then. The significance that religious ceremonies have for the people who celebrate them changes over the years, depending in part on the historical situation in which they find themselves. Whatever the Seder may once have meant to the earliest Christians, the vast majority of them stopped celebrating it a very long time ago. And in the meantime, during many centuries of Christian dominance, the Seder became one of the ways in which Jews quietly declined to be absorbed into the major religious culture. For Christians to dilute the distinctiveness of the Seder by using it in a Christian context, however generous the impulse might be, does not necessarily move the still touchy relationship between Jews and Christians to a higher plane. Gentiles are sometimes welcomed to Jewish Seders. I believe we should attend them whenever we are invited and even ask to be invited if we are not. But in this historical moment, let us not appropriate for Christian purposes — however worthy — something that belongs to Jews.[5]

Throughout the Seder, an extra wineglass has been sitting on the table. Now, as the hour grows late, it is filled for the prophet Elijah, who, custom says, may appear at the door and ask to be admitted. In the Jewish tradition, Elijah is the prophet of good news who reconciles children to their parents ("a family values kind of guy," one of our guests suggested) and who is also the immediate predecessor of the messiah. Someone, usually one of the children, is dispatched to fling open the door. If no one is there, none of the dinner guests seems too upset. From a Jewish perspective, the wait has already been a long one. There are smiles and jokes, maybe in part because the adults have already consumed the Seder's requisite four cups of wine. But the light touch cannot fully obscure my recognition that here we come to a great divide.

Or do we? Elijah does not appear, and neither does any messiah. What does it mean? In thinking about this seemingly light but actually quite significant part of the Seder — that there is no one at the door — it is time to look again at the contentious term "messiah." The word simply means "one who is anointed by God to accomplish a particular task." Jews and Christians, it has been said over and over again, differ on whether the title "messiah" can legitimately be applied to Jesus. Jews point out that he obviously did not accomplish the things that at least some Jews expected a messiah was to do at that time, namely, to liberate them from their Roman captors and usher in an era of peace and justice.

Recent historical research has cast some helpful light on this question. It now seems certain that not all Jews at the time of Jesus expected a messianic figure at all. Among those who did, there were many different hopes and expectations of what such a figure should accomplish, and some of them contradicted others. There was no firm consensus.[6] Still, Jesus did not seem to achieve anything that any of them expected. He did not lead a successful revolution against the Romans. He did not throw out the corrupt priests who had sold out to the Romans. True, he chased some small-time swindlers ("money-changers") out of the Temple, but that was a symbolic gesture, and the racketeers were undoubtedly back the next day. He did not purify or rebuild the Temple. He was, as far as anyone at the time could see, completely miscast, a consummate fiasco as a messiah. So why would anyone give him this title, as his earliest followers — all Jews — clearly did, despite his spectacular failure?

Shelves of books have been devoted to this question. One plausible explanation is that after he was crucified, Jesus' followers, who were convinced he was still alive, were forced to begin working with a completely different definition of "messiah." Given the circumstances of his death, they had to discard the theories that called for a visible and obvious historical success story. They embraced instead an understanding of "messiah" that combined it with another powerful old Jewish concept, that of the "suffering servant," who takes the pain of the whole people on himself. Both the Messiah and the suffering servant were seen as God's representative to human beings, and both demonstrated the manner in which Israel serves God. For the earliest Christians, the fusing of these two concepts meant that it was precisely Jesus' suffering and humiliation, vindicated by God's raising him from the dead, that confirmed his messiahship. His power was proven by his powerlessness, his victory for God by his defeat at the hands of an evil empire.

But the earlier concepts of what a messiah should be never died out, and as history unfolded, the term itself became a point of contention. As a child in Sunday school, I was taught that the main difference — sometimes it was put as the only difference — between Jews and Christians was that "they believe the messiah is yet to come." I do not recall that this was ever said in a deprecating way. It was just a difference, an interesting or even curious one, but nothing more than that. This distinction, however, stuck in my head, and when one of my dormmates at college told me he was Jewish (the first Jewish person of my age I had ever met) during my second week, it was the first thing that came to my mind. "Oh yeah," I said, smiling, "you believe the messiah is yet to come. Right?"

He seemed a little taken aback but recovered quickly. "Well," he offered, "that's what they say. But to tell you the truth, I don't believe he's ever coming."

I was temporarily taken back by his answer. If he hasn't already come, and he is not yet to come, then where does that leave us? I thought. But I was far too polite to say so.

That was over fifty years ago, and it was a quick exchange between two new freshmen in Ashurst dormitory at the University of Pennsylvania. But I have thought about it many times since. Imbedded in that elliptical chat between two adolescents in a third-floor hallway lie a host of perennial riddles about human life and history. In two quick sentences we had covered all the ground tracked over for centuries of theological brow-knitting. One of my favorite theologians, Reinhold Niebuhr, in his masterpiece *The Nature and Destiny of Man*, divides all human cultures into those that expect a messiah and those that do not. The questions are anything but trivial. Does history have a direction or doesn't it? The cultures that "expect a messiah," Niebuhr wrote, inhabit a time sequence that goes from past to present to future and for which some ultimate fulfillment is expected or hoped for. Those that "do not expect a messiah," according to Niebuhr, see time as fundamentally cyclical. We live through long epochs of growth and decay, but then the great wheel simply turns again. This is indeed a great divide, but it puts Jews and Christians and Muslims (along with an array of secular "messianisms") on one side and all the rest on the other.[7]

In more recent years I have grown uncomfortable with Niebuhr's neat distinction. For example, even within the Jewish-Christian-Islamic view of history, there are important differences. If the ultimate meaning and purpose of history has indeed already begun to appear in history (as biblical faith suggests), albeit in hidden form, then how open — really — is the future? Are we free, in some measure at least, to shape it? Or are we just slogging along a defined path toward a goal that has already been set? Some Christians seem to believe we are simply enacting a divine scenario. On the other hand, if we have no clues within history of God's intention for the creation, then how are we to recognize that intention as it unfolds and eventually comes to fruition? Or is there no divine intention? We may not be able to answer these questions, but they are hardly trivial.

"Already come and coming again?" Or "yet to come?" These different interpretations of the messianic idea seem irreconcilable. But neither should the divergence be exaggerated either. Religious Jews, like Christians, also believe that God has manifested himself within human history, through the patriarchs and prophets to be sure, but principally through the Torah. So we do have clues. It is often remarked that Moses does not play the central part in the Passover story. That role is assigned to God. But Moses, as the prophet through whom God acted to liberate an enslaved people and through whom God later bestowed the Torah on the Israelites at Mount Sinai, is still an indispensable figure in the narrative. Like the other prophets, he reminds us that God works through human beings, both accomplishing his purposes and revealing something of the divine nature. Some religious Jews even allow that Jesus can be understood as a part of this divine self-revelation, but not the central one Christians believe him to be. Similarly, Christians believe that God revealed himself in the centuries before Jesus. "In many and various ways," writes the author of the Letter to the Hebrews, "God spoke of old to our fathers by the prophets, but in these last days he has spoken to us through a Son [who] reflects the glory of God and bears the very stamp of his nature" (Hebrews 1:1–3). Also, the Christian creeds, echoing the Jewish belief that something important is "yet to come," include a hoped-for ultimate fulfillment, a "coming again," which will involve this same figure. These are obviously different beliefs, but they are variations of a common underlying "messianic" understanding of history.[8]

But what if my classmate's flip response to my inept question actually hints at a truth neither of us had in mind at the time? I have come to look forward to the opening of the door for an Elijah who is always a no-show, and I have come to believe that precisely by not appearing, that great prophet is teaching us something we need to know. What does it mean that there is never anyone at the door? What if, for all practical purposes, no messiah can be counted on? Would that make any significant difference in the way we engage in the present human enterprise?

This idea is not as alien to Jewish history as it may first sound. Discussions among Jewish thinkers about the messiah and the coming age of *shalom* have sometimes hinted at just this possibility. In his classic work *The Messianic Idea in Judaism*, Gershom Scholem includes a chapter on the messianic idea in Kabbalah, the Jewish mystical tradition. In this vein of thinking, the critical human task is that of repairing and mending the world (*tikkun*). This redemption of the world is not a spectacular intrusion from beyond but rather the "logical consequence" of the history of the world. Further, Scholem continues:

> The Messiah himself will not bring the redemption; rather he symbolizes the advent of the redemption, the completion of the task of emendation. . . . Galut [exile] and redemption are not historical manifestations peculiar to Israel, but manifestations of all being, up to and including the mystery of divinity itself.[9]

In this fascinating school of Jewish thought, Scholem continues, the hope for the redemption of Israel "was widened and deepened by making it the symbol of the redemption of the whole world, the restoration of the universe to the state it was to have attained when the Creator planned its creation."[10] This insight calls to mind the idea, shaped by Saint Paul and developed by later Christian theologians, that not just human beings but the cosmos itself is somehow flawed or defective, that sin and estrangement infect the entire creation. In a soaring passage in his Epistle to the Romans, Saint Paul declares:

> The created universe is waiting with eager expectation . . . It was subject to frustration [but] is to be freed from the shackles of mortality and to enter upon the glorious liberty of the children of God. Up to the present, as we know, the whole created universe with all its parts, groans as if in the pangs of childbirth (Romans 8:19–22).

Further, according to the Kabbalah, it is not just the universe that suffers pain and exile. God himself feels the pangs too. God is in exile. And human suffering and striving serve not only to repair the broken cosmos but to restore God to God's original perfection.

True, the idea that God needs anything, or that human beings can help restore God, has been deemed totally unacceptable by many Jewish and Christian scholars. Some of the Christians have stressed the "impassibility" of God (the idea that he is incapable of suffering or feeling emotion) as one of the marks of his divine perfection. They strenuously insist that God needs no help at all. But, if the life of Jesus tells us something about the nature of God, then the question of whether God needs help from human beings can be answered in a very different manner. Christians believe that God was fully present in a tiny, helpless infant who needed someone to change his diapers. Jesus asked people for water to drink and cried when a friend died. And eventually he had to be gently eased down off the cross, a scene that is movingly depicted in so many *descendamientos.* I think this means we cannot imagine God as never needing human hands. Jesus tells his followers very distinctly that when they feed the hungry, clothe the naked, or visit the prisoner, they are doing it for him.

Also, the kabbalistic interpretation of the messiah that Scholem describes represents a strain in Judaism that the rabbinical establishment has often viewed with disfavor. But it has been rediscovered in recent years, thanks in part to the brilliance of Scholem's own work, and it is gradually assuming a more accepted place in the halls of intellectual respectability, though it is still hotly disputed. As an outsider, I hesitate to advocate one Jewish view against another, especially on an issue as sensitive as the meaning of the messiah. Still, I cannot help airing my excitement in discovering the Kabbalah, the rich and powerful, if not quite mainstream, voice within the wide spectrum of Jewish speculation. Besides, if Saint Paul himself was a kind of proto-kabbalist, or a kabbalist before his time, this would open a whole new venue for Jewish-Christian dialogue.

The boldness and imagination of the Jewish kabbalists set me to wondering what a comparable approach to Christian ideas of the messiah might yield. Already many Christian theologians — most of whom know nothing at all about Kabbalah — insist that it is impossible to understand Jesus without the centerpiece and content of his message, the dawning of God's age of *shalom.* Liberation theologians, in particular, point out that Jesus only rarely points to himself, but constantly points his hearers to the hidden signs of the reigning of God in their midst. I would like to carry this a step further. What if Jesus' intention was not to be a cosmic deliverer? What if his intention was to "play the messianic card" — including riding into Jerusalem and symbolically purging the Temple — so that no one could mistake what he was doing, but then taking it upon himself to subvert the whole idea? What if Jesus, by confronting the power elites nonviolently and then being betrayed by his friends and executed by the Romans as a dissident, was actually trying to put an end to extravagant messianic fantasies? He played part of the script as written but then tore it up. As I have suggested in Chapter 4, he demonstrated the strength of fragility. He acted for a while as a conqueror-messiah was supposed to act but then declined to play the role of a cosmic champion. He revealed a God who, rather than dispatching legions of angels, chooses to struggle and suffer along with human beings.

The difficulty is that just as Jesus was misunderstood and betrayed by his followers before his death, we have continued to betray and misunderstand him afterward. Some of this misunderstanding found its way into the pages of the New Testament itself. But the idea that he will come again in power and glory, like a vanquishing warrior, contradicts what he did and said during his lifetime. It is true that here and there the New Testament portrays a grandiose, even vengeful, Second Coming. But that is not the only way, or even the most frequent way, that the New Testament speaks of Jesus' continuing and future role. Some early Christians spoke, rather, about the "appearing" of Jesus, the making more visible of someone and something that is already present.

This reading of how Jesus both played and subverted the "messianic" script is not original to me. It is espoused by a growing number of Christian scholars today. But even if it were the majority view, it would not solve all the long-standing disagreements about the messiah either among Christians or among Jews or between Jews and Christians. Still, if it were more widely preached and taught, it might provide a welcome opening.

The same might be said about the cliché that claims what separates Christians from Jews is that Christians believe Jesus was the Son of God while Jews do not. How many times have I heard this confidently voiced by people who ought to know better? Even a cursory awareness of both traditions, however, indicates that this trite distinction is misleading. Using "son" to describe Jesus' relationship to God need not cause as much dissension as it often has. Both Jewish and Christian scholars agree that the words "Son of God" were widely known during the period in which Jesus lived, and Jews used them to designate one who represents God or for one who represents the people of Israel to God. Also, the whole people of Israel is sometimes spoken of in Jewish texts as God's "son." For example, when instructing Moses on what to say to the pharaoh to obtain the release of the Israelites, God says: "And you shall say to Pharaoh, 'Thus says the Lord, Israel is my first-born son, and I say to you, 'Let my son go that he may serve me'" (Exodus 4:22, 23).

What complicates the title "Son of God" when it is used to refer to Jesus is not its usage in the Old Testament or during the period of Jesus' life but in the later absorption of the word "son" into Trinitarian theology. That is indeed a quite different use of "son" and one on which Jews can hardly be expected to agree since there have been a considerable number of disagreements even among Christians about it. It is possible that some Jews may not object to seeing in Jesus a "representative" of God or even a "child" of God if that did not carry all the Trinitarian baggage with it.[11]

So, when Elijah does not appear year after year, where does this leave us? Saint Paul had a useful way of understanding this issue. He saw Jesus as a messiah, one who is sent by God. He saw him as the one in whom God had reached out to include the Gentiles in a covenant previously restricted to the descendants of Abraham. As for the Jews themselves, Saint Paul had no doubt that they would be included in the salvation God intended for all peoples. Indeed, in the Epistle to the Romans, he makes this point quite emphatically. "All Israel will be saved," he says. ". . . they are beloved for the sake of their forefathers. For the gifts and the call of God are irrevocable" (Romans 11:26, 29). Simply put, this means that Jesus is the representative God sends to open the door to the gentiles to worship and serve the God of Abraham, Isaac, and Jacob — the God Jews serve. I strongly agree with the biblical scholar Krister Stendahl that this passage rules out Christian missions to the Jews. If Jews are already part of God's people "for the sake of their forefathers," then it is mainly for the gentiles (what the Bible calls "the nations") that God has manifested himself in Jesus.

There is more. If Elijah, and the messiah, are indefinitely delayed, what does that mean for Niebuhr's nice distinction between those cultures that do and those that do not "expect a messiah"? I think what it opens is an even wider ecumenical door. It means that the barrier between the "Abrahamic" faiths (Judaism, Christianity, and Islam) and the others, such as Buddhism, Hinduism, and the various indigenous religions, becomes a little lower. It suggests that we are all in this together. Does the absent Elijah's message that no Hand-from-the-Sky is going to clean up our human mess mean that we humans are the only actors in cosmic history, that history has no direction, no meaning, except what we manage to give it? This is an honest option that appeals to many people. It is the underlying impulse of existentialism, humanism, and Marxism, the main surrogate religions of the twentieth century. It is also an option that commends itself to many nominal Christians and Jews. But it is not the only answer implied by no-Elijah-at-the-door. Another possibility has been suggested by Rabbi Irving Greenberg's thoughtful interpretation of the Holocaust. Greenberg believes that through that unprecedented evil, God makes it clear that we cannot rely on divine intervention to redress our human injustices. If God did not reach down to smash the gas chambers and destroy the ovens at Auschwitz, does it make any sense to expect God to intervene at some future time? I agree with Greenberg. It is now up to us, but we are not alone. God suffers with us and sustains us. There is no deus ex machina, as in the ancient Greek dramas,[12] but there is God-with-us ("Emmanuel"). Greenberg's words remind me of those of Jesus when he told his followers, "I will be *with* you until the end of the age." There is a difference between one who promises to be with us and one who is expected to do what needs to be done for us.

Now our Passover Seder is almost over. The children have raced around the house searching for the *afikoman,* the half of the piece of *matzah* that was concealed (this time hidden behind a piece of music on the piano) at the beginning of the dinner. The closing blessing is said. Everyone raises a glass and says, "Next year in Jerusalem" — although we know that next year we will probably be gathered right here. Now there are coats to put on, dishes to wash, sleepy children to tuck into bed, and *matzah* crumbs to sweep up. A little groggy myself, I nonetheless recognize that I have just taken part in a ceremony that goes back in history to the time before my own religion came to birth. This was a night different from all other nights. It always is.

9

After All the Apologies

Yom ha-Shoah

Ever since Rosh Hashana, the New Year, the question had been bitterly debated all over the camp. Fasting meant a quicker death. Here everybody fasted all year round. Every day was Yom Kippur. And the book of life and death was no longer in God's hands, but in the hands of the executioner. The words *mi yichye umi yamut,* "who shall live and who shall die," had an immediate bearing.

— Elie Wiesel[1]

THE NAZIS, TOO, knew about the Jewish holidays, and celebrated them in their own way. On Yom Kippur of 1940 they locked the Jews into the Warsaw ghetto. On Tisha B'Av 1942 they began to deport six thousand Jews out of Warsaw. They scheduled what they thought would be the final destruction of the ghetto for Passover 1943. Josef Mengele was familiar with the tradition of the divine trial at Yom Kippur. He scheduled special "selections" of who would be retained for more slave labor and who would be shipped to the gas chambers immediately so that, as he put it, he — not God — could decide "who shall live and who shall die." In one camp the guards served extra food with rich soup and noodles on Yom Kippur, the day many Jews fast. The Holocaust was not just a nearly successful attempt to annihilate the entire Jewish people, it was also a deliberate effort to destroy the Jewish religion.[2]

Yom ha-Shoah is a new Jewish holiday that was first inaugurated by the Israeli Knesset on April 12, 1951, as Yom ha-Shoah U'Mered ha-Getaot (Holocaust and Ghetto Revolt Remembrance Day). Since then it has spread around the world. It comes on the twenty-seventh day of the Jewish month of Nisan, late April or early May on the Western calendar. It is intended to commemorate, not only those who were deliberately starved and frozen to death or gassed or shot by Einsatzgruppen, but also those who managed to maintain their dignity and teach their children under horrendous circumstances, as well as those — like the Warsaw ghetto fighters — who died resisting the atrocity.

Because it is a relatively new holiday, the liturgies of Yom ha-Shoah are still taking shape and vary from place to place. The events are often held in public places, not just in synagogues, and public figures frequently speak. Almost always prayers such as the mourners' Kaddish are recited. Sometimes survivors are invited to speak, and there are readings of accounts and testimonies from those horrendous days. But suggestions for how best to mark the day are constantly being put forward. One Jewish writer has suggested that it could be the occasion to bring back the medieval kabbalistic custom of what was then called *tzom shtikah*. This is a fast, like the one on Yom Kippur, only in this one the people refrain from speaking, not eating: it is a fast of silence. During such a silence, he proposes, the questions posed by the Shoah, for which there are simply no satisfying answers, can be pondered. Also, as Strassfeld says, "an aura of silence creates an appropriate space in which to ponder the silence of the world and the silence of God during those awful years."[3]

As a Christian husband with a Jewish family, the memory of the Shoah causes me a particular kind of ache. Not as intense, surely, as the distress of those who suffered it directly or those whose families were killed, but an inward hurt nonetheless. It arises from my recognition that the Holocaust, although it was perpetrated by a neo-pagan ideology, did not occur in a vacuum. It took place on soil prepared by more than a thousand years of Christian derogation of Jews and Judaism. In recent decades, little by little, many Christians have come to realize this complicity. Church after church has made a statement of apology, penitence, and regret. At present, however, this recognition remains for the most part on an intellectual level. Most American Christians who know the ghastly history regret it, but few feel any personal responsibility. After all, "we" were not there, and didn't the United States fight a war against Hitler? There is even the temptation to find some convenient scapegoat like (the hardly blameless) Pope Pius XII, in part, I suspect, to make the rest of us feel a little better. Rarely does the full import of Christianity's involvement in this epochal iniquity penetrate to the spiritual level. Books are written; conferences are held; statements are issued; but only a few real changes have been made in the theological formulations and liturgical practices that fostered anti-Judaism. Still, the truth is that anti-Judaism is not peripheral to Christianity. It is imbedded in the scriptures, liturgies, and even the art and architecture of the churches. It is perpetuated in painting, sculpture, and literature. Can we do anything about it?

I am convinced that before there can be any substantive Christian response, the painful awareness of this ugly fact must touch us personally, at the core of our lives. But I am equally convinced that, once this happens, neither breast-beating nor bouncing into a myopic ardor for all things Jewish is an appropriate response. Guilt, like fear, seldom produces responsible moral action, and it is too easy for some Christians to luxuriate in their guilt. As for philo-Semitism, it has in the past too easily mutated, like a spiritual Dr. Jekyll and Mr. Hyde, into anti-Semitism when the Jews did not live up to all that was expected of them.

I remember to the day, almost to the hour and minute, when my largely intellectual awareness of the role of Christianity in the Holocaust sank from my head into my entrails. It happened during one of those years when Easter and Passover occur in the same week. It was a few years after Nina and I had married, and we had gone to New York to celebrate Passover with her family. After partaking in the extended family's Seder and basking in their expansive hospitality at Nina's mother's ample apartment, I slipped away the next afternoon to attend the Good Friday service at a nearby Episcopal church of the "high" Anglo-Catholic coloration. I vaguely knew that churches in this tradition sometimes continue to practice rituals that the Roman Catholic Church has discarded. But I was not prepared for what I would find.

Ever since I first heard about the crucifixion of Christ as a small boy, I have always approached Good Friday with a sense of awe and gratitude. The idea that God himself, in the person of Jesus, was willing to taste death, the ultimate terror of the human condition, stirred me intensely. It still does. I therefore entered the church, which I had never been in before, with a sense of expectation and gratitude. I was not disappointed — at least not at first. As is the custom during the forty days of Lent, the cross on the altar was veiled with a diaphanous black cloth. The congregation joined in the prayers and hymns with sober intensity. The pageantry, the solemn music, and the ancient narrative all carried me along. But then, about an hour after the service began, came the dénouement that marked me indelibly.

The priest quietly announced that the time had come for the annual Adoration of the Cross. I had read about this ritual but had never seen it before, so I watched attentively. First, a deacon gently removed the veiled cross from the altar and carried it to the priest who was celebrating the Eucharist. He, in turn, removed the veil and placed the simple wooden cross just outside the altar rail at the head of the central aisle. He then invited the congregation to "contemplate the mystery of the cross and of the world's salvation." With that, the people removed their shoes and, one by one, walked forward, knelt, kissed the cross, and returned to their seats. To my surprise, I felt strongly drawn to join them, but I did not know quite why. In the mixture of Quaker and Baptist traditions I was raised in, kneeling in front of crosses and kissing them would have been viewed with a mixture of distaste and revulsion. But in more recent years I had seen Russians in Moscow reverently kissing icons and Jews kissing their prayer shawls and prayer books after they had touched the Torah with them. I had even watched with surprise as many of the Jews at a Yom Kippur service fell to their knees at one point and prostrated themselves toward the Torah scroll. (I had been under the mistaken impression that Jews never knelt.) So, ironically delivered from my boyhood biases by Russians and Jews, I unlaced my shoes, went forward, knelt, and kissed the replica of the Roman gallows on which Christ had died. Somehow the tactile encounter with this symbol of innocent suffering spoke to me as words never had. The old spiritual "Were you there when they crucified my Lord?" came to mind. We are, after all, creatures of our senses as well as our minds.

I returned to my pew to meditate. But then, as more people went forward, I began to notice what the choir was singing; the words had been printed so the congregation could follow. I was immediately startled and dismayed. They were chanting something called the Re-proaches, historically a principal locus of liturgical anti-Judaism, which I thought had been removed from Good Friday services years before. But here it was, being chanted on the Upper West Side of New York City in the 1990s. As I listened, I began fidgeting in my seat. I felt myself becoming angry, even feeling betrayed. How had I been snared into an elegant service commemorating the central event in my faith, only to be lured into a ritual denunciation of the Jews? It was especially personal because I knew that for me now "the Jews" referred not only to millions of people around the world and through the centuries but to my wife, our son, and to Suzanne, Em-manuel, Benjy, and the whole crew that was ready to fling open the apartment door and hug me later with the cheery inquiry, "Well, how was church?" At first I bit my lip and stayed. But within a few min-utes the contradictions became unbearable, and I got up and strode out into the welcome noise of the taxis on West End Avenue.

The next morning, I hurried directly to the nearest branch library to brush up on what I had once learned, many years before, about the Reproaches (which are still often referred to by their Latin name, the Improperia). The only edition of *The Catholic Encyclopedia* in that branch had been published in 1913. What I discovered made me feel even worse. The verses the choir sings are torn out of context from the Jewish prophets. First they quote Jeremiah (2:21): "Yet I planted you as a choice vine, from the purest stock. How then did you turn degenerate and become a wild vine?" Then they cite Isaiah 5:4: "What more was there to do for my vineyard, that I have not done for it? When I expected it to yield grapes, why did it yield wild grapes?"

How, I wondered, and when, had this numbing misuse of the Jew-ish scriptures against the people who produced them found its way into the Good Friday service? Further reading made me realize that the Reproaches had first appeared in Christian liturgies in the ninth or tenth century, but traces of them can be found three hundred years earlier. The article states that while the Adoration of the Cross proceeds, the choir chants the words which "the Savior is made to ut-ter against the Jews, who in requital for all the divine favors and par-ticularly for the delivery from the bondage of Egypt and safe conduct into the Promised Land, inflicted the ignominies of the Passion and cruel death."[4]

"The Savior is *made* to utter"! In other words, Jesus never said these things. The phrases are simply lifted from the original setting and placed in his mouth. Then "the Jews" are singled out for "the ignominies of the Passion and cruel death." It would be hard to imagine a crueler distortion. This description then goes on to exult in the "unsurpassed . . . simple beauty" of the musical setting, composed by Palestrina in 1560, and to praise its "dramatic feeling and depth of expression." It concludes with the information that the Reproaches in this "exquisite" musical setting may still be heard in the Sistine Chapel on Good Friday each year.[5] When I got back to Cambridge, I went to a library and tried a more recent edition of the *Catholic Encyclopedia* (1967), hoping it might offer better news. But it did not help much. It says the Reproaches are "directed against God's own people, and appear as utterances of Jesus during the adoration of the Cross." Softer language, but the same damage is done.[6]

In *The Last of the Just*, Ernie Levy writes, "The Christians say they love Christ, but I think they hate him without knowing it. So they take the cross by the other end and make a sword out of it and strike us with it."[7] The Reproaches constitute a particularly grotesque example of twisting the cross into a sword. Literally, to put words condemning his own people into the mouth of Jesus Christ while worshipers are venerating the cross constitutes the nadir of Christian liturgical anti-Judaism. The thought that they were used for a thousand years on the holiest day of the Christian year stuns the spirit. But on that particular Good Friday the Reproaches served at least one good purpose. They pushed my realization of the depth of Christian anti-Judaism from my mind into my marrow.

After that, I began trying to discover just how widely the Reproaches are still used. I knew that Pope John XXIII had removed the phrase "perfidious Jews" from the Good Friday liturgy. But what about the Reproaches themselves? Specialists in Catholic liturgy told me they were no longer obligatory; whether to use them was up to local bishops and parishes. One said that to his knowledge they had not been used in Roman Catholic churches in the United States for years. Although they still appeared in the actual text, he said, the rubric covering their use states that either the Reproaches "or some other suitable songs" may be sung during the liturgy, but some Catholics I spoke with told me they had not heard them for years, even decades.[8] When I mentioned to one colleague that it was in an An glo-Catholic — not a Roman Catholic — church that I had heard the Reproaches, he told me that Anglicans often continue liturgical practices that have been abandoned by Roman Catholics, especially, he added, smiling ruefully, if they are set to beautiful music.

Krister Stendahl, the Swedish Lutheran bishop who has spent a lifetime engaged in Christian-Jewish dialogue, had a different view of the matter. He helpfully reminded me that I might be hearing the Reproaches differently from the way other people hear them. He suggested that for most Christians the words placed in Jesus' mouth call them, the Christians present, to sorrow and repentance and do not refer to the Jews. I had to concede that whenever I have heard sermons about the crucifixion, the preacher always emphasizes that it is we — those in the congregation — who crucify Christ by our coldness and indifference, that he died for our sins. But I cannot fully escape the suspicion that the Reproaches can be too easily misunderstood. Besides, in addition to the Reproaches, there is the traditional reading for Good Friday from the Gospel of John, which, time after time, speaks collectively of "the Jews" as those who demand the death of Christ. It is certainly essential for priests and ministers to point out that this Gospel was written a hundred years after the events it describes, at a time of fierce controversy between churches and synagogues. But this is at best like one of those corrections or apologies newspapers dutifully publish after a false headline has misinformed its readers. The people tend to remember the first message. And one should never forget that it was after Good Friday services that furious mobs in Russia and other places poured from the churches to beat the Jews, who learned the hard way to stay inside, behind closed doors, on the holiest of Christian days.

Christians still face an immense theological task. If we want to divest our theologies and our liturgies of anti-Judaism, we must also rid them of what used to be called supersessionism. This word describes one particularly perverse theory of the relationship between Christians and Jews. It means "to take the place of," and the idea is that after the coming of Jesus, Christianity displaced the Jewish people as the covenant partner of God. Consequently, the term used more often now is displacement theology. This theory held sway for centuries but has, in recent decades, been disavowed by almost every Christian church. One example of such a statement is the one made by the United Church of Christ:

We in the United Church of Christ acknowledge that the Christian Church has, throughout much of its history, denied God's continuing covenantal relationship with the Jewish people expressed in the faith of Judaism. This denial has often led to outright rejection of the Jewish people and to theologically and humanly intolerable violence. Faced with this history, from which we as Christians cannot, and must not disassociate ourselves, we ask for God's forgiveness.

The statement continues with commendable intentions. It asks for grace that will enable Christians,

> to turn from the past of rejection and persecution, to affirm that Judaism has not been superseded by Christianity; that Christianity is not to be understood as the successor religion to Judaism; God's covenant with the Jewish people has not been abrogated. God has not rejected the Jewish people; God is faithful in keeping covenant.[9]

It could hardly be clearer. But merely disavowing displacement theology does not go nearly far enough. Christians have to be made sufficiently aware of the damage this idea has done over the centuries so that they feel the need for the kind of repentance that leads to actual changes in ritual and practice. Here the churches have not been nearly as forthcoming. For example, the long-awaited and much-heralded statement "We Remember," issued by the Vatican in March 1998, left most Jewish and many Christian readers disappointed and disheartened. The frustration was even sharper because Pope John Paul II had announced that he hoped the document would begin a healing process. I remember how dismayed I was myself when I first read it. By its abstruseness, and what appears at times to be a calculated vagueness, it manages to relieve the church itself of all responsibility. While expressing regret about "erroneous and unjust" interpretations of the New Testament, it states that these were held by individuals and never by "the church as such." It attributes Nazi anti-Semitism to a "neo-pagan regime with roots outside Christianity" but does not mention the undeniable fact that centuries of Christian anti-Semitism, in Germany and elsewhere, sowed the seeds this neo-pagan movement reaped. It also voices regret for the failure of "sons and daughters of the church" to do more to resist the Holocaust, but this wording again seems to exculpate the church itself, institutionally and theologically, from any real complicity. When I finished reading "We Remember," I recall thinking that it was not only bitterly disappointing, it was almost worse than nothing since it claimed to be something it plainly was not. It was clear that a far more forthright and penetrating statement was still needed.

It is doubly regrettable that the Vatican statement turned out to be so weak when one remembers that within the Catholic Church itself a much stronger document had already appeared — the official apology released by the French Catholic bishops less than a year before, in October 1997. In contrast to the Vatican's statement, the French bishops speak about the Church's disobedience of divine laws and its "ecclesiastical docility." They also suggest, correctly in my opinion, that if the French church had spoken out distinctly it might have helped other institutions to speak as well. The proof that this earlier document touched a nerve was indicated when it was immediately attacked by the usual right-wing Catholic groups as a blatant betrayal. The response of Jewish groups, on the other hand, was positive and welcoming, thus undermining the complaint one sometimes hears that no matter what the churches say, the Jews will never be satisfied.[10]

Undoubtedly Pope John Paul II made a highly significant gesture when, during his trip to Israel in March 2000, he visited Yad Vashem, the Holocaust memorial, and later prayed quietly at the Western Wall. Whatever this might have meant to Jews, it sent a powerful message to Catholics and to many other Christians. It seemed to signal a fundamental redirection in Catholic thinking about Judaism. But then, unfortunately, just a few months later, the Vatican released a document entitled *Dominus Jesus*, which was intended to clarify the Church's position toward other churches and other religions. It is an acutely distressing statement. Not only does it take two steps backward in its judgment of other religions, including Judaism, it is also bound to make Catholic-Protestant relations more awkward. It retreats to the "one true Church" terminology that I often heard in my youth but thought had been abandoned after Vatican II, and it explicitly refuses to permit churches such as the one to which I belong even to be called churches.

Dominus Jesus also leaves many behind when it claims that it is God himself who has designated the bishop of Rome as the supreme teacher and authority for all Christians everywhere. I am happy to recognize the pope as the head of the Catholic Church, and I admire much of what Pope John Paul II has done, especially, ironically, in the area of Christian-Jewish relations. But, along with about one billion other non-Catholic Christians, I respectfully decline to believe that God has given him supreme authority over all of us or that other faiths must be viewed as congenitally flawed.[11]

Why does it take so agonizingly long to make the changes in Christian theology the experience of the past so patently requires? Why after so many statements by so many church bodies does so much Christian anti-Judaism persist, both in liturgies and at the popular level? As late as 1992, for example, Professor Hillel Levine of Boston University discovered that the small Bavarian city of Deggendorf had only recently stopped celebrating an annual pilgrimage based on a legend that typifies the many local anti-Jewish Christian canards that are still thriving. The story recounts how, during a crop failure in 1337, the Jews of the town convinced a Christian woman to steal a sanctified Communion wafer and secretly bring it to them. They then tortured the wafer in several ways, including with a large thorn — probably reminiscent of the crown of thorns — and plotted to burn the town down. Then, however, the night watchman had a revelation of the Virgin Mary weeping and urging the townspeople to do something about the suffering that was being inflicted on her son. They did. They killed the town's Jews. Then they allegedly retrieved the stolen wafer from its tormentors, and it was displayed for centuries in a gold case on the altar of the town church. Each year a pilgrimage and festival, called the Deggendorf Gnad, took place, and for many years the church was adorned with fourteen murals depicting the story in detail.

As other Germans became more aware of Deggendorf — and many other local anti-Jewish traditions — voices were raised in protest. As early as 1961 Günter Grass, who in 1999 won the Nobel Prize for Literature, labeled the murals "painted anti-Semitism" and once even announced that he intended to walk into the Deggendorf church and spit. Still, both town and regional Catholic officials were reluctant to act. The annual pilgrimage and festival continued until eventually, in 1992, a new bishop stepped in and substituted a Glaubenswoche (Week of Faith) in its place, and put the murals in deep storage.[12]

But Deggendorf is not the only place in the world where Christian anti-Semitism persists decades after churches at the highest levels have denounced it, as I myself discovered on that momentous Good

Friday in New York. Sometimes the situation appears as daunting as a religious Augean stable, which will require Herculean efforts to cleanse. It is imbedded not only in liturgies but in painting, literature, and architecture. Even if the art were taken off the walls and the literature off the library shelves — which is not only highly unlikely but not even advisable — what about the statuary that is an integral part of Western cultural heritage? The historian Grover A. Zinn reminds us that in many of the great cathedrals of Europe, the church and the synagogue are symbolized by two paired female figures. The "church" stands erect, often holding a chalice, a crown firmly on her head. The "synagogue," on the other hand, is slumped, her crown has fallen off (and sometimes lies at her feet), and she is blindfolded. These twin statues appear, for example, in the cathedrals of Reims, Strassbourg, and on the main facade of Notre Dame de Paris.[13] No one will seriously contend that these cathedrals, or even their facades, be dismantled. That would not only be an inexcusable desecration, it would simply succeed in papering over an ugly part of the history we as Christians must recognize. Rather than obliterating the art, Christians might well be taught that seeing such things should always remind us to utter a quiet prayer that in the future we avoid the sins of our forebears. There is so much to do. Where do we start?

Christian anti-Judaism is rooted in the deluded theory that Christianity has displaced Judaism. Therefore, we must begin by asking how and when this peculiar notion got started, and why. Is it rooted in the Gospels and the rest of the New Testament? If not, where did it come from? These questions have stoked a fierce debate among Christian scholars. Rosemary Ruether set out her position two decades ago in her influential book *Faith and Fratricide*.[14] She argued, eloquently and disturbingly, that both anti-Judaism and displacement theology follow inevitably from the Christian claim that Jesus is the awaited messiah, because this claim implies that Jews are blind to the real meaning of their own sacred texts. Since Christians have the "correct" interpretation, not only of the New Testament but of the Hebrew scriptures as well, Christians have obviously displaced the Jews in God's plan for the ages. The church has become, to use a theological term I find distasteful, the "new Israel." Therefore, Ruether suggested, any Christian claim that Jesus is the "Christ" (which derives from the Greek word for "messiah") inevitably carries within it the logic of displacement theology and should be discontinued.

Not surprisingly, many Christian scholars disagree with Ruether on this point. Some argue that her reading of the New Testament is too monolithic, that it actually contains a variety of different understandings of who Jesus was, and that some New Testament passages, for example the latter part of Paul's Epistle to the Romans, argue explicitly against displacement. One scholar, Paul Van Buren, who devoted a lifetime to these questions, argued with an eloquence equal to Ruether's that God had in fact created two covenants, two parallel paths, and Jesus could be understood as the messiah *of the Gentiles*.[15]

As I have already said in Chapter 4, I find elements of Ruether's arguments compelling. If "messiah" carries with it some suggestion of discernible success in a project, then Jesus was certainly not one. But he did seem to use messianic actions and imagery, and he did so, I believe, in order to subvert the standard messianic scenario. According to that script, the messiah could not be defeated. If he was defeated, then he was ipso facto not the messiah. But Jesus both assumed a messianic role and was defeated. Once, in conversation, Rabbi Irving Greenberg told me that he did not believe Jesus was "a false messiah," as many Jews have asserted for centuries, but rather "a failed messiah." He seemed a bit surprised when I agreed. But, I added, Jesus' "failure" forces us to reflect deeply about what we mean by failure — or success — in human life. Jesus was without a doubt the most influential "failure" in history. Sometimes the deepest truths can be expressed only in paradox. Therefore I believe Christians can use "messiah" for Jesus, but only if we realize we are talking about a crucified messiah, a failure. This may be what Ivonne Gebara is trying to say with her idea of Jesus as "anti-messiah."

I am also attracted by Paul Van Buren's idea that God created a first covenant with Israel and then "a second covenant" with the church. In another of his many provocative contributions, Rabbi Greenberg has suggested that God may well have created innumerable covenants with each of the peoples of the earth. This helps respond to the resentment that some people, including some Christians, have felt about the traditional Jewish assertion that God made a covenant with them and with no one else, that they and no one else are God's "chosen people." Dr. David Gordis, a respected Jewish scholar, makes an intriguing suggestion. "I myself use a different formulation from the one of chosenness, which I discard," he says. "I'd like to substitute the notion of uniqueness: each of our traditions is unique in its particularity but universal in its humanity."[16] Still, I have never had any real difficulty with the Jewish claim to chosenness so long as one remembers that the Jews were not chosen to enjoy special privilege and power but for service and witness: to be "a light to the nations." Besides, even God has to start somewhere. Consequently, I prefer to think of the widening of God's one covenant to include gentiles (which means all non-Jews, not just Christians) rather than the creation of a second, third, and hundredth one.

The debate among Christians about how to construct a credible theological basis for religious pluralism continues, and it will undoubtedly go on for a long time. It is not, however, just a squabble among the monks. It has immensely serious implications. It is especially pressing, however, for Christian relations with Jews, with whom we share a large portion of the Bible and with whom there have been endless disputes about which is the right interpretation of an Old Testament passage. On this issue, my own hope is that we can one day soon lay aside contests about who has "the" correct interpretation of scriptural texts altogether. We can do this by appreciating what modern literary critics now take for granted — that texts can and should be open to multiple meanings and that one reading does not invalidate another. As with poetry, music, and paintings, we also bring to scriptural texts a variety of cultural and personal backgrounds, and the scriptures invite a variety of interpretations. To some this may sound too much like a "postmodern" way out. But it is actually a very old method of reading the Bible. The rabbis have operated with it for centuries, rarely settling on a single authoritative interpretation, but recording their disagreements and inviting successive generations of readers to enter into the never-ending conversation. It is mostly Christian exegetes who have striven to discover a univocal and authoritative meaning for each text.

Displacement theology is the deformed child of this lamentable element in a certain kind of single-minded Christian mentality. And, although the connection may seem elusive at first, it has much to do with Yom ha-Shoah. In fact, the logic is all too simple. The understandable controversies between those early Christian congregations and their Jewish neighbors (who had their own arguments with one another) were frozen into some New Testament texts, then read in churches — totally out of context — for centuries. The displacement idea, too, set in very early and became a part of the intellectual foundation of subsequent Christian theology. The consigning of Jews to ghettos and pales of settlement meant that fewer Christians could become personally acquainted with them, so stereotypes flourished and were often fused with negative Christian religious images. Then racial anti-Semitism, sometimes cloaked in pseudo-science, lit the spark that spread through the Church, and the popular culture it spawned, like a fire through a dry forest. This is why Christian theologians must go back to these earliest pathogens, trace how they still infect our liturgies and practices, and begin all over.

We have made a real start in the past forty years. But much work remains. After Christians recognize the complicity of their religion in the Shoah, there follows a nettlesome set of questions. Is there anything at all Christians can do or say, or is the proper response — as some Christian and some Jewish scholars contend — silence and repentance? These questions continue to gnaw at me even when I am not fully conscious of them. But now and then, usually unexpectedly, they leap to the surface and lash out.

One such occasion occurred a few years after my disconcerting encounter with the Reproaches. It was at a commemoration of Yom ha-Shoah sponsored by the Human Rights Commission of the City of Cambridge, Massachusetts, where we live. Along with a few other citizens, both Jewish and non-Jewish, I had been invited to speak briefly. I had never spoken at any such occasion and wondered what I could possibly say that would not sound thin and trite. But eventually I accepted. It was one of the hardest talks I have ever prepared, and it wasn't made any easier when, as we climbed into our car, a neighbor asked where we were going. I told him we were going to attend an event, sponsored by the city, commemorating the Holocaust. He looked a little puzzled. Then a glimmer of recognition appeared. "Oh, yeah," he said. "That's when the Jews remember the concentration camps and all. Right?"

I was bothered by his remark, and I answered perhaps a bit too curtly, "No. It's when we all remember those things and see what we can do to make sure they don't happen again." With that I slammed the car into gear and drove away. I was still upset when we arrived, ten minutes later. By then I had realized that it was not really my ingenuous neighbor who was making me testy. It was another eruption of my own disturbing, unanswered questions, which I had thought were safely under control. It even crossed my mind that I was feeling a little righteous attending, even speaking, at this event. Another way to keep the wraiths in their cages.

I did my best with my short talk, assuring those present that — albeit very late — we were all finally confronting the bitter reality of the Holocaust. That this commemoration was sponsored not by a synagogue or a church but by the city demonstrated how widely it had penetrated our common consciousness. I also included a few words about the caution we should exercise in dismissing so-called marginal hate groups, since the Nazis had started out in Germany as a tiny party that many people had ridiculed.

When I finished, I felt I was beginning to regain my equilibrium. But then the next speaker, a gray and wrinkled Lithuanian Jewish survivor, shuffled to the podium. At first he simply squinted hesitantly at the audience through thick steel-rimmed glasses. Then he began to speak, barely audibly. He said that what the previous speaker had described was not his experience at all. In his village in Lithuania, he said, it was not Germans or Nazis who had rounded up and shot his whole family, including the children. It was their neighbors, people they had known and lived with for years.

I listened in horror. No arrests, no deportations, no sealed trains, no selections at the station, no barbed wire, no gas, no ovens. Just neighbors arriving one day with hunting rifles, pushing whole families ahead of them out into the woods, forcing them to dig shallow graves, and killing them all. He himself had escaped when a bullet grazed his forehead, causing the loss of a lot of blood and knocking him unconscious. He was left for dead, but he later crept away and escaped. He described this memory with little outward emotion in broken English. He offered no explanation for why it had happened and no suggestion for how to prevent a recurrence. He spoke for less than five minutes, then was helped back to his seat, sat down, and stared straight ahead.

A klezmer band played Jewish music, a town official spoke, and the event was over. Soft drinks and cookies were served in the basement. People milled around. Many thanked me for my remarks. But the wraiths were back, and they were biting and gnawing at my stomach like a badly digested meal. I had to face again the question I thought I had gone beyond. Do Christians, in fact, have anything to say about this most colossal of twentieth-century crimes against humanity? Or are silence and penitence the only appropriate responses?

The tentative answer I have come to embrace is: penitence, yes; silence, no. But that is only the beginning. Remembering the Shoah and asking the hard questions about it are things Christians have to do. But the point is not to make ourselves feel sorry. It is to realize that the Shoah was not fated, it did not have to happen, and the main purpose of remembering it is to make sure it does not happen again. In that sense, my cranky answer to my neighbor was right. That the Yom ha-Shoah event we were attending was sponsored by the city (as in many cities) may not be as reassuring as I implied in my talk, but it means something. It is one indication, among others, of the position the Shoah has assumed in American life today. Not only is it — along with the founding of Israel — a definitive event in the religious identity of contemporary Jews, but there are many indications that it has also assumed a significant place in American identity. Since it opened in 1993, more than two million people have visited the United States Holocaust Memorial Museum in Washington, D.C. Every year there is a Holocaust commemoration in the rotunda of the Capitol. Millions of people saw Steven Spielberg's *Schindler's List*. A high school curriculum growing out of the need to make a new generation aware of the Shoah, called Facing History and Ourselves was introduced in 1976 in Brookline, Massachusetts, and is now used in schools all over the country. Its goal is "to engage students of diverse backgrounds in an examination of racism, prejudice and anti-Semitism in order to promote the development of a more humane and informed citizenry." In the past decade, more than 11,000 teachers have attended its workshops, and each year over 600,000 students participate in its programs.

When I think about all this, it is hard for me to believe that when I was a college student in the late 1940s, and then a divinity student in the middle 1950s, I heard virtually nothing, in class or outside, about the Holocaust. I don't even remember hearing the word. What changed this for me, however, was one man: Elie Wiesel. I still remember exactly where I was during the afternoon and evening in which I read *Night* in one sitting. It was one of the few books I have read in my life that left me a different person. Reading Wiesel, I knew that I had been overlooking — not ignoring but overlooking — an event that had enormous repercussions for how I or anyone else was to think about my own faith and my vocation. I even had to ask myself whether it was still possible for me to study theology. When I later read Richard Rubenstein's *After Auschwitz*, in which he flatly states that a belief in the God of the Bible is simply no longer feasible after the death camps, it was hard for me to imagine any plausible theological response.[17] The Shoah poses a staggering question: How could a people who had produced Goethe and Mozart and Bach devise and nearly carry out a comprehensive plan to murder every Jew in Europe — and if they had their way, every Jew in the world? It seems inconceivable. But it happened. How?

Studying for my doctoral degree, I became absorbed in the work of Dietrich Bonhoeffer, the German pastor killed by the Nazis for his role in the attempt to assassinate Hitler. This sharpened my growing interest in the sources of the Holocaust. When I finished my degree in 1962, I received an unexpected invitation to spend a year in Berlin. I accepted, and I lived the whole time in the shadow of the Wall, which had been built a year earlier. I spent every spare moment trying to answer my questions about the Holocaust, but never did. I returned home with the problem still lodged in my mind. It seemed odd to me that few of my colleagues shared my concern or my curiosity. But a few years later the situation began to change dramatically. Beginning in the 1960s and 1970s, then burgeoning during the 1980s, interest in the reasons for the Holocaust and questions about its implications became widespread. For reasons that still remain disputed, the Holocaust became a part of nearly every American's mental landscape. Why did this happen, and why did it happen then and not earlier?

Some think the widely publicized trial of Adolf Eichmann in Jerusalem in 1961 started the process. Others suspect it began when the survivors began passing away. Still others believe that several decades were required before the sheer scope and horror of the Holocaust could sink in on people, including Jews. Others believe the Holocaust was purposely raised to a higher level of consciousness by Jewish leaders who wanted to use it as an emotional appeal for the support of the state of Israel. There are also those who think that because ritual laxity and intermarriage were gaining in America, Jewish religious leaders purposely brought the Holocaust to the forefront to shore up Jewish identity as a bulwark against assimilation and mixed marriage: "Don't give Hitler a posthumous victory."

I doubt that this debate will ever be fully resolved, and it may well be that many factors were involved in the near-disappearance and eventual reemergence of the memory of the Holocaust. Nevertheless, the Holocaust now stands like a towering rebuttal of much of the religious and humanistic thinking of the nineteenth and twentieth centuries. The SS commandant who could listen to Beethoven quartets in the morning and murder Jewish women and children in the afternoon shatters any lingering notions one may have about the civilizing power of culture. As Rabbi Greenberg has written, "On the rock of Auschwitz, the classic assumptions of modern culture are broken."[18] I would add, however, that on that same rock many of the assumptions of Christian theology were also broken. To continue to cling to the same Christian theological ideas that imply the erasure or dismissal of Judaism was always wrong. Now it is unthinkable. To live or to think and write today without reference to the primal evil that has shown its face in the twentieth century is to dwell in a fantasy land. The test of any theology or philosophy today, one Jewish writer has said, is whether it can be taught or spoken in the presence of burning children.

Still, the way the memory of the Holocaust is framed will inevitably influence what someone thinks or says about it. And the emphasis placed on it, especially in American Reform and Conservative congregations, has begun to raise difficult questions in the minds of many Jews. Does equating Jewish identity so closely with the Holocaust and Israel shortchange other sources Jews have treasured in the three thousand years of their history? Some Jewish and Christian thinkers try to interpret the Holocaust as a redemptive event, but I find this hard to stomach. Does it have any sacred significance at all? Who is to say?

Perhaps the most tormenting and divisive issue about the Shoah centers on its uniqueness. Among Jews there was a long, and at times acrimonious, discussion about whether to create a new holiday to remember the Holocaust or to include it in the existing day of mourning, Tisha B'Av. It was finally decided that, even for a people who have experienced so many and such devastating tragedies, the magnitude of this one made it impossible simply to subsume it with the others. A separate day was needed. Both inside and outside the Jewish community there has always been the question about the millions of "others" who also perished. Gypsies, Communists, homosexuals, Poles (especially the priests and intellectuals), and the political opponents of the Nazis were also packed off to the camps. When Ehud Barak, as the new prime minister of Israel in the fall of 1999, visited Sachsenhausen, the concentration camp nearest Berlin, historians noted that of the 200,000 people who had died there under the Nazis, only a few had been Jews. In its principal focus, the Holocaust was surely a crime perpetrated against Jews because they were Jews. Fully 30 percent of the Jews who were alive in 1939 were dead by 1945. Ninety percent of three of the main Jewish communities of the world — in Poland, western Russia, and the Baltic states — were eradicated. It must be possible to acknowledge the vast crime perpetrated against all the "others" without diminishing the enormity of the crime against the Jewish people.

This is an intricate question, and it sharpens the issue of who has any warrant to speak about it and who does not. I learned this lesson nearly two decades ago when I was teaching what is known at Harvard as a Freshman Seminar, a course for a small number of freshmen given by a senior professor. We were reading spiritual autobiographies, and when we came to Elie Wiesel's Legends for Our Time, I took the whole class (a dozen students) to discuss it with Rabbi Ben-Zion Gold, a concentration camp survivor and a man whom I admire intensely. At the time, Rabbi Gold was the director of the Hillel Foundation at Harvard. One of the students was a sandy-haired, freckled, and impressively bright Jewish freshman who was proud of his identity and was one of the first students to wear a yarmulka all the time (now many do). After remaining uncharacteristically silent for the first several minutes of the discussion with Rabbi Gold, the young man finally ventured, "Well, the main thing I get out of this book is 'never again.'"

The rabbi looked at him. "You're right," he said, "and do you know who the Kurds are?"

The youth looked puzzled and embarrassed. "Well, no I don't," he admitted.

"Well, then, how can you say 'never again,'" he asked, "because they are facing extermination as we speak."

I thought it was strong medicine for a freshman, but I'm sure he never forgot it. Later, as I reflected on the exchange, it became clear to me that although Rabbi Gold could make such a remark to this young man and be heard, I probably could not. It was not yet time for Christians to enter the conversation.

But has that time now come? My grappling with this subject has been clarified recently by the historian Peter Novick's lucid and controversial book *The Holocaust in American Life*. Novick contends that the memory of the Holocaust is no longer a uniquely Jewish cultural reality (if it ever was) but has become part of the received American tradition.[19] This is obviously true, and it is not just the American cultural landscape, either. Within a few months after I had read Novick's book, virtually every day's newspaper carried yet another example of just how common Holocaust references have become and in how many ways these references are deployed in current debates. It was clear that Pat Buchanan's quest for the Republican nomination for the presidency had been dealt a lethal blow when he seemed to imply that the United States had no moral obligation to fight the Nazis in World War II. But apparently right thinking about the Holocaust, or the appearance of right thinking, can also provide positive political leverage. In a story about the inclusion of the far right party of Kurt Haider in a coalition government in Austria, it was reported that one of the party's leaders denied it has fascist tendencies. As proof, he pointed out that he had taken his children to visit the Holocaust Museum in Washington. In October 1999, the dean of the (Episcopal) Cathedral of St. John the Divine in New York rejected the decision of the advisory committee, which decides on which American poets will be honored with a plaque in the cathedral's Poets' Corner (modeled after the one in Westminster Abbey), when it nominated Ezra Pound. In the face of much criticism, the dean refused because of Pound's open anti-Semitism. In March 2000 the Anti-Defamation League publicly criticized an artwork by Hans Haacke, which the Whitney Museum of American Art in New York had accepted (apparently without knowing its precise content) to display in an exhibition. The work consists of three quotations from New York's mayor Rudolph Giuliani, printed in the heavy fraktur

Gothic type favored by the Third Reich, juxtaposed with framed quotations from the First Amendment. The artist planned to have the display accompanied by the sound of marching jackboots. A spokesman from the Anti-Defamation League complained to the museum's director that the effect was to denigrate the memory of those who were killed by the Nazis and thus to trivialize the Holocaust.[20]

Allusions to the Holocaust and debates about its interpretation and misuse seem to go on ceaselessly. The implications are far-reaching. One historian, Michael Dintenfass, has suggested that its brutal reality totally undermines the former established practice of writing history from a neutral point of view. He contends that historians have striven to present "what is true," but this massive iniquity suggests that they should also strive for "the good."[21] In other words, to try to describe the Holocaust in a disinterested manner is to miss its essence entirely. Even the inner deliberations of the Roman Catholic Church are not exempt. Think of how astonished Hitler's victims would be to know that their fate would someday cause a major upheaval in the Vatican. Or how the caution and spinelessness of Pope Pius XII, when he learned what was going on would — more than half a century later — derail the efforts of some high-placed Catholics to have him canonized as a saint. Furthermore, this fierce debate within the Catholic Church has even polarized the upper reaches of the curia and the hierarchy into factions competing not only over Pius XII's attitude toward the Holocaust but also over his entire philosophy of severe centralization in the Church.[22]

Whatever else all this means, it suggests that pondering the significance of the Holocaust — what it was and what it means today — cannot be left to Jews. We all do have to think about it, and therefore we have to talk about it. In fact, this process has been under way for some time. Lately, however, it has been expressed in new and daring forms. Until recently, no one could have imagined a comic treatment of such an event. But then two such versions appeared. In 1999 *La Vida Est Bella*, by the Italian filmmaker and comedian Roberto Begnini, won the first "Best Picture" Academy Award ever given to a foreign movie. Then Robin Williams appeared in a similar vein in *Jacob the Liar*. The Shoah is the theme of hundreds of novels, plays, short stories, memoirs, and poems. In the fall of 1999 it was the subject of a "dance drama" by Suki John, especially for urban young people, using waltz, tango, ballet, jazz, and swing.[23] The term "final solution" is frequently used as a rhetorical basis for American foreign policy, most recently to justify the war in Kosovo. As I have just shown, it has become a major stimulus for Christians to reformulate long-standing theological definitions of Judaism. It seems undeniable that — for good or for evil — the generalization of Holocaust rhetoric is already a fact. I can understand why Jews may occasionally wonder whether they really want this many people poking fingers into the scar tissue of the deepest wound they have ever sustained — with the possible exception of the destruction of Jerusalem and the exile of 70 C.E. But it is too late to squeeze this genie back into the bottle.

Still, even though it now seems allowed, maybe even mandatory, for Christians to join the discussion about the meaning of the Shoah, the question of what to say remains. It will take a long time to work it out. Decades ago, when I first explored the theology of Dietrich Bonhoeffer, I became convinced that the human race has now reached a stage at which we can no longer look to God as a deus ex machina who will intervene to save us from our folly. Sitting in his Gestapo cell, Bonhoeffer came to believe that humankind had now "come of age" and that God had in fact allowed Jesus to be "pushed out of the world and onto a cross" rather than negating our human freedom. The moral is that it is now up to us. The problem is that although we have come of age, we have not yet grown up. If we destroy one another with nuclear war or make the planet uninhabitable by poisoning our life support systems, God will not appear from the clouds to rescue us. I have written about the changes in our theology this requires, especially in *The Secular City*.[24] In recent years I have come to see that if the Holocaust has any "lesson" at all for us, it is the same one. Rabbi Greenberg writes: "To the question, 'Where was God at Auschwitz?' the answer is: God was there — starving, broken, humiliated, gassed and burned alive, sharing the infinite pain as only an infinite capacity for pain can share it."[25]

For Greenberg, that God did not intervene to stop the Holocaust means that God was telling us something as human beings. He was saying, "You stop the Holocaust." We did not. But now we know that, in a terrifying sense, the future of our planet and of our species is in our own hands. It still seems terribly wrong to talk about "the lesson of Auschwitz." Its evil was too colossal to be thought of as a lesson. But Yom ha-Shoah forces us at least to think about it. And we can reassure one another that God's withdrawal does not mean that God is dead. It means that God is present in a more demanding way, as a partner who suffers and struggles along with us. We should expect no miraculous deliverance from crosses or gas chambers or an endless nuclear night. It is now up to us.

10

The Meaning of the Land

Yom ha-Atzma'ut

> When the Lord restored the fortunes of Zion,
> we were like people renewed in health.
> Our mouths were full of laughter
> and our tongues sang aloud with joy.
> Then among the nations it was said,
> "The Lord has done great things for them."
> Great things indeed the Lord did for us,
> and we rejoiced.
>
> — Psalm 126:1–3

JEWS ARE ENORMOUSLY RELUCTANT to tack new holidays onto their calendar; very few have been added in the past two thousand years. But, in addition to Yom ha-Shoah, another one was created in the twentieth century: Yom ha-Atzma'ut, Israeli Independence Day, celebrated on the fifth day of the Jewish month of Iyyar, which falls sometime in May or June. In Israel itself, it is like an American Fourth of July or a French Bastille Day, hailed with fireworks, parades, and parties. Among Jews in other countries, including the United States, it is not marked with as much fervor. Even though an Israel Day parade does take place in New York City, Jews who live elsewhere hardly notice it.

Religious Jews do not consider Yom ha-Atzma'ut a major holiday, and it took some years before the rabbis created a set of rituals for it. Today the synagogue service consists mainly of celebratory selections from the Bible that, although written in a different context, are also meant to call to mind Israel's victory in the 1948 War of Independence, as exemplified by Psalm 98:

Sing a new song to the Lord,
for he has done marvelous deeds;
His right hand and his holy arm have won him victory.
The Lord has made his victory known;
He has displayed his saving righteousness to all nations (1, 2).

Or they read Psalm 126, quoted at the start of this chapter. They also sometimes read Isaiah 11, in which the prophet foresees, not only the deliverance of the Israelites from all their earthly enemies, but a time when "the wolf will lie with the lamb, and the leopard will lie down with the kid; the calf and the young lion will feed together" (11:6).

All these biblical readings seem to blend the emergence of an independent Israel in the twentieth century with the ancient prophecies of return from Babylonian exile and the longed-for messianic era. They interpret Israel's victory over the Arabs in 1948, and the resulting establishment of a Jewish national state, as a religious event, a miraculous act of God. I doubt that many of the early Zionist pioneers, most of them secular and agnostic, would see it that way. Certainly no Palestinians did. But the very presence of Yom ha-Atzma'ut on the Jewish calendar makes a clear statement about the importance of Eretz Yisrael (the Land of Israel) in the self-understanding of most Jewish people today. In fact, one of the most important things I had to learn as a Christian husband, is that it is impossible to understand Jews or Judaism today without trying to comprehend the complicated set of loyalties that link them to a tiny country five thousand miles away.

After the Holocaust, it should be clear to everyone why Jews around the world so insist on the immense importance of Israel. As the severity of the German repression of the Jews heated up in the 1930s, most countries, including the United States, still refused to admit Jewish refugees in anything but insignificant numbers, even when the fate of those who were rejected became painfully clear. This bitter experience taught Jews that they could not rely on anyone else for a safe haven in time of desperate need. It revived the idea of an independent Jewish state, which had languished after Theodor Herzl, the founder of political Zionism, had defended it so energetically a half century before.[1] Jews realized they needed a state they could govern themselves, not so that every Jew could live there (although some Zionists thought they should), but so that every Jew who needed a safe place to live would have one.

The Land of Israel figures prominently in Jewish legend and prayers. According to the ancient story, it was the land God promised to Abraham, the land "flowing with milk and honey," the one the Israelites set out for from Egypt, the one where David and Solomon and their successors established their kingly rule. Even after their massive exile after the Roman destruction of Jerusalem in the first century c.e., some Jews have always lived there. It is mentioned every year in the prayer that ends the Passover Seder, "Next year in Jerusalem." But despite its centuries-long place in the Jewish cultural memory, there is no single religious definition of the significance of the Land of Israel. Indeed, it is a matter of heated and continuing dispute.

Since the birth of the Zionist movement in the nineteenth century, many Orthodox Jews, including some who live in Israel, have refused to give the state any religious significance at all. Some even assign it a negative meaning. A rabbi who leads one such group in Jerusalem makes it a practice of raising a black flag on Israeli Independence Day because in his view that event marked a despicable abandonment of what traditional Judaism had always held. He contends that the rabbis had always taught that Jews should wait with patience for God to deliver them from exile and persecution. Jews of this persuasion see Zionism and the state of Israel, not as some kind of fulfillment of centuries of Jewish hopes and prayers, but as idolatry and betrayal. It is the result of mere human beings arrogantly trying to do what only God can do.

On the opposite wing, but oddly similar in some curious respects, are the secular Jews, who — for the obvious reason that they are not religious — also attribute no religious significance to the state of Israel. Although he was never entirely consistent, Theodor Herzl himself was mainly of this opinion. Born in Budapest and living in Vienna, he was a highly prescient observer of his times. He could see even in the last decade of the nineteenth century that the assimilation of Jews into European countries was not turning out well and that hard times were coming. Also touched by the nationalist revivals going on all around him, he was convinced that the Jews, like all other peoples, needed a national state of their own. His belief that it should be in Palestine was not particularly religious. It was based in part on historical and traditional grounds, as well as on his pragmatic recognition that current political circumstances made it the most likely place. The Ottoman Empire, which included Palestine, was in a state of collapse, and Herzl believed he could convince both Germany and England that having a Jewish state there would be in their interests. He wanted Jews to get out of their urban ghettos and isolated rural villages. Like many Israeli Jews today, he wanted them to become a "normal people," like the other peoples of the world. Something of a skeptic, he rarely if ever spoke about a "promised land" and had little interest in Jerusalem itself, which he considered a backwater. He once informed the Ottoman sultan that "Jerusalem will be extraterritorial. It will belong to nobody, and to all — a holy place in the joint possession of all believers."[2]

After the spectacular Israeli victory in the 1967 war, a third view of the religious significance of the Jewish state emerged, based on the thought of Rabbi Abraham Isaac Kook (1865–1935), the first Ashkenazi chief rabbi in Palestine. Rabbi Kook believed that even though many of the early Zionists were atheists, they were nonetheless doing God's will without knowing it. God led them to take a major step toward the long process of redemption by using them to reclaim the Land of Israel, thereby providing a staging area for the next climactic phase, the redemption of the Jewish people and of the whole world. Rabbi Kook had voiced these ideas even before 1967, but in the aftermath of the war many Orthodox Jews and even some secular Jews began to share his interpretation. Today, this view of the religious meaning of the Land informs the passion of many of the "settlers" who establish Jewish outposts in what they believe is terrain God gave to the Jews even if it falls within the territory of the Palestinian Authority and outside the political borders of the state of Israel. These settlers turn to the biblical Book of Joshua, which they believe chronicles the original conquest, and use it as a kind of handbook for their present activities, and they are convinced that the divine command to "conquer and occupy" the Land is the most important biblical mandate today.

There are many shades and mixtures of opinion within these three options. For example, Rabbi David Hartman and Yeshayahu Liebowitz, both Orthodox Israeli scholars, argue that the Land of Israel is enormously important for Jews, but that as such it has no redemptive or theological significance whatever and to imbue it with such meaning risks idolatry. Liebowitz in particular greeted the Jewish national renaissance that produced the state of Israel. But he warned that giving it a religious significance was dangerous because it obscured the moral ambiguity, the danger of corruption, xenophobia, and jingoism, that are inherent in all nationalisms. It even poses the danger, he cautioned, that Jews might make Israel, not God, into the God they worship and serve. His thinking recalls for me Reinhold Niebuhr's constant reminder of our seemingly ingrained tendency to identify what we do with God's work, which he saw as an expression of "original sin."

This debate is fascinating, but it is also frustrating. With so many contending Jewish views about the meaning of the Land in play, how can this discussion be anything but confusing to outsiders, Christians in particular, who are listening in? Does being a Christian require one to have any special attitude toward the Land of Israel? Should Christian concerns for Israel be principally humanitarian or political? Or should they have a specifically religious dimension? Is there any real reason, other than custom, why we should speak of it as "the *Holy* Land"?[3]

The vast majority of Christians do not think about this very often. When they do, they probably agree that it is the "promised land," and that Jews should have it, without being at all clear about what "it" is. Unless, of course, they are among the many thousand Palestinian Christians. They think about this a lot, and they find it incredible that the God they worship would give what they consider to be their land to another people. But other Christians deny that Christians should have a particular religiously informed attitude toward the Land of Israel. As among Jews, there is considerable disagreement.

My own sentiments about Jerusalem and the Holy Land began early, with the songs I was taught and the stories I was told in my Baptist Sunday school. As a small child, I probably heard as much about Jerusalem as about any other city in the world, and the words "Holy Land" reverberated with celestial overtones long before I had any idea where it was. Years later, I understood right away when I read David Ben-Gurion's recollection of his childhood in a Polish *shtetl*, where the only two cities he knew about were the one he lived in and Jerusalem. Many decades later I still remember a song the tenor soloist in our church choir used to sing. "Last night as I lay sleeping," he would croon, "I dreamed a dream so fair. I stood in old Jerusalem, beside the Temple there." The text goes on to mention songs of angels, hosannas, and "the shadow of a cross." Then the whole choir would join with "Jerusalem, Jerusalem, lift up your voice and sing." I still recall sitting in my grandmother's pew and being transported by the romance and tragedy of it all.

I am not alone. For millions of American Christians, Jerusalem and the Land of Israel — even after more than fifty years of Israeli statehood — still radiate a mythical, dreamlike quality. They glisten, like the Camelot of King Arthur and his knights, on that misty plain where legends guard the gates. This is understandable. What other patch of rock and dirt has been fought over so stubbornly for so long, then rhapsodized so lavishly and mythologized so imaginatively? "If I forget thee, O Jerusalem, may my tongue cleave to the roof of my mouth," intones the psalm composed while the Jews fretted in captivity in Babylon. Is it any wonder that the actual city that stands on a rise some seventy miles east of the Mediterranean Sea often disappears completely into a haze of fantasy. For this reason I had no problem believing a woman who once told me about trying to place a call to Jerusalem from a city in the southwestern United States and being told by a friendly operator that she must be kidding because "Jerusalem isn't a *real* city, honey, it's only in the *Bible!*" Jerusalem is a holy city for three religions, but the curse the city and the Land around it bear is that while they are "in the Bible," they are also real.

I think we have this mixture of myth and history in all of us. But it assumes a special and highly determinative place in the Jewish collective memory. This may be because the most intense collective memories tend to be either religious or national, those preserved by the rituals of a faith tradition or those sustained by the epics and anthems of a national community. The Jews, however, are both of these. Not only that, the duty to "remember" is deeply imbedded in Jewish thought. Indeed, hardly any category is more central. The word for "remember" is used on 169 occasions in the Bible. It is significant that not only are the Israelites told to remember but God himself is so told. In fact, if God does not remember he too can be reprimanded. The writer of Psalm 44 seems to scold God for not remembering what he has done for his people in the past, even suggesting that he must have fallen asleep.

But urgent questions still remain. What are the Israelites supposed to remember? And why? And how are they supposed to remember it? It has often been observed that for centuries the Jews have been absorbed, not to say obsessed, with history. Someone has said that Herodotus may have invented historical writing, but the Jews invented meaning in history. While some of their neighbors in ancient times viewed their gods as contending with one another in a transcendent world, with occasional sorties down to earth, the Jews saw historical events as the theater of God's activity. History was important to them as the arena of God's disclosure of himself. What the Jews were exhorted to remember was what God had done for them in the past. Why? So they could continue to trust him in the future. And the way they were to remember was through the recurrent recital and ritual reenactment of the events in which God had acted. It was not curiosity that turned the Jews toward history, it was their faith in a God whose locus was there.

This emphasis on collective memory can be a strong unifying force in the life of a people. For a people who have lived through so much defeat and dispersion, it is especially essential. But it also presents some serious problems. Memory, whether individual or collective, is notoriously treacherous, often inaccurate, and sometimes fickle. It also, by its very nature, must be selective. Psychologists tell us that we can remember coherently only by blotting out a huge percentage of the thoughts and experiences that occur to us. In his classic work on memory in Judaism, Josef Yerushalmi refers to a story told by the Argentine writer Jorge Luis Borges called "Funes el Memorioso." It concerns a man who, due to a riding accident, has become incapable of forgetting anything. Every minute of every day in his past, all the conversations and all his thoughts about them, remain vivid in his memory. He can only go over them time and again, grinding them into ever smaller pieces, then remembering even the grinding process. The moral is that to remember everything is to remember nothing in particular. One would be better off to forget.[4]

Memory has to be selective. And what we remember is determined by why we remember it. The Jews did not turn to history out of mere inquisitiveness but because their survival as a people depended on it. The ritual reenactment of previous events in which God had come to

their aid kept their hopes alive. It replenished their spirits and renewed their determination. This is why Yerushalmi criticizes modern
historical writing as an inadequate pathway to the past. He believes
that the assumptions informing the way modern historians write
need to be reexamined. Their determination to tear fact from myth,
to sever what happened from what it means, renders history sterile.
There is a danger that when history is no longer perceived as the
sphere of God's activity, every event becomes equally significant —
and therefore equally insignificant. Such a way of telling history is no
longer capable of inspiring hope or renewing the spirit.

My first visit to Israel was a painful lesson in how solidly fused historical "fact" and human meaning have become, not just for Jews,
but for all of us. Since my college days, I had been trained in the
modern, "critical" approach to history. I had been taught to be suspicious of myths and to scrape away legendary encrustation. But no
one arrives in the Holy Land (the phrase — Terra Sancta — was invented by Christians, not Jews) as a blank slate. Everyone brings
along a cargo of emotions and expectations, and I am no exception.
Still, this visit, which took place years before I married Nina, did surprise me and left me with a mixture of admiration and awe, of anger
and futility, and with many questions that I still carry with me. It did
not answer my puzzlement about whether there should be any distinctive "Christian" view of Israel. But it did cause me to ask myself
some of the questions about history, memory, and meaning that
Yerushalmi asks. It made me reconsider my commitment to "critical"
history, which I soon noticed I had been clinging to quite uncriti-
cally.

I had not yet landed in Israel when I received a dose of the no-
torious mixture of hospitality and rudeness that so many visitors
have found among Israelis. Flying into Tel Aviv from Rome, I wanted
to be anonymous, a kind of secret pilgrim, not a writer or a theologian. I had told no one I was coming and had not even made a hotel reservation. It was early evening as the plane approached Ben-
Gurion Airport and I heard my name crackle over the loudspeaker
system. On arrival, it said, I was requested to introduce myself at the
airline desk. I asked the flight attendant what it was about, but she
didn't know. Maybe someone had seen my name on the passenger
list, she said, and wanted to give me a special welcome. She then
scurried off to make sure everyone's seat belt was fastened.

I was tired and wanted a good meal and a bath more than a special welcome. But I was also curious and a little apprehensive. After I was waved through customs I reported to the airline counter, waited until the four people ahead of me had done their business, then told the agent I was reporting as requested. He seemed puzzled, rifled through some papers, and shook his head. He knew nothing about it. I should go to the next building, second floor, and inquire at the airport authority's office. Dragging a large suitcase in the days before wheeled ones were available, I made my way, inquiring twice and being hurriedly pointed down hallways and around corners. Finally reaching the door with the right sign I knocked. No one answered; the door was locked. I sat on my suitcase for a few minutes pondering what to do, then returned to the airline counter, which, by this time, was also closed. When I asked a custodian where the shuttle bus to Jerusalem was, he told me it had just left. What could I do now? I asked him. He told me that a regular bus would come by in about forty-five minutes; the bus stop was over there, a few hundred yards away.

It was quite dark when the bus arrived. I was obviously the only tourist on it. The rest of the passengers seemed to be weary Arabs on their way home from work. I could not understand either the driver or the route sign inside the bus, so I peered out the window, hoping for the best. If this was a special welcome, I was ready to settle for an ordinary one. After an hour of stops and starts, I saw that we were approaching what were surely the walls of the Old City of Jerusalem. In that part of my brain where myth mixes with history the synapses sparked. We pulled to a stop at the gate and I got out. The bus disappeared. I entered the city neither dancing before the ark like David, nor riding a donkey like Jesus, nor walking ahead of a military escort in a pretentious show of humility as the British general Sir Edmund Allenby had in 1917. I walked in annoyed, hungry, and exhausted.

Burdened by my suitcase, I began to look for a place to sleep or eat or both. But the whole area seemed ominously dark. Turning a corner, I saw a tiny sign on a dingy building: "Hotel." I knocked at the door. There was no answer. I knocked again. This time a small Arab boy opened it and looked up at me with surprise, as though it were somehow unusual for visitors to knock on a hotel door. I told him I was looking for a place to sleep and eat. He clearly did not understand me. I mimicked sleeping, with my head leaning sideways on my hands, and then eating. He nodded and ran off, leaving the door ajar. I stepped in.

The lobby was dimly lit and deserted. Crates, cardboard boxes, and empty Coca-Cola bottles were piled on the table that appeared to be the closest thing to a reception desk in sight. I took a few more steps and noticed a small group of men playing a game of cards. A pitcher and glasses sat on the table. The boy ran up to one of the men and said something to him, pointing to me. The man waved the smoke of his cigarette away from his eyes and peered at me, not hostile, just curious. Finally he said something to the boy and held up his palm to me as a signal to wait. The boy scampered off and returned in a few minutes with an older boy, who walked over to me and asked, in confident English, if there was anything he could do. He appeared to be about fifteen and wore jeans, a white shirt open at the collar, and horn-rimmed glasses.

I told him I needed something to eat and a room for the night and said that I had seen the "Hotel" sign on the door.

"Hotel?" he asked, a little surprised.

"Yes," I said, "hotel," and felt as though I should open the door and show him the sign, which was only about ten feet from where we stood.

"Oh," he said, "ho-*tel*, yes, hotel, hotel," as though the word was a little unfamiliar to him. "Yes," he said, "here, just sign this, uh, guest book. Yes, guest book." He rummaged through a drawer in the table under the crates and bottles. "Let's see, yes, guest book. Yes, hotel."

By now the suspicion had long since come over me that despite the sign, this place — whatever it was — did not function very often as a hotel. Something told me I should thank him and walk out into the cold night to look for something else. But his smile was reassuring, and by now I was terribly tired, so I decided to stay. He fished out a looseleaf notebook and brushed the dust off the cover, opened it, and pulled a plastic ball-point pen from his pocket. As I signed, he sent the younger boy off with a quick command in Arabic. Then I asked if I could get something to eat. He smiled again, nodded, and raised his palms in the universal "Why not?" gesture. He seated me at a small table in the lobby and told me to wait. Out of the corner of my eye I saw a young woman climb the stairs carrying a bundle of linen. I surmised it was the sheets and pillow for the bed I was going to sleep in. I looked around the table but there was no sign of a menu. I was now convinced that not only was this not a hotel, it was also not a restaurant. But within a few minutes yet another young man appeared with a tray of food: falafel, rice, sliced cucumbers, a bottle of orange soda, a small dish of figs, and a paper napkin. I thanked him and ate heartily. Given the speed with which it appeared, I'm sure it was artfully assembled from the remains of the family's dinner.

When I finished eating, the young man in the horn rims sidled up and said he would show me to my room. He picked up my suitcase and led the way up the stairs to a room on a short hallway, pushed open a door that did not seem to have a lock, and put my case down on the floor next to a narrow bed. He pointed across the hall and said "WC," the international cipher for bathroom. I tried to hand him a dollar but he shook his head, smiled, and left, closing the door behind him. I stepped across the hall to the tiny WC, performed a minimum of late-night ablutions, then came back and crawled gratefully into the hard bed. There was no pillow. It occurred to me that no one had told me how much this "hotel" room was going to cost me, but at that point I didn't really care. I fell asleep instantly, awakened only partially now and then by a shout from below which erupted briefly — apparently when one of the card players drew three aces.

Early the next morning I woke up to what sounded like a phonograph needle scraping a record that was terribly old and scratchy but turned up to ear-splitting volume. The noise went on for about fifteen seconds. Then I heard, so close it seemed to be in the same room, "*Allahu akbar, 'ashhadu alla ilaha illallah*" — the Muslim call to morning prayer. I had never heard it before, but even coming from a scratchy recording it nearly overwhelmed me with its sonorous elegance. No wonder it is said that Muslims sometimes weep uncontrollably at the very sound of the words. It was Arabic, of course, which I do not understand. But from my reading I knew what it was saying: "Allah is great. Allah is compassionate." I pulled up the green shade and looked out. Immediately next door stood a small mosque, its tower within twenty feet of my room. Truly an innocent abroad, I realized only then that I had obviously stumbled into the Muslim quarter of the Old City, the part where tourists are sometimes warned not to venture. Allah, I am told, has a special sense of compassion for children and fools.

I got up, washed and dressed, picked up my suitcase, and walked downstairs. My watch told me it was 7:15 A.M. The card game was over, but empty bottles and full ashtrays still cluttered the table. No one seemed to be around, but just then both the small boy and the older one in glasses appeared and smiled. I thanked the older one and asked him how much I owed.

To my amazement, he extended his hands palms down and moved them back and forth, shaking his head. "Please, nothing," he said, "my pleasure." I tried again, but it seemed the matter was closed, so I shook hands with both of them and walked out past the "Hotel" sign, realizing that what I had just imbibed was not the kind of hospitality Conrad Hilton offers but the kind for which the Middle East in general, and Arabs in particular, are justly famous. As I wandered through the already sun-drenched streets of the Old City, I thought of the announcement on the plane and the special welcome the flight attendant thought it might suggest. I will never know what it was supposed to be, but I was sure it could not possibly have surpassed the one I actually, if quite accidentally, received.

I spent the remainder of that first five-day visit in Israeli hands. It began with a three-day minibus excursion north to the Galilee, making all the required tourist-pilgrim stops. I sloshed ankle-deep into the Jordan River at the "exact place" where Jesus was baptized, or so our loquacious driver-guide insisted authoritatively. (I was amused some years later to have an equally prolix driver point out a very different spot with equal authority.) The politics of contending holy places in the Holy Land is never easy to negotiate. When Pope John Paul II visited in March of 2000, he tactfully paid respectful visits to two different sites of Jesus' baptism. But I was growing restless when we stopped at the alleged site of the miracle of the loaves and the fishes, and by the time we reached Gerasa — where, we were assured, Jesus had healed the young man named Legion, who was possessed by demons — I felt that the factual side of my brain was in danger of being overwhelmed by the mythical. I was ready for something with at least a little more historical basis.

I found it when the vehicle parked in the village of Capernaum, just north of the Sea of Galilee, where both the Bible and archaeology agree that Jesus spent many months of his life after leaving his home in Nazareth. His reason for moving there had always interested me. "Now when he heard that John [the Baptist] had been arrested," reports the Gospel of Matthew, "he withdrew into Galilee; and leaving Nazareth he went and dwelt in Capernaum by the sea" (4:12). In other words, Jesus left home when it got too hot for him, when John, the shaggy prophet from the desert with whom he had cast his lot, was picked up by Herod's police, who were undoubtedly also on the lookout for his compatriots. The New Testament also reports that it was in Capernaum that the young prophet from Nazareth began to organize his own band of followers, selected the twelve disciples, and began his teaching. Like any pious Jew, he prayed in the synagogue and sometimes preached and taught there. Archaeologists say the city dates back to the second century B.C.E., and they have uncovered the remains of a synagogue that dates from the fifth century C.E. Many of them believe that further digging could uncover the first-century synagogue of Jesus' own time. Meanwhile, fragments and broken columns of the more recent one are still standing. One column carries an inscription in Aramaic, the language Jesus spoke, that reads: "Alphaeus, Son of Zebedee, son of John, made this column as a blessing to himself."

It was a warm day, and I sat down on one of the fragments to sip a tepid Coke. It was then that the surge of unanticipated realization struck me: He was really here. Right *here*. Under this very sun, on this spot. I had wondered, before I left home, whether "walking where Jesus walked" might wear down my critical faculties and sweep me up into some sentimental religious euphoria. This had not happened, but something else had. Here in Capernaum fact and myth had colluded in a wholly positive way. The result was a calm but deep-seated recognition that this place was not just any place. I could hardly finish the Coke. After years of looking down with condescension on the pious souls who became weepy and mawkish over "holy places," here I was reduced nearly to tears, my stern Protestant skepticism melting under the Galilean sun and the associations this spot evoked. Ever since, although I still remain suspicious of sacred sites, especially when people kill one another over them, I can at least understand why they may be moved to do so.

My temporary lapse into ecstasy was interrupted by the horn of the minibus, summoning us to press on to the next stop. Dragging my feet, I was the last one back on board, earning some frowns from my impatient fellow tourists. Our next stop was the Golan, where we climbed out and gazed across the demilitarized zone into Syria. On the way up and back we stopped overnight at two different kibbutzim with inn facilities.

When we got back to Jerusalem the next day, I decided to walk the whole way around the Old City, following the path on top of the walls. I bought some fruit, bread, cheese, and an orange drink, packed them in a shoulder bag, and started. It took longer and required more effort than I had anticipated, but it was a walk I will not forget. From the eastern section of the wall, I could look over at the Mount of Olives and then behind me onto the silvery dome of Al-Aqsa mosque and the golden dome of the Qubbet el-Sakhra (the Dome of the Rock), which towers above the Temple Mount over the site (it is said) of both Abraham's near-sacrifice of Isaac and of the Prophet Muhammad's heavenly journey. Farther away, but still in the Old City, I could see the pink stone and two domes of the Church of the Holy Sepulcher and near it the higher tower of the Lutheran Church of the Redeemer, dedicated by none other than Kaiser Wilhelm II in 1898. Beyond that lay the opposite wall and the incongruous modern buildings of west Jerusalem.

I remember being bothered by the noise of cars and buses. In the fabled Jerusalem of my childhood fantasies there were no motor vehicles, only camels and donkeys. Still, I was impressed — and surprised at how small the Old City is and how close the edifices of the different religions stand to one another, literally in each other's shadows. It was a memory that would often come back to me, especially after what is now called Intifada II continued to drag on. It had broken out after Ariel Sharon, who was then merely an aging Israeli politician, walked up to the Dome of the Rock accompanied by a huge military escort. His visit touched off storms of rock-throwing attacks by enraged young Palestinians and their lethal suppression by the Israeli army. (At this writing, Sharon has become prime minister of Israel, and the Intifada shows no sign of abating.)

After my solitary circumambulation of the Old City, I strolled into a small shop off King David Street to buy more film for my camera. There I noticed a man standing next to me wearing a neatly pressed summer suit, a flamboyant tie, and reflecting sunglasses. In what was clearly an American accent from somewhere south of the Mason-Dixon Line, he introduced himself to me and extended a hand on which he wore three rings. He had apparently picked me out as a countryman when he heard me speaking English to the clerk. Smiling broadly and removing his shades, he asked me what I was doing in the Holy Land. I hesitated. Somehow I did not appreciate being interrogated by a stranger before I had sorted through the jumbled impressions of my walk. I told him I was there as a pilgrim. He glanced at his expensive watch, stretched his neck to relieve it of what must have been a slightly restrictive tie, then told me he was here to bring the full Gospel to the land God had given to the Jewish people. "I love the Jewish people," he said. "They are the apple of God's eye. And the Lord has given me a ministry to them, right here in the Holy Land." He seemed to savor the words "Holy Land," using them in almost every sentence. He had a disconcerting habit of glancing over my shoulders as he talked, as though he were expecting someone, and of swiveling his jaw from right to left. He told me he was convinced we were drawing near to the End Times, that the Last Days were nearly upon us, and when the end came it would start and wind up "right here in the Holy Land."

I was beginning to feel awkward standing with this overwrought pulpiteer while he proclaimed his theology in a voice twice as loud as I needed to hear. I backed out of the shop but he followed, continuing to talk. The unpleasant thought came to me that he might be trying to gather a congregation and I was to be the first recruit. But no more listeners materialized. A few pedestrians glanced at him, but no one paused. I was still uneasy, however. I glanced at my Timex and told him I had to go. He asked if I needed a place to eat or to stay overnight. I told him thanks, but no, and walked away.

During the years since our brief, uncomfortable conversation, his face and voice have often come back to me. I know that one reason I was so fidgety around him was that his viewpoint was one I was already familiar with. It is a Christian theology of the Land. But I had never liked it much, and since that day I have come to like it even less. I had heard it in my Sunday school as a child. Dating from the nineteenth century, it is called "dispensationalism," and it is still alive and powerful — albeit in a modified form — today. It purports to be a Christian theology of the Land, but it is not one I can accept. Not only does it transform the Bible into a kind of Nostradamus, packed with cryptic predictions waiting to be decoded, it also represents one of the many ways Christians try to absorb Jews into what is clearly a Christian religious scenario.

The feature of dispensationalism that spells out a theological view of the Holy Land was originally called restorationism but is now spoken of more frequently as Christian Zionism. It has deep roots: its sources can be seen in the millenarian movements of the Middle Ages. Some trace its current expression back to the Fifth Monarchy Men, the radical millenarian Protestants who gathered in Cromwell's army during the seventeenth century. They were convinced the End of the Age was coming and that the Jews should therefore return to Palestine, as foretold (so they believed) by the Old Testament prophets. These ideas gained more popularity in America during the nineteenth century with the publication, in 1878, of *Jesus Is Coming*, by one William E. Blackstone.[5] The book was later expanded, and in its various versions and editions sold over a million copies, an astonishing number for that time. Its message was clear. The second coming of Jesus Christ was imminent, but before it could occur, the Jews would have to return to the Promised Land and the Temple, destroyed by the Romans in 70 C.E., would have to be rebuilt.

Blackstone never had a formal theological education but was a self-taught student of the Bible. He was also active politically. In 1891 he sent a Memorial to Benjamin Harrison, then president of the United States, and to the secretary of state, James G. Blanton, imploring them to use whatever influence they could to "secure the holding at an early date of an international conference to consider the condition of the Israelites and their claims to Palestine as their ancient home."[6] Blackstone was very persuasive, and his Memorial was endorsed by no less than 413 dignitaries. The historian Paul C. Merkeley in his informative book on Christian Zionism reports that among the signatories were "the Chief Justice of the United States, the Speaker of the House of Representatives, the Chairman of the House Foreign Relations Committee, prominent Members of Congress, several of the greatest industrialists of the day (including Rockefeller, Morgan, and McCormack), famous clergymen, Christian and Jewish, writers, journalists and the editors of several of the great newspapers of the day."[7]

Blackstone was careful not to bolster his public political appeal with too much overt theology. But in the letter he sent along with it he summarized the apocalyptic worldview that is spelled out in detail in *Jesus Is Coming*. The final paragraph reads:

There seem to be many evidences to show that we have reached the period in the great roll of centuries, when the everlasting God of Abraham, Isaac and Jacob, is lifting up his hand to the Gentiles (Isaiah

49:22) to bring his sons and daughters from afar, that he may plant them again in their own land, Ezekiel 34, etc. Not for twenty-four centuries, since the days of Cyrus, King of Persia, has there been offered to any mortal such a privileged opportunity to further the purposes of God concerning His ancient people.[8]

A number of elements in this compact paragraph help explain why the Christian restorationism it presents appealed to so many people. First, amid the dizzying social change that seemed to accelerate as the new century approached, it reassured large numbers of bewildered Christians that God did, after all, have a purpose for what appeared to be the meaningless onrush of history. Second, even though the Jews remained God's chosen ones, gentiles were to be given a real role in the fulfillment of the divine purpose for them. Third, the time was now. Everyone likes to think he or she lives in a particularly critical and unique period, and this theology assured them that they did. Indeed, not for twenty-one centuries had anyone had such an opportunity to help the hand of the Almighty to fulfill eternal promises. Furthermore, Christians in small-town America, who had never met a Jew and knew Jews only from the Bible, now had a chance to step into the pages of that big black book and become a part of the greatest story ever told. It was an offer many found hard to refuse.

Still, Christian restorationism might have remained within a relatively small coterie of dispensationalist aficionados if it had not been lofted into orbit by a publishing event of epochal significance: the publication, in 1909, of the so-called Scofield Reference Bible, an edition of the classic King James translation interspersed with notes, charts, and cross-referencing that delineated the dispensationalist restorationist theology. This Bible quickly became the edition of choice, first largely among conservative and revivalist Christian groups, but eventually throughout the entire American Protestant population. When as a boy I was solemnly presented with a Bible for my excellent attendance at Sunday school, it was the Scofield Reference edition I received. Its attraction was that, by virtue of its elaborate cross-referencing, it seemed to tie the Old Testament and New Testament together, and to a novice, the footnotes seemed to make the difficult passages easier to understand. Its theology taught that God had a plan for human history which divided it into seven dispensations. We were, of course, in the last one. The grand climax was coming soon. And the return of the Jews to the Holy Land was both a sure sign that it was coming and an absolute prerequisite.

There were, of course, debates within the movement about the specifics of the End Time. Most taught that there would be a "rapture," when all true Christian believers would, without warning, be gathered up to meet Christ without going through the unattractive process of dying. This would have the added advantage of enabling them to escape the Great Tribulation (the Time of Jacob's Troubles), which would come before the End. That was good news because those Last Days, according to this script, were not going to be pleasant. There would be plagues and earthquakes and wars. Then, after the rebuilding of the Temple and the reinstitution of animal sacrifice by a restored Jewish priesthood, the King of the North with his cruel allies would make war on God's chosen people. This king used to be identified with Soviet Russia. "Moscow," the Christian Zionists loved to point out, "is *due north* of Jerusalem!" Now, however, the villain is more often equated with Islam. Finally a titanic battle would be joined at Armageddon. The situation would appear hopeless. But then Jesus Christ would appear on a white stallion, save the day, and the mass conversion of the Jews would take place. The Final Judgment would follow, complete with scorpions, hailstones, and a lake of fire. Not a pretty picture.

The European version of this theology was not as vivid or detailed. But it did insist that the prophecies were being fulfilled and that it was the obvious duty of all Christians, especially the heads of states, to help the Jews return to Palestine according to God's revealed plan. The fact that the land was part of the Ottoman Empire, they suggested, should not pose any problem. The empire was decaying anyway, and since this was a time when European powers were buying or otherwise acquiring countries all over the world, surely this tiny patch of sand and stone could be procured without much difficulty. Few of the Christian restorationists seemed aware of an indigenous population in Palestine — to say nothing of an ancient Arab Christian community, which already thought of Palestine as its homeland.

Among Jews, the leaders of the Zionist movement were both gratified and puzzled by this theology. On the one hand, they resented Christians who tried to convert them. On the other, they wanted help, from whatever quarter, to support what was first viewed by many as an unlikely, utopian scheme to settle Jews in Palestine. But Louis Brandeis, who became the main spokesman for Zionism in America, seems to have valued Blackstone's work and even referred to him once as "the true founder of Zionism." Brandeis kept in touch with the maverick but influential theologian until Blackstone's death. Some believe his ideas influenced President Woodrow Wilson, the son of a Presbyterian minister who liked to refer to himself as "a son of the manse." Wilson's support in 1917 of the Balfour Declaration, in which the British government pledged its support to a Jewish homeland in Palestine, was probably critical in getting it through the British cabinet. Harry Truman, a Southern Baptist, was undoubtedly influenced by Christian restorationist ideas. This helps to explain why, against the near-unanimous counsel of his secretary of state and the State Department's Middle East experts, he insisted on the immediate recognition of the new state of Israel on May 14, 1948. Clark Clifford, a close adviser, wrote in *Counsel to the President*: "From his reading of the Old Testament he felt the Jews derived a legitimate historical right to Palestine, and he sometimes cited such Biblical lines as Deuteronomy 1:8: 'Behold I have given up the land before you; go in and take possession of the land which the Lord hath sworn to your fathers, to Abraham, to Isaac and to Jacob.'"[9]

There is no reason to doubt Clifford's memory, and there is ample evidence elsewhere that Truman was an assiduous reader of the Bible. But it would be a mistake to think there were no other factors influencing his decision. Throughout his life he valued his friendship with Eddie Jacobson, the son of Jewish immigrants from Russia. The two served together in the army and then went into the haberdashery business together. Jacobson later became a friend of Chaim Weizmann's, the Zionist leader who became the first president of Israel. Historians have little doubt that Jacobson, one of the few people who could drop in on the president without an appointment, encouraged Truman's inclinations to support Israel. But those inclinations themselves were anchored in his own understanding of the Bible. Thus, when he was introduced to some of the faculty at the Jewish Theological Seminary a few months after he left office as the man who had helped create the state of Israel, he denied it. No, he said, "I am Cyrus. I am Cyrus," referring to the Persian king who had restored the Jews to their home after their captivity in Babylon.[10]

Perhaps the most compelling example of the influence of Christian Zionism on a president, however, is the case of Ronald Reagan. In his chatty but enormously informative *President Reagan, Role of a Lifetime*, Lou Cannon contends that the idea of Armageddon "appealed to Reagan's adventurous imagination and met his requirements of a happy ending."[11] Reagan also came to believe that events occurring in his own time indicated the imminent coming of the Last Days. At a banquet for a California senate president, he told his startled dinner companion that the end of the world was nigh. "For the first time ever, everything is in place for the battle of Armageddon and the second coming of Christ," he said. One of the omens, he observed, were the "strange weather things" that were going on.[12] Cannon believes Reagan picked up some of these ideas from the Sunday school he attended as a child, but that they were often reinforced by evangelical ministers he met and to whom he apparently listened with fascination when they talked about the coming of the Last Days.

Obviously Christian restorationism has played a significant role in the larger history of Zionism. But neither restorationism nor Blackstone receives more than scant mention in most standard histories of Zionism. Maybe the authors would prefer to forget about this peculiar part of the story. Still, Blackstone himself is not completely forgotten. His Bible, with the prophetic passages underlined, is displayed in the reconstituted study of Theodor Herzl in Jerusalem, and — although many visitors do not know about it — there is a Blackstone Memorial Forest in Israel today.

In Europe, the story was a little different. Herzl, who began as a journalist and playwright in Vienna before he became the acknowledged champion of the Zionist movement, nurtured a close relationship with a pietistic Anglo-German biblical interpreter named William Hechler. Hechler, who seems to have had valuable contacts with the German nobility, had written *Die Bevorstehende Ruckkehr der Juden nach Palestina* (*The Imminent Return of the Jews to Palestine*) in 1893, three years before Herzl's own *Der Judenstaat* (*The Jewish State*) appeared. Hechler's theology focused on the prophetic promise of the return of the Jews to Palestine without the baroque End Time element found in American and British dispensationalism, but he did not believe in trying to convert Jews. It was he who arranged for Herzl to meet some of the most influential rulers in Europe, including the German kaiser. Both Blackstone and Hechler believed whole-

heartedly in the eventual conversion of the Jews. But unlike more recent Christian Zionists, like the one I met after my walk around the
Old City walls, they did not push for immediate conversion. It would
happen, but in God's own good time.

Christian Zionism is a grotesque example of how myth can sometimes swallow history and an inventive theology can descry a pattern
of meaning in anything it turns its mind to. But Christian Zionism is
anything but a dying movement. Every September on the Jewish holiday of Sukkot, thousands of Christians who subscribe to this view
converge on Israel from the United States and Europe. This has been
going on for twenty years now; by 1999 their number had reached
five thousand. That year they prayed at the Western Wall, held political rallies to support the Jewish settlements on the West Bank, and
staged a march through Jerusalem. They constitute the largest single
group of pilgrims to visit Israel each year. Their trip is coordinated
by the International Christian Embassy, a Christian Zionist group,
whose spokesman, John Luckhoff, told a reporter, "We are here to
witness the miracle of Israel and the restoration of the Jewish people,
exactly as it was spoken by the prophets thousands of years ago." The
International Christian Embassy is a formidable presence in Israel.
According to the New York Times, it now has sixty-five employees,
several foreign offices, and an $8 million annual budget, half of
which is contributed by Americans.[13] As might be expected, Jerusalem's Christian population, which dates back to the earliest decades
of Christianity, is not happy with the influx. Made up almost entirely
of Palestinians, most of these local Christians are opposed to Israel's
rule over East Jerusalem and the West Bank. They especially resent it
when the pilgrims (some of whom seem surprised to learn that there
is, in fact, an indigenous Christian community), claim that they represent the Christian view of these matters.[14]

Jewish Zionists have always been uneasy about Christian Zionism.
On the one hand, they recoil at the thought that someday, which according to this scenario is coming soon, they and all Jews will recognize the true messiah and leave their ancestral faith behind (or simply "complete" it, as the Christian Zionists put it). On the other
hand, they operate on the premise that Zionism and Israel both need
all the support they can get. Sometimes, among Israelis, this ambivalence divides along party lines. The jubilant Sukkot pilgrims were
welcomed in 1998 by Ehud Olmert, the Likud mayor of Jerusalem.

The previous year they were addressed by Benjamin Netanyahu, then the prime minister. But in 1999 the new prime minister, Ehud Barak, a member of the Labor party, declined to meet with them. When Netanyahu visited the United States in 1998, he rushed from the airport to embrace Jerry Falwell and some Southern Baptist leaders at an Israel First rally in Washington even before he was driven to the White House to see President Clinton. The gathering he attended represents another incarnation of the original Christian Zionist movement. However, the Southern Baptists Netanyahu hugged had recently announced a massive effort to convert American Jews, which was publicly attacked by a wide spectrum of American Jewish organizations. Does this make any sense?

It does. It seems mind-boggling, but from the perspective of Christian Zionists, one can believe that Jews who do not accept Christ as the messiah are doomed to hell, while at the same time lobbying Congress on behalf of Israel and urging the Israeli government not to give back one square inch of the Holy Land to the Arabs. They believe Israel is the setting for the last act of their apocalyptic drama, and the stage must be prepared according to the script. Apparently some Israeli politicians, and some American Jewish leaders, believe they can simply ignore this bizarre "goyische" theology to retain some dependable friends. Indeed, these days in Israel, when many describe their country as entering a "post-Zionist" era, one Israeli told me, with only a trace of sardonic humor, that the Christian Zionists may be the only real Zionists left.

The day after I met the evangelist I left Tel Aviv on an early flight. As we climbed, I looked down on the shining Mediterranean Sea and the coastline and thought about the hodgepodge of peoples who had swarmed through this area during its tortured history: Canaanites and Phoenicians, Jebusites and Hebrews, Muslims and Crusaders, Ottomans and Brits, and now — once again — Jews and Palestinians. I wondered why destiny had introduced me to this Holy Land by first plunking me down in the Muslim quarter, then sending me off with a sermon from a Christian Zionist. There had been many memorable moments in between, including my unfinished Coca-Cola at Capernaum, which were following me home to ponder anew the relationship between memory and history. Was I supposed to be learning something from all this?

I knew then and I know now that I am not a Christian Zionist. I cannot separate their eccentric theology from their politics. I cannot reject one and embrace the other. They are both of one piece, and I think anyone with a modicum of intellectual honesty should recognize this. I simply do not believe that the prophecies of the Old Testament refer to Theodor Herzl and David Ben-Gurion and their fellow Zionists (and their biographers insist neither Herzl nor Ben-Gurion believed it either). I find myself closer to the views of those early Zionists who hoped Palestine could be what they called "a land of two peoples." And I agree with Rabbi Arthur Green, who writes:

> The state of Israel is a great historic achievement of the Jewish people. Its role in the survival and renewal of Jewish life, especially in the aftermath of the Holocaust, cannot be overestimated. But the state as such has no *theological* significance. . . . How do we live in a holy land in our time? . . . The answer is that we do so by *sharing* it with others [italics in original].[15]

But even this formula does not quite satisfy me. As I left Israel after that first visit, I could not seem to get either the hospitable Arabs or the synagogue where Jesus taught out of my mind. And I had to ask myself why the eager evangelist had bothered me so much. I slowly realized that although I could not accept the Christian Zionist version of the meaning of the Land, neither could my understanding of Israel and Palestine be merely geopolitical. I felt I needed a genuinely theological framework to make sense of it all. I could see no reason to celebrate Yom ha-Atzma'ut, Israeli Independence Day, any more than I would the Italian or French equivalent. Before I could, I needed to understand the spiritual meaning of the Land. But it would take two decades, two more visits to the Holy Land, and a series of conversations with Israelis and Palestinian Christians before the lineaments of this understanding began to appear.

11

"Next Year in Jerusalem"

Jerusalem the golden,
With milk and honey blest,
Beneath thy contemplation
Sink heart and voice opprest.
I know not, O I know not
What joys await us there;
What radiancy of glory!
What bliss beyond compare!

— Bernard of Cluny (fl. 1150)[1]

I DID NOT RETURN to Israel for eighteen years. Even after a decade of marriage to Nina I had never made the trip. There were so many other places we wanted to visit. But gradually the desire to visit Israel together grew. Then Nina's last surviving aunt on her father's side moved to Tel Aviv from Washington after her husband died. She went, not because she had either Zionist or religious inclinations (which she did not), but because her only daughter, Helen, had moved there ("made *aliyah*") thirty years before as a young woman. Now Aunt Natasha had become too old to travel, so if we were going to see her before she died, it would have to be there. We decided to go.

I tried to prepare myself for this second trip better than I had the first time. Each year at the end of the Seder I had heard the traditional "Next year in Jerusalem," but I still did not comprehend the nearly mystical feeling so many Jews, including nonobservant ones, have for "the Land of Israel." After a lot of reading and inquiry, I began to think that the mystique can be understood only in terms of the collective Jewish memory of centuries of exile (called *galut* in Hebrew), the repetition of countless prayers about "return," and years of copious rabbinical speculations about the inner meaning of *galut.*

For thirty-five hundred years, in history, myth, and imagination, the dialectic of exile and return has throbbed in Jewish thought like the theme of a symphony. It has colored Jewish thinking about history, human nature, God, and the cosmos itself. First there was the exile in Egypt and the return to Canaan. Then there was the captivity in Babylon and the return under the Persian king Cyrus in 539 B.C.E. Then there was the defeat by the Romans and the forced dispersion around the world that has lasted for nineteen hundred years. Now there is the state of Israel. It is understandable, then, that the Jewish literature on the spiritual meaning of *galut* is enormous. There is no comparable body of thought on the subject by Christians since, though at times they have undergone exile as well, it has not been their central and defining experience.

But what does the inner experience of *galut* feel like to the exiled person? What is the spiritual meaning of exile? Here the rabbinical analysis is particularly acute. The Hasidic teachers, for example, held that exile is both corporate and individual. They believed that just as the Jewish people, however dislocated and mistreated, always retained a core of dignity and freedom, so individuals also bear within themselves a nucleus of freedom that can never be eradicated. They suggested that Torah and the prayers of Jewish worship nourished this inner flame. The people's exile became a paradigm for the individual soul of all Jews, and ultimately of all people. Rabbi Arthur Green is substantially influenced by the Hasidic tradition in his thinking. In his explication of the exile in Egypt and the deliverance, he writes, "Each of us has been to (and often revisits) our Egypt. We have to learn to see this Egypt — even in the fury of our daily struggles with our own desires — as a purifying furnace. . . . Remembering that Egypt and transforming its meaning is a process vital to our religious lives."[2]

Rabbi Green focuses here on the personal meaning of exile. But in the long Jewish discussion of the subject, some rabbis ventured an even more daring proposal. It is one with which many Jews and nearly all Christians are unfamiliar but which I find immensely suggestive. They began with the recognition that since God has a special link to his people, their exile means that God himself is in exile too. Therefore the reality of God is itself in a state of crisis. Exile is not only a disaster for the Jews, it is also a disaster for God and for the cosmos. God, too, is homeless and is suffering the same estrangement that human beings suffer. By engaging in *tikkun olam*, the mending of the broken world, we are actually helping to heal a wounded God as well.

This is a bold idea. It is also a suggestive opening for further interfaith conversation, since many Christians also believe in a God who can be wounded and who suffers in the suffering of human beings. It also brings to mind "the absent Jesus" of some contemporary Christian poetry, both the explicitly religious verse of T. S. Eliot's "The Waste Land" and the inverse Christian imagery of Samuel Beckett's *Waiting for Godot*. In her recent book, *The Poets' Jesus: Representations at the End of a Millennium*, Peggy Rosenthal suggests that this exile-like theme appears with particular poignancy in the poetry of Czeslaw Milosz, whose meditations on "the presence of God's absence" inspires him to write about a "Jesus Forgotten"; not a Christ about whom one could harbor doubts and skepticism, but one who seems distant, elusive, and far beyond the reach of human definition.[3]

The long Jewish controversy about the meaning of exile — of the Jews, of humanity, of God, and of the cosmos itself — is astonishing and sometimes disturbing in its imaginative reach. Still, for anyone reading it today, whether believer or nonbeliever, this literature — from ancient, medieval, and modern times — sounds strikingly contemporary. This may be because in our own era the pangs of exile and homelessness have become so common. The great Jewish philosopher Franz Rosenzweig once wrote that exile is not just about geography. It has a profound psychological dimension: it is about estrangement, the sense of being an alien among people who seem at home. It is about nostalgia, the vague but powerful aching to "return" to somewhere or something, even when we do not know quite what it is. It is about my terror of losing my grip on who I really am in a faceless mass. These themes were discussed for centuries by the Jewish sages as they contemplated exile, the longing to return, and the threat of assimilation. But now they have reappeared in contemporary existentialist philosophy and literature. They recur time and again in the philosophy of Heidegger and Sartre, in writers as diverse as Jack Kerouac and Franz Kafka, in current films and even in rock music. The sociologist Peter Berger has written that in the modern world, "identity ceases to be an objectively and subjectively given fact, and instead becomes the goal of an often devious and difficult quest. Modern man . . . is ever in search of himself."⁴ Rosenzweig once wrote that "there is no one today who is not alienated."

This may be another case of a very old idea that has become very contemporary. Jewish speculation on *galut* speaks to us today, not just because so many millions of people are homeless refugees, but because the contemporary human plight as such is one of spiritual exile and estrangement. Consequently, the Jewish experience speaks to nearly everyone. In the frontispiece of his book on exile and memory, the Jewish thinker Josef Yerushalmi quotes these lines from the modern Greek poet George Seferis:

> Having known this fate of ours so well
> wandering around among broken stones, three or six
>   thousand years
> searching in collapsed buildings that might have been
>   our homes
> trying to remember dates and heroic deeds:
> will we be able?⁵

Poets always seem to be prescient. Now even professional historians suggest that the era of national histories may be over and that the next generation of scholars will concentrate on border crossing, diaspora, migrants, and frontiers.⁶ But Jews did not set out to create a metaphor for our postmodern world. Their speculation did not begin on such a universal or philosophical scale. It began with specific and unavoidable questions about why these exiles have occurred; what their inner meaning was; if they ever would end; and if so, how? Jewish efforts to grapple with these questions went on century after century, with the sages suggesting many different answers. Some of them addressed the sense of Jewish exile in particular, but others went on to explore the reality of exile as a facet of the human condition. In the early centuries, for example, the rabbis' answers to the why of Jewish exile were very straightforward. They taught that exile was God's way of punishing his chosen people for their failure to obey his laws. But they soon had to go deeper than that, partly in re-action to constant Christian accusations that the misery of exile was visible proof of their punishment by God for rejecting his son — and indeed, some Christians loved to perpetuate the image of the "wan-dering Jew," homeless, despised, and rootless, as a living demonstra-tion of God's displeasure. But the rabbis also thought deeply about *galut* because they were driven by their own questions.

Century after century, the deliberation continued. Not content with the punishment explanation, Jewish thinkers searched for a more positive meaning of exile. Some discerned a deeper purpose in their dispersion around the world. Perhaps God had allowed his people to be scattered among foreigners so they could better be the "light to nations" that he wanted them to be. Exile could be seen as a kind of spiritual mission. Even their suffering might eventually in-spire and purify the gentiles. The Jewish mystics gave this interpreta-tion a more esoteric twist. They declared that Jews had been strewn to the far corners of the globe in order to gather the divine sparks of holiness that had been sprinkled there at the Creation.

These various views spawned different ideas of how, and if, exile would end. All agreed that it would end sometime, although for cen-turies many Jews firmly held that it would happen only with the coming of the messiah. Others said it would conclude when Jews and Gentiles were reconciled in the various lands to which the Jews had been scattered. This view gained support when, during the late eigh-teenth and early nineteenth century, Jews were granted full citizen-ship in many European countries. Still other Jewish thinkers held that exile would end only when the spiritual mission of Judaism had been accomplished. Then, in the late nineteenth and throughout the twentieth century, as persecution and pogroms returned, another option arose. The Zionists proclaimed that exile and the anguish that goes with it would end only when Jews physically returned from their dispersion back to the Land of Israel and established their own national state.

The argument still goes on. Most Orthodox Jews still devoutly be-lieve that only the messiah can bring an end to *galut*. For some Jews, the Holocaust demolished the contention of those who hoped the exile would end with the reconciliation of Jews to their non-Jewish neighbors. But the idea of reconciliation is by no means dead, and the political, economic, and cultural success of Jews in so many countries has once again made it more plausible. Nor has the establishment of a Jewish state closed the discussion; it may even have intensified it. If the existence of such a state was supposed to end the exile, why have more than half the Jews in the world decided not to "return"? Why do some of the Jews who live in Israel believe they are still living just as much in exile as ever? What is the relationship between physical *galut* and "return" to the Land, on the one hand, and spiritual *galut* and the return to God on the other?

These were some of the questions on my mind when I arrived for the second time at Ben-Gurion Airport. This time Nina and Nicholas were with me, and there were no announcements about some mysterious welcome awaiting me. But Nina's cousin Helen was waiting and whisked us immediately to Aunt Natasha's apartment in Tel Aviv. On the way I noticed that the reading I had done on the history of Palestine and Israel since my previous visit helped orient me a bit. At least now I recognized some of the street names — like Jabotinsky, and Nohdau, and I also noticed that Tel Aviv exudes a decidedly European or New York flavor. It reminded me of the remark made by Theodor Herzl, who said he wanted the capital of the Jewish homeland to be "the Vienna in the Middle East." The sidewalk cafés could have been along the Champs-Élysées or Columbus Circle. The bookstores carried titles in several languages. The traffic was hectic. It was only the Hebrew letters on the shops that reminded me where I was. Natasha's apartment fit right in. It resembled Nina's mother's apartment on the Upper West Side. Here was another layered depository of stages in the life of a cultured, well-to-do, and highly "russified" Jewish woman. Books and paintings recalled her early years in St. Petersburg, the period in France, the final decades in America. And here it was: another *galut*, ending in a strange mixture of exile and return.

Much of our initial conversation had to do with how Natasha, already in her mid-eighties, was getting along in this new environment. She did not speak a word of Hebrew and had little interest in learning any. But since my visit in 1979 a big change had come over Israel with the arrival of hundreds of thousands of Russian Jews. The joke in Tel Aviv now was, "What is the second most frequently spoken language in Israel?" The answer: "Hebrew." Russian was now spoken everywhere — in the restaurants, in the shops, and at the grocery store. And, since Natasha spoke Russian, she was feeling quite at home, especially since she could watch the news on television in either English or Russian. But she still felt displaced.

We slept that night at the lodge of a health resort near Tel Aviv called Kfar Maccabiah, which had been built to house the athletes during the Maccabean games. Contented-looking older Israelis were now using it as a swimming pool, spa, and convivial gossip center. The breakfasts, abounding with fresh fruits, nuts, salads, and yogurt, were superb. We slept well. The next day we stayed in and around Tel Aviv and ate dinner at A Propos, an elegant French-style restaurant that made a specialty of Thai cuisine. I didn't know it then, but we were to hear a lot more about A Propos within a few days.

Most Israelis are aware of the touchy and acrimonious question of the "holy places" and want visitors to see that they are handling these sites evenhandedly. Nina's cousin Helen is no exception — in addition to being an unusually hospitable person. She had made bookings in advance, then took nearly a week away from her work to drive us up and down the length of Israel. She wanted to make sure her Christian cousin-in-law saw the Galilee, where Jesus lived most of his life, and all the sites a good Christian tourist-pilgrim should visit. With one glaring exception. She did not want to take us into the walled Old City of Jerusalem, warning us that we should avoid going there ourselves. "For your own safety," she said. I didn't argue. I knew we would be in Jerusalem on our own for a few days after our jaunt around the Galilee with her, and I fully intended to visit the Old City. So we set off for the same Galilee I had stopped at under such different circumstances eighteen years earlier.

One of the first pilgrimage sites we visited was a spot on the Jordan River where, the sign assured us, Jesus had been baptized. I took one glance and saw that it was obviously not the place I had been shown before, but I took it in good humor. One cannot be literal about holy places. Besides, an enterprising Israeli kibbutz had set up a completely furnished set of tourist facilities on this spot. There was an ample parking lot, a coffee and snack bar, a souvenir shop, and well-kept restrooms. There was a wooden shelter so that one could view the rippling waters of the holy place even in bad weather. There was an obliging photographer who would gladly snap pictures of you while you were being baptized. Most impressive, however, was how the kibbutzniks had equipped the site with a sturdy railing and graduated platform so that disabled people and those in wheelchairs could also make their way into the waters. I thought to myself that Jesus would have appreciated that touch.

As we arrived, a group of forty or more Romanian seasonal workers were filing in and out of the water while a fully vested Orthodox priest touched each one with a small tree branch, swishing it in the muddy water between each application. It was the first time I realized that a large number of Romanians were working in Israel. When the Romanians were finished, a more prosperous-looking and smaller group of Russian tourists began wading into the stream. One of them, a middle-aged man, stood beside me filming his wife, who was sloshing in up to her thighs with her clothes on. It was obviously a sound camera because, as Nina translated for me, he was saying, "And now, Ivan and Anna, here you see Grandma, getting blessed by the holy waters of the Jordan River, just as Jesus Christ did and in the very same location, the *very same* location." It was hard for me not to be touched by the display of simple piety mixed with tourist gullibility. I decided after a few minutes that I wanted to wade in too, at least up to my knees. (Galilee has a way of melting sophisticated skepticism very quickly.) I rolled up my trousers, took off my shoes and socks, and splashed into the cold current. Nina and Nicholas were pleased and amused, but Helen was very pleased indeed. See, her smile seemed to say, not only were she and her fellow Israelis taking good care of the sacred sites, they were actually improving them.

The other holy places in the Galilee were not nearly as impressive. There was the tasteless church built over the spot where Jesus is said to have fed the five thousand, an ultramodern shrine over the place in Capernaum where Peter's house supposedly stood, and the cliff just below the Golan Heights where Jesus healed the Garasene demoniac and the swine rushed over the precipice to their destruction. Each spot had its coffee bar, souvenir shop well stocked with colorful postcards, and, of course, sponged and scoured restrooms. I'm afraid I showed a little less enthusiasm than I had at the Jordan. But I appreciated Helen's intentions. She seemed to want me not to miss even a single spot that a Christian pilgrim would yearn to take in. Still, after a day or two I was beginning to feel a little jaded. I mused fondly about the raucous wayfarers in *The Canterbury Tales* who spent their evenings whooping it up, getting drunk, and telling bawdy stories. But under the circumstances, this was hardly an option for me.

Then things changed. We had circled back to Capernaum to visit the ruins of the same fourth-century synagogue, built over the one that had stood there in the first century, that I had visited on my previous trip. As we approached, I remembered how I had toured this town in the minibus and been unexpectedly moved by it. It was here that I had suddenly gotten the sensation many people seek and some even find in the Holy Land. I recalled how I felt that first time when I realized that I was standing where Jesus stood, or very close to it. I'm not always a stickler for historical accuracy in these matters. Still, I knew this site was "real" in the sense of modern historical accuracy. Every biblical scholar agrees that Jesus did indeed pass a good deal of time in Capernaum, and there can be no doubt that he prayed in the ruined synagogue that supports the present one. This made a difference to me then. I had come away doubting that even the most hardened low church Protestant, suspicious as we all are of the magic of holy places, could have avoided being at least a little awed. Now, as we parked in the lot next to the synagogue, I wondered whether it would happen again, whether this place could once more cut through the armor of a weary scholar-pilgrim.

It did. But this time I think it was for a different reason. I was now visiting the site with a Jewish wife and son and cousin-in-law. As we ambled around the ruins, I became more clearly aware than ever that what linked me to Jesus here was a synagogue, not one of the kitschy churches in the area. It was a place Jews had gathered to pray and to study Torah. I was sure at that moment that if Jesus himself climbed off the next tourist bus or strode into town with a knapsack searching for a place to pray, he would look for a synagogue. It was not an insight I felt like sharing with Nina or Helen at that moment. But it became clearer to me than ever before that my wife's Judaism need not be a barrier but could be a bridge between us. Now Capernaum became for me a holy place twice over. I was a bit reluctant to leave. I even decided that I could probably do without the miller, the cook, the wife of Bath, and the other rambunctious characters with whom Chaucer populated his tales.

I was still a happy pilgrim that evening when we stopped at an Arab restaurant in Tiberias, next to the Sea of Galilee. We all, of course, ordered Peter's Fish, which local custom insists is exactly the species the disciples were pulling from the sea when Jesus called them to be "fishers of men." It tasted like normal lake trout to me, but I savored the pseudo-historical spicing. After supper we attended a multimedia show, "The Galilee Experience," produced in a lakeside auditorium by an evangelical Christian organization called the Christian Embassy. It was a straightforward presentation of the Christian Zionist perspective on Israel and the Galilee that I described earlier. Beautifully executed technically, it walks the viewer through centuries of Jewish history, relying heavily on Old Testament prophecies of the coming of a messiah to be born in Bethlehem. It leaves a curious impression. The Jewish Zionist movement itself is scarcely mentioned. Theodor Herzl does not make an appearance. And no Arabs are seen from beginning to end. It seemed that the strange slogan of some Zionists, "A land without people for a people without land," though now discarded by most Israelis, was still being nurtured by the Christian Embassy.

Nazareth was our next stop, an Israeli city with an Arab majority, most of whom are Christians. It is not an attractive city, nor is the Roman Catholic Church of the Annunciation anything special. But according to the Gospel, it was in Nazareth that the angel Gabriel made his announcement to Mary and she conceived; so it was here, not in Bethlehem, that the Incarnation took place. Understandably, the church is dedicated to the Virgin Mary, and the courtyard around it is ringed with statues of her in different national costumes, representing her various apparitions in countries around the world. Unlike many Protestants, I have a strong interest and even some affection for Mariological piety, so I looked at it all with real appreciation. It was in Nazareth, a few years later, that ugly tensions broke out when a local radical Islamist group erected a small temporary mosque on the edge of the courtyard here. But even before we left the town that day, we were to experience a taste of the simmering tension that would break out later.

The incident occurred just after we left the Catholic church. Still fascinated by Jesus and synagogues, I suggested we look for yet another church, the one said to be built over the synagogue where Jesus preached the homecoming sermon described in the fourth chapter of the Gospel of Luke, one of my favorite parts of the New Testament. This passage says that Jesus "came to Nazareth where he had been brought up, and went to the synagogue on the Sabbath as he regularly did." At the appropriate place in the service Jesus was asked to read from the prophet Isaiah, so he opened the scroll and read:

"The spirit of the Lord is upon me
because he has anointed me;
he has sent me to announce good news to the poor,
to proclaim release for the prisoners
and recovery of sight for the blind;
and to let the broken victims go free,
to proclaim the year of the Lord's favor" (Luke 4:18, 19).

My guidebook indicated that this church was at the end of a narrow alley that functioned as the bazaar on weekdays. As it happened,
it was Sunday, and the shops and stalls along the alley were closed. I
was walking a few steps ahead of Nina, Nicholas, and Helen, peering
back and forth between my guidebook and the empty shops ahead.
Then three young Arab boys on bikes appeared in front of us, zigzag-
ging back and forth across the alley. When they got to me they rode
entirely too close, shouted in an unfriendly tone, and one of them
appeared to spit. Then they continued on behind me. A second or
two later I heard Nicholas say, "Hey, Dad, that kid just spit at me and
tried to run me down." Then Nina, from farther behind me, suggested in no uncertain terms that we get out of there and return to
the main square, where our car was parked. I agreed.

As we left Nazareth, Nicholas, who was ten at the time, said, "Dad,
I didn't like Nazareth. Why did those kids spit at me?" It was obviously time for a talk, and since Helen was driving, Nina and I tried to
carry the ball. Those kids, I told him, were obviously not demonstrating very good manners, but they had nothing against him personally. Israelis and Palestinians, I said, were living through a lot of
turmoil. They were Palestinian kids who had no idea who we were
but knew we were not from Nazareth. Maybe they thought we were
Americans and believed Americans were not being fair in the argument between Israel and the Palestinians. But who knows what they
thought. In any case, to visit Israel, where both Jews and Arabs live
together with a lot of unrest every day, and not to undergo any of
that uneasiness, would be to miss something very important. Didn't
he think so?

I had obviously not persuaded him. Sitting with his lips pressed
together, he told me he understood what I was saying, but he *still*
didn't like Nazareth. Two years later, when Intifada II broke out, I was
distressed but not surprised to read of the clashes between Jews and

Palestinians in Nazareth and in some other Israeli towns where the two peoples live close together.

We drove in silence for a while. Then Helen's cell phone buzzed. A friend was calling to say that an explosive device carried by a suicide bomber had just blown up in a restaurant in Tel Aviv. Six people had been killed, including the bomber, and several others wounded.

"What restaurant was it?" Helen asked.

"It was A Propos."

"*Which* A Propos?" she asked quickly. (I had not realized there was more than one, but it seems there was a small chain of them.) Her caller told her it was the one on Eliashiv Street. It was not where we had dined two nights before; it was four blocks away.

I had been annoyed and a bit upset by the spitting incident in Nazareth. Maybe, I thought later, I did not want my son — or my wife — to carry away a bad impression of the town where Jesus' family lived and where he grew up. But now it seemed like a minor irritation. When I heard that a restaurant with the same name, and so close to the one where we had eaten forty-eight hours earlier, was now a shambles of broken glass and torn bodies, the spitting seemed insignificant. I had been told many times how nerve-racking it is for both Jews and Arabs to live in a country in which you never know when you climb onto a bus, walk to the market, or sit down to a restaurant meal when a bomb may explode. I had occasion to think about this more than once during the rest of our visit.

After our personal tour of the Galilee, Helen drove us to Jerusalem and dropped us off in front of what must be the grandest and most architecturally elegant YMCA building in the world. The "Yimkah," as everyone calls it, first opened its doors in 1933. It was designed by the American architect Arthur Loomis Harmon, whose firm also designed the Empire State Building. But although the New York skyscraper still stands as a marvelous example of the Art Deco style, Harmon had something else in mind for the Holy Land.

Scholars who criticize Western "orientalist" stereotypes of the Middle East are right when they contend that when we arrive, we often see what our mental images have prepared us to see. One reason is that the architecture of Jerusalem, so much of it invented by Western planners, has for decades pasted over the landscape with exotic concoctions that express what the architects imagine the Holy City should look like. But even this hall-of-cultural-mirrors effect is fascinating, especially since to understand the sad history of Jerusalem is in large measure to understand how people have imagined it.

The Jerusalem YMCA is an exquisite example of this echo-chamber syndrome, but it is also a remarkable building by anyone's standards. Even though Nina and Nicholas were eager to hurry inside and unpack, I insisted we stand for a few minutes and drink it in. Harmon, of course, could have settled for a European style, a basilica or something with a touch of Gothic. God knows, Jerusalem is saturated with such derivative structures. Instead, he tried to combine several local traditions, and he very nearly succeeded. He chose white stone. On either side of the central edifice he placed square halls topped by low Byzantine domes, connected to the main building by arched loggias in pink and white stone. The central tower rises 120 feet and is always crowded with tourists who have heard about the superlative view it affords. In the middle of the tower a six-winged seraph, drawn from the vision of the prophet Isaiah, is keeping permanent guard over the city — or simply enjoying the vista along with everyone else.

After a few minutes we hoisted our suitcases and started up the stairs to the entrance. But I appealed for one more brief stop. Still outside the main entrance stands a sarcophagus on the right and across from it an inscription in Hebrew, English, and Arabic, drawn from the dedication speech in 1933, made by General Allenby during the period of the British mandate over Palestine. "Here is a place," it says, "whose atmosphere is peace, where politics and religious jealousies can be forgotten." I'm sure that what Allenby had in mind was what still goes on within the YMCA itself, not the city of Jerusalem as a whole. Here Jews, Christians, and Muslims — Israelis, Palestinians, and visitors from dozens of countries — do in fact mix amicably in the restaurant, on the tennis courts, and in the pool. A day care center holds children carefully selected to represent a cross section of the city. A few days later, the director of the Y told me that friendships are constantly being formed between Israelis and Arabs on the handball court that, he assured me, pay off richly on the government level. At the time I took his word for it, but later, after the eruption of violence in Jerusalem in the fall of 2000, I wondered whether those friendships had survived.

Directly across the street from the YMCA stands the historic King David Hotel, a sober reminder that Jerusalem itself is hardly a place where, despite Allenby's ingenuous words, either politics or religious jealousies are ever forgotten for very long. I remembered that Menachem Begin, who later became prime minister of Israel (and made peace with President Anwar Sadat of Egypt) was one of those who blew up an entire wing of that hotel during the final months of the British Mandate. Today the King David, like the YMCA, is also an example of cultural image projections, demonstrating how yet another architect, the Swiss G. E. Hufschmid, tried to invent what he hoped would be a "local" style. While my family napped, I sauntered across the street to visit.

The King David imitates the profiles of the historic grand hotels, including the once-famous Shepherd's Hotel in Cairo, owned by Jews. Inside, it is crammed with motifs that Hufschmid believed represented Assyrian, Hittite, and Phoenician styles, in the lobby, lounge, and dining room respectively. The total effect is a dizzying plushness that is oddly comforting. "Don't worry," it seems to say, "the good old days are not gone forever. Here you are right in the midst of them." On a less historical note, I also remembered that it was on the terrace of the King David that Paul Newman and Eva Marie Saint had a rendezvous in the 1960 film *Exodus*. The aggregate, I thought, is yet another demonstration of how hard it is to extricate actual history from mythology in this city, which is loaded to the brim with both.[7]

I decided to sit on the terrace, overlooking the Old City, and sip a cup of coffee. The city walls, the tower of David, assorted steeples, domes, and minarets paraded across the horizon like some incongruous ecclesiastical procession. But at the next table three people were loudly discussing the A Propos suicide bombing. I was annoyed at first, but then, the terrace of the King David Hotel is not an inappropriate place to think about the history of terrorism that has scarred Jerusalem. It did not start with the bombing of this hotel in 1946, for the entire history of Jewish-Arab relations is drenched in the blood of terrorist acts. As soon as the British Mandate began, tensions arose as more Jews began to immigrate and Arabs began to fear being overwhelmed. Random beatings and killings, mostly of Jews, started to spread. By the late 1920s and into the 1930s riots often broke out. One exploit of terror always evoked another, and the response sometimes came almost instantly. In March 1937, for example, an Arab tossed a bomb onto the Jaffa Road, injuring three Jews.

Within the hour, members of the Irgun, the military wing of the re-visionist Zionists, threw two bombs into Arab cafés in Jerusalem, killing one Arab and wounding twenty others. In 1938, as the Jews were becoming impatient with British policies, the Irgun exploded more homemade bombs in Jaffa, then an Arab town, killing five people and wounding twenty. Two days later the same group struck again, this time killing twenty-three Arabs and wounding seventy-nine. Two weeks later they carried out another attack in Jerusalem it-self, killing ten more.

Not only did Arabs and Jews kill each other. More and more, both groups directed their fury toward the British. The Arabs believed the British were intent on "Judaizing" Palestine. The Jews were enraged by the British limitations on immigration, especially as the plight of German Jews became more intolerable. The culmination of this ter-rorism, was the bombing of the King David. Not only was it particu-larly gruesome, but it has become a landmark in the whole grisly his-tory of conflict since it involved two future prime ministers of Israel, Menachem Begin and Yitzhak Shamir. On July 22, 1946, Jewish mili-tants disguised as Arabs delivered explosives hidden in milk churns to the hall outside the hotel's Regence Café, where solicitous waiters were even now pouring my coffee. At that time, the five floors above the café were being used by the British as their headquarters. A woman telephoned the switchboard anonymously to warn that the hotel should be evacuated immediately. No one followed her warn-ing. The explosion occurred shortly after noon. It demolished the lower floors, and the five floors above collapsed into smoking rubble. Among the ninety-one dead were Arabs and Jews as well as Britons. A passerby was killed by a large safe thrown from the hotel by the blast.[8]

Terrorism is highly contagious; it almost always provokes more terrorism. In February 1948, British deserters placed a bomb in the Ben Yehuda market, one of the busiest in the Jewish section. More than fifty people died. The situation was becoming ever more com-plicated. Two months later, Jewish militants attacked and destroyed the Arab village of Deir Yassin and killed more than a hundred of its inhabitants, including women and children. This happened only five weeks before Israel declared its independence; it was apparently in-tended to demonstrate to Ben-Gurion's government-in-the-making and the rest of the new government that the Jewish terrorists he had opposed were still a force to be reckoned with. Ben-Gurion's response was to apologize to the king of Trans-Jordan and to crack down on the diehards.

After the establishment of the state of Israel, the government tried to end all terrorism, but never with success. Terrorism is the weapon of the weaker party, and Jerusalem continued to be virtually the terrorist capital of the world. The Arabs, who considered the partitioning of Palestine a "catastrophe," renewed their attacks, and in November 1969 the open-air Mehane Yehuda market was their target. Twelve people were killed by the blast, including two Arabs, and fifty-three wounded. Terrorism is also an inexact weapon. In January 1970 Arabs flipped a grenade at an Israeli military jeep making its way through the Arab market near the Holy Sepulcher. It missed, and five Arabs died. When a huge bomb, hidden in a refrigerator, exploded outside a shop on Zion Square in July 1975, the dead and wounded included both Jews and Arabs.[9] Sometimes both the facts and the symbolism are almost too much to bear. When, in 1986, members of the Islamic Jihad murdered a young religious Jew in the Old City, his mourners turned the funeral procession into an assault on the Muslim quarter. The Israeli writer Naomi Shepherd recalled it: "At one stage, the bearers of the corpse, carried in a winding sheet according to Jewish custom,[10] on a stretcher, set the stretcher down and took part in the riot; as they passed the Basilica of the Agony of Gethsemane, they tried to break into the grounds."[11]

The Basilica of the Agony of Gethsemane! The place where nearly two thousand years ago a young Palestinian Jew wept tears of blood as he anticipated a death by torture at the hands of Roman terrorists. The French artist Georges Rouault once created a searing painting entitled *Christ Will Be in Agony Until the End of the World.* Some thoughtful Christians dismiss this idea because, they say, it does not reflect with sufficient clarity the hope of Easter. Some Protestants say it is "too Catholic." But I think it contains a profound insight. Christianity teaches that, one way or another, God shares the deepest pain of human beings. I believe this myself. But I do not believe that this divine empathy lasted only the thirty-three years of Jesus' earthly life. The incident at the Basilica of the Agony of Gethsemane demonstrates that both the Jews and the Arabs involved were spewing out their own rage and pain. Who could be drawn to any God who does not feel that torment today just as he did centuries ago?

I was aroused from my reflections when Nina and Nicholas breezed onto the terrace of the King David to remind me it was time to head for the Old City, just a few blocks away. I was glad to be interrupted. Even after a bombing incident in Tel Aviv, even when everyone is unusually tense, even when the borders between Israel and the territory of the Palestinian Authority have been closed by the Israeli authorities, even after being cautioned by a worried cousin, it was impossible for me to be in Jerusalem and not visit the Old City. We walked and looked and shopped along with hundreds of other visitors, who also seemed to be ignoring the warnings and the scrutiny of the Israeli Defense Force troops at every other corner with their shiny Uzis at the ready. We visited many places in the Old City, but two in particular brought up significant thoughts for our family. The first was largely positive, but — like everything else in Jerusalem — somewhat ambiguous. The second was, at least for me, mostly negative. The first was the Western Wall, the second, the Church of the Holy Sepulcher.

It is hard not to be impressed by the Wall. If you enter the Old City through the Jaffa Gate, which opens toward West Jerusalem, you walk along David and then Chain Street, then make a right and left turn. There it is, a structure of huge, off-white stones standing sixty feet high and fifty-two yards wide. Its different names conjure up its tortuous history. It was constructed by Herod around the time of Jesus as a retaining wall on the southwest side of the Temple Mount; so — contrary to what some believe — it was never actually a part of the Temple itself. After the Romans destroyed the Temple in 70 C.E., they decided to allow this fragment to remain as a stern reminder of their awesome power. For years Jews were allowed to enter the city only once a year, on the ninth day of the month of Av, to lament the destruction of the Temple. They would gather at this fragment of the Wall to weep and tear their garments — hence the centuries-old name the Wailing Wall. After the Israelis captured the Old City from Jordanian forces during the Six-Day War in 1967, it once again became possible for Jews to pray at the Wall. But many felt their prayers should now be psalms of gratitude, not laments, so they wanted to stop calling it the Wailing Wall. Old photographs show it towering over a dark narrow alley, but soon after they captured this section of the city, the Israelis bulldozed an Arab residential quarter that stood there; the approach to the Wall is now a wide courtyard, filled day after day by crowds of Jews praying, as well as hundreds of tourists and sightseers. A fence running at a right angle to the Wall indicates the separate areas in which men and women are to pray.

I approached the Wall with a deep sense of irony. I was acutely aware that as a gentile-Christian father I was permitted to escort my Jewish son to this holiest place in his faith but that his Jewish mother would have to pray on the other side of the barrier. I knew that this "first visit to the Wall" would be a marker in our family's history. No subsequent visit would be like this first one. An enormous sense of responsibility and a strange joy came over me. When we got to the barrier, Nina gave us both an ambiguous little wave, then Nicholas and I pressed toward the towering stones, edging past dozens of male Jews dressed in everything from the severest of Orthodox black to casual tourist denims. When we reached the Wall itself Nicholas, following an old custom, placed some prayers scrawled on tiny bits of paper by the boys and girls in his Hebrew school class between the cracks in the stones, then said a short prayer in Hebrew he had learned especially for this occasion. I could see he was impressed. He would not forget this moment. I knew I would not forget it either.

When Nicholas had finished his prayer, I tucked a slip of paper with a prayer of my own into a crack in the rock. I had written on it simply: "For the Peace of the City." It seemed trite and unimaginative, but there it was. And I certainly meant it seriously. When I finished, I saw Nicholas looking at me with the expression I had come to recognize as "Can we go now?" How much holiness and history can one ten-year-old — or anyone else — take all at once? As we turned to leave, a breathless young man stepped toward us quickly and asked me if we were Jewish. Off guard, I answered, accurately enough, "Well, I'm not, but he is." Nicholas looked at me uncomfortably, although he also knew it was the correct answer. Still, I sensed some resentment in myself that anyone should separate me from my son in any way at this majestic moment for us both. "Well," our eager interrogator continued, "would you like him to have a blessing from the rabbi?" He jerked his head toward a bearded gentleman in a *tallit* standing a few feet away. I agreed, though I still resented the interruption. We followed him the few steps to the rabbi, who led Nicholas back to the Wall (indicating discreetly that I should stand a couple of paces back), placed his hands on Nicholas's head, and uttered a few words of Hebrew in a distracted tone. It was over in ten seconds.

I thanked the rabbi's assistant, but evidently that was not enough. "Some money for the rabbi," he said, extending his hand while his eyes searched the crowd, presumably for the next recipient of the rabbinical benediction, "a hundred shekels?" I calculated quickly; it was about $35. That seemed a little steep, even for a blessing at the Wall. Besides, I had felt a bit put upon by his intrusion and therefore not terribly generous. I handed him thirty shekels, about $10. He seemed grateful, and as he tucked the money in his pocket, he was already offering the rabbi's services to a young man wearing sandals, a *yarmulka*, and a New York Yankees T-shirt.

When Nina rejoined us outside the fence between the men and women, I found it hard to articulate the maelstrom of emotions that had assailed me during our visit to the Wall. On the one hand, I felt unspeakably grateful for the opportunity to be the one to accompany my son to this place. On the other, I was sorry that Nina could not be with us. And I resented the intrusion of the blessing hawker, not so much because I dislike the merchandising of religion in any tradition, but because I felt he had shattered a magical mood between my son and myself, a rare and sweet opportunity that I had wanted to cling to a little longer, a moment that could never be reconstituted.

As we walked back through the Old City, then stopped for a soft drink, I could not get it out of my mind. All kinds of thoughts came to me. I remembered Goethe's famous line *"Verweile euch, du bist so schon"* ("Linger awhile, you are so lovely"). It is his acute characterization of both the impossibility of slowing down a precious moment and the way we always try to do it anyway. I also remembered how many other transcendent moments in my life had been interrupted or cut short before they ran their course. For example, after receiving the news of my father's death, I immediately returned home from my job in another state. Just as the taxi pulled up at our front door and I saw my mother open it and extend her arms to embrace me, I also saw a black car pull up and my father's boss — with a bouquet of flowers in hand — leap out and run toward her, cutting me off. By the time she had received him and handed the blossoms to my sister, the mixture of sadness and affection I had felt when the taxi arrived had melted into resentment and annoyance. Why had he appeared at just that instant?

Heaven rarely grants us unalloyed moments of transcendence or ecstasy. I have certainly had few enough myself. Maybe God had planted that blessing dealer at the Wall to remind me that just as all idols have feet of clay, even the most rapturous moments in life are subject to the need to urinate or to fend off someone who is tapping you on the shoulder. Maybe these musings themselves were crawling up from the soul of a more Kierkegaardian Protestant and would not be as upsetting to my Jewish wife and son. At least the two of them seemed to be enjoying their Oranginas without any evidence of angst. This observation pushed me into an even deeper layer of paradox. How is it that Jews often seem to take their religion so lightly and yet so seriously at the same time? At one moment they can poke fun at it with a wryness that would shock a devout Presbyterian, but in the next they are willing to die rather than give it up. When I eventually told Nina about the enterprising rabbi's assistant at the Wall, she thought it was amusing and didn't see why it should have disturbed the sanctity of the visit.

When we had finished the Orangina we made our way past the T-shirt and religious kitsch vendors who line the cramped alleys toward our next destination, the Church of the Holy Sepulcher, about halfway between the Jaffa Gate to the west and the Damascus Gate to the north. Having had my fill of alleged holy places in the Galilee, I approached what some people call the holiest of all Christian sites with many reservations. Besides, I continued to chafe over the slapdash mingling of history and legend in the Holy Land, and I had read something about the questionable credentials of this one as well. Still, Nina was stalwartly fulfilling her interfaith and marital duty by accompanying me with Nicholas in tow. We had been to the Wall. Now it was my turn, time to visit the principal Christian holy place in the Old City. So I tried to stay in a good mood, even though I had a sense of foreboding.

The foreboding soon won out. What perturbed me about the Church of the Holy Sepulcher was not the historically dubious claim that it covers the spot where Jesus was crucified and buried, but that the history of the church itself is hardly one to be proud of. In the fourth century c.e., Jerusalem was still part of the Roman empire and called by its Roman name, Aelia Capitolina. Christian worship in the city was barely tolerated. But early in that century everything changed. Emperor Constantine first embraced Christianity and then convoked a council of the bishops at Nicaea to hammer out a consistent policy for the church and a uniform creed. His motives were largely political. He wanted the empire to have a religion that would unify, not divide it; but the Christians were already bickering over doctrine and jurisdiction. At this time, the bishop of the tiny Christian congregation in Jerusalem was an ambitious man named Makarios, who resented being subject to the metropolitan bishop of Caesarea, fifty miles north. Makarios hit on a splendid idea to increase the prestige of his city. At the meeting of the Council of Nicaea he pushed through a resolution, rarely mentioned in histories, to tear down the Roman Temple of Aphrodite, which had been built by the emperor Hadrian two hundred years before, in order to uncover the tomb of Christ, which he claimed lay underneath it. Constantine loved the idea. A connoisseur of any monumental architecture that would bring more glory to his rule, he saw this as a golden opportunity to raise an imposing edifice at a central location, indeed the central holy place in the Christian story.

There were two problems, however. First, the vast majority of the residents of Aelia Capitolina were pagans who still worshiped the gods of the Roman pantheon, and the Temple of Aphrodite was the main architectural focus of their devotion. Second, it was not at all certain that the tomb of Christ actually lay beneath the pagan temple. There was a good chance that it might, and some legends confirmed the belief. But for Bishop Makarios and the emperor, ecclesiastical and imperial considerations far outweighed archaeological theorizing. Thus began the first chapter in the long and dubious history of religiously inspired digging in and around Jerusalem, and both the emperor and the bishop were determined that it was going to be a success.

It was. Just in time for the celebrated arrival in Jerusalem of the emperor's aged mother, Helen, who pioneered pilgrimages to the Holy Land, the pagan shrine was demolished and the tomb — or at least what Bishop Makarios insisted was the tomb — unearthed. Helen, who had become a Christian in 327 C.E. and who was one of the first but not the last of the credulous and enthusiastic pilgrims in Jerusalem, was duly impressed. Then her joy soared even higher when she discovered, or was given (it is not at all clear), a section of what she was assured was the true cross on which Christ had died. Enough slivers of the "true cross," someone once wrote, can now be found in the reliquaries of European churches to provide the ties for miles of railroad tracks.

But I felt edgy as we drew close to the church for another reason. I knew I was supposed to be impressed, maybe even touched, by standing at the very spot where Christ was crucified. Having just been to the Wall with me, Nina and Nicholas were ready to appreciate my holy place as well. But it was not to happen. The pathetic truth is that for centuries, the Church of the Holy Sepulcher has been a battleground among warring factions of Christians who today share an uneasy truce, each claiming a corner, an aisle, or a side chapel as their exclusive turf. The Greek Orthodox church owns the Katholikon (the nave), the northern part of the cliff of Golgotha (which is actually inside the church), and something called Christ's prison, where Jesus is said to have been held after his arrest. The Roman Catholics — or Latins, as they are known in Jerusalem — own the choir between the Rotunda and the Katholikon as well as the Chapel of the Apparition. The Armenians have the Place of the Three Marys and the chapel dedicated to Saint Helen (the imperial mother whose pilgrimage and discoveries started all this). The Coptic Church controls a chapel on the western side of the sepulcher itself; the Syrians own the western chapel in the Rotunda, and the Abyssinians own the Tomb of Joseph of Arimathaea, the rich man who the Gospels report made the tomb available for Jesus. It is a relief to learn that at least the Holy Sepulcher itself is owned in common by all the sects. Still, the friction among the contending Christian churches over the place has been so severe at times, and the distrust among them so venomous, that for centuries a Muslim family, the Nuseibehs, has functioned as the custodian and the keeper of the keys. These people were the only ones, it seems, who could be trusted to be fair by all parties concerned. The irony of this arrangement deepens when one understands that although Muslims honor Jesus as a prophet, they reject the accounts of his crucifixion.

Admittedly, I am ambivalent about the mystery of any holy place, but I was unusually wary about this one from the outset. Still, I wanted to give it a chance. My attempt to keep an open mind was not helped by a slight case of claustrophobia, which makes me jumpy in enclosed places, and by my distinct distaste for being squeezed by crowds. But try I did, and Nina and Nicholas did their best to help. We entered under a Corinthian cornice that dates back to the original church erected under Constantine. From there we were pressed along by the crowd to the spot where Jesus was nailed to the cross, the spot where Jesus' mother, Mary, stood by the cross, and the stone in which the cross itself is said to have been implanted. Next to it is the fissure in the rock that is identified as the one that opened up when Christ died.

By this time we had been in the church less than ten minutes, and I was entirely ready to go. Nina and Nicholas were in no hurry, however; they even seemed to be enjoying themselves. Nicholas, with the morbid curiosity of the young, stared in fascination at all the evidence of torture and death. Nina, I darkly suspected, was probably saying a silent prayer of thanksgiving that this gloomy necropolis, its obscurity punctuated every few seconds by a flashbulb, was not a part of her tradition. One corner of the site did attract my attention, however, or at least my curiosity. On either side of the entrance to the Chapel of Adam (which gets its name from the legendary claim that the skull of our original ancestor was found under the cross) stand two stone benches. They mark the tombs where Godfrey of Bouillon (1058–1100) and Baldwin I (1058–1118), the first two rulers of the kingdom the Crusaders founded in Jerusalem, were once buried. Neither of these gentlemen is one of my favorites. Godfrey had allowed his soldiers to rape and plunder Constantinople on the way to the Holy Land. After Jerusalem fell, he was designated its ruler but unctuously refused the title of king, choosing instead Defender of the Holy Sepulcher. After he died, his brother Baldwin, less cramped by religious humility, accepted the title of king. It was he who with the help of the Genoese and the Venetians captured the ports of Palestine. His alliance with Venice helps explain why St. Mark's Cathedral is so crammed with the booty, much of it Greek, picked up along the way to Jerusalem. The Muslims removed the remains of these two Crusaders when they recaptured the city in the thirteenth century. In 1808 the empty tombs themselves were broken to pieces by Greek Orthodox monks. One historian identifies these monks as "fanatics" — and they probably were. But it is not hard to imagine why any Greek, then or now, should harbor any fondness for these two brothers from Boulogne. Still, defacing a tomb is a nasty business, so when I found myself sympathizing with the monks, I decided it was clearly time to leave. I gave the signal to my wife and child, whose puzzled expressions indicated their surprise that I wanted to shorten the time allotted to "my" holy place. But leave we did, without paying tribute to either the Chapel of St. Helen or the grave of Joseph of Arimathaea.

Even the jostling crowds of peddlers and pilgrims and tourists that choke the narrow alleys of the Old City seemed a distinct relief after the suffocating atmosphere of the church. It was clearly time for another Orangina. Once again, as we sat and sipped, my Jewish family tried to be sympathetic. Sensing that I had not been overwhelmed by tears of piety in the holy place, they gently asked me what I didn't like about it.

How could I explain? I did not want to rehearse my quaint Protestant prejudices against such places. Besides, what had I expected? We were in Jerusalem, in the Holy Land, the apogee of the fusion of myth and history. But I was too embarrassed to admit that if I had been there alone I might not have found the Church of the Holy Sepulcher so repellent. Christianity, after all, is still fraught with bitter internal divisions, and it drags along with it a sordid record of conquest and pillage. Maybe this church is an all too accurate emblem of that reality. I felt so ill at ease because, I think, I was there *with* my Jewish wife. Naturally, in the city of the three faiths, I had wanted to hold up my end of the bargain. I had hoped that they might get some deeper appreciation for my religion just as I was getting a deeper feeling for theirs. But the Church of the Holy Sepulcher had not done it. Would there still be an opportunity?

As it turned out, there was. But for me, not for them. As we had planned, on the Saturday of our last week in Israel, Nicholas and Nina flew back to Boston. It was Holy Week, at least according to the "Western" Christian calendar. Nicholas had to return to school on Monday, but I wanted to be in Jerusalem for Good Friday and Easter Sunday. After I said good-bye to them, I checked out of the YMCA and took a taxi to the ecumenical study center called Tantur, on the road to Bethlehem. Originally founded by Roman Catholics, Tantur is now administered by an ecumenical board and has become a free space where Christians of various denominations, Jews, and Muslims can gather for study, conversation, and prayer. I had arranged with Father Thomas Stransky, the director, to give a lecture in exchange for a few days' room and board. I thought it would be a good place to collect my thoughts and digest all I had seen and heard during my visit. I was also hoping that it might enable me to reclaim something of my own faith tradition, which had been badly dented by our dispiriting visit to the Church of the Holy Sepulcher.

Tantur did all I hoped it would, but not in the way I expected. The pleasant room I was shown to looks out to the south on the barbed-wire fence that separates Jerusalem proper (as defined by recent Israeli annexations) and the territory that Israelis speak of as "under the jurisdiction of the Palestinian National Authority" and Palestinians refer to simply as "Palestine." Just to the left of the window, perhaps two hundred yards away, was the checkpoint where all vehicles crossing the border in either direction must stop and be inspected by the Israeli Defense Forces. Farther off to the left, about a half mile away, stood the controversial hill called Har Homa in Hebrew and Jebel Abu Ghneim in Arabic. The Israelis had recently announced that they intended to build a new housing project on this hill for Israeli Jews, even though it is in what has traditionally been an Arab section of Jerusalem. Earlier that week, there had been a demonstration at the hill, in which both Arabs and Israelis had participated, opposing the project. The next day the *Jerusalem Post* had carried on its first page a photograph of a young Palestinian tied to a wooden cross — crucifixion-style — to dramatize the protest. (Since then, the project has been completed.)

It was a clear, warm day, and the windows in the room were open. I had not even unpacked my suitcase when I heard the first thuds of the tear gas guns and the thunks of the rifles firing rubber bullets. Looking toward the checkpoint, I could see clouds of tear gas and crowds of Palestinian boys throwing stones toward the guards, then running back as the tear gas missiles hit the ground and the spume spread. Just down the hill, less than a mile away, was Bethlehem. How could I possibly avoid thinking of the grim irony of one of the most popular Christmas carols: "O little town of Bethlehem, how still we see thee lie."

Today Bethlehem is not little, and that weekend it was anything but still. As I watched the white puffs slowly dispersing in the breeze and heard more *thuds* and *thunks*, I thought at first that this was a strange place to try to meditate on Good Friday, the day Christians remember the crucifixion. But almost instantly I realized that there was probably no better place in the world to ask myself what, if anything, the event that had happened so close by almost two thousand years ago had to do with what was happening today.

I continued to watch. As the sun was setting, I began to notice cars and vans pulling up in the parking lot behind Tantur, on the side next to the fence facing Bethlehem. From each vehicle four or five people, both men and women, jumped out quickly and scurried down the shrubbery-covered hill toward the barbed-wire fence. Because it was getting dark and the bushes were so thick, I couldn't see where they were going. I wandered out into the parking lot and asked one of the other guests. "They're Palestinian workers," he said. "The border has been closed to them because of the bombing at the A Propos in Tel Aviv. But they need the work, and their Israeli employers need them, so they drive them here when it gets dark. Then they slip over the border."

"But how do they get over?" I asked in all innocence.

"Go look for yourself," he said.

A bit cautiously, I stumbled down the hill, wishing I had brought a flashlight but aware that I would probably not want to use it anyway, for fear of attracting the attention of the border guards no more than a hundred yards away. Soon I came to the fence, but I noticed a trail on the Israeli side that led to a convenient break in the wire, big enough for someone to slip through easily. When I climbed back to the main building of Tantur I told my fellow guest what I had seen, and he winked.

"But don't the guards over there know there's a huge hole in the fence?" I asked. "Don't they ever check?"

"Of course they know," he answered. "But, like I say, these people need the work and their employers need them, so the soldiers look the other way."

It was my first but not my last lesson in the curious mixture of competition and complicity that characterizes the relations between Israelis and Palestinians.

The next day was Easter Sunday. I set out with Father Stransky to drive the short distance to the checkpoint and then into Bethlehem, a predominantly Christian Arab town. As we slowed down for the road barriers and pulled up to the point where the bored Israeli soldiers stood, languidly smoking cigarettes, the collars of their unpressed uniforms open, I tensed. Father Stransky, however, was either nonchalant or wanted to appear so. He did not wear a clerical collar, but his brown wooden cross was visible on its leather cord around his neck. He showed an American passport to the guard, who glanced at it distractedly while he looked at me and then scanned the backseats of the van. Father Stransky was speaking to him in Hebrew, but I

heard "church" and wondered idly if there was any Hebrew equivalent. The guard took only thirty seconds, then stepped back and
waved us on without a word.

"A Russian," said Father Stransky. "Probably doesn't know any Hebrew anyway."

I was slightly relieved, but not for long. As soon as our car crawled
out of the actual checkpoint area, we were surrounded by a crowd of
about fifty Palestinian boys and young men. Three or four of them
danced slowly in front of us so that we could proceed at only about
five miles an hour. The others grouped themselves on the side of the
car away from the Israeli guard station and hurled stones over the car
toward the soldiers. I had seen this many times on television at
home, but I suddenly realized that this was a lot closer than I wanted
to be. I must have looked a bit nervous.

"Don't worry," Father Stransky muttered while the car lurched forward, stopped, and lurched again as he tried to avoid hitting the
dancers, "they're not aiming at us. They're just using us as a moving
shield."

I nodded, not entirely reassured.

"Anyway," he added, almost casually, "it might be a good idea to
wind up your window. The Israelis sometimes fire tear gas at them."

Trying not to appear hurried, I wound it up. Quickly. The next instant I heard the same *thud* I had heard from a distance. Only this
time it was very close and very loud. At the sound, the boys and
young men scampered away. Two more *thuds*. We sped up just a bit.
Then two more, and I saw the spumes of tear gas rising from the can-
isters and — even though the windows were closed — felt a sharp
prickling sensation in my eyes and throat.

"They're gone now," Father Stransky murmured in a philosophical
tone as he shifted into a higher gear, "but they'll be back. And then
the Israelis will shoot the tear gas again. And then they'll run away
again. And then they'll be back again. It's a scenario. And everybody
knows the rules. Mostly."

I have thought about that word, "mostly," many times since. In
October 2000, the pantomime gave way to a real and hideous drama.
After Ariel Sharon's foray onto the Temple Mount, the rock hurl-
ing, mixed with gunfire, spread all over the territories and into the
towns in Israel itself where Jews and Palestinians live uneasily side by

side, as we had discovered in Nazareth. The Israeli army responded with tanks, live bullets, helicopter gunships, and M-16s. Ritual confrontation turned into real death. Instead of watching with fascination from a balcony, the whole world watched in horror.

In contrast to the fury that exploded in the fall of 2000, that Easter Sunday two years earlier now seems almost idyllic. Leaving the border roadblock, we drove along at a normal speed and, within three minutes, entered the city of Bethlehem. It was then that I learned it was not only Easter Sunday on the Western calendar, it was also what the Palestinians call Land Day, an annual occasion for speeches, demonstrations, and protests against the Israeli annexing of Palestinian land. There was no place to park in Manger Square, the central plaza. Father Stransky poked the car through some back streets and finally found a spot. As we left the car, I noticed he placed a black burnoose, the traditional Arab headdress, on the dashboard above the steering wheel. I knew he never wore a burnoose, and he saw my quizzical expression.

"We do have Israeli plates, after all, and we're in a Palestinian town," he explained. "This helps."

We walked the three blocks to Manger Square, decked out with hundreds of white folding chairs in rows facing a temporary platform, where musicians were already tuning up for the Land Day program. Huge posters of Yasir Arafat and banners with slogans were hung from stores and balconies. The police of the Palestinian Authority, sporting their racy black berets, patrolled in pairs. My priestly companion, his shirt open but his cross still in sight, seemed to know everybody we met. Each one greeted him with a smile, usually toothy and sometimes flecked with gold. He chatted with them briefly in Arabic. One friend invited us for coffee, but Father Stransky politely declined. We were on our way, he told him, to the church.

The church was, of course, the famous Orthodox Church of the Nativity. The service was just ending in a burst of praise as we entered. Clouds of incense were still wafting through the crowds. I wondered if ever again I would sniff both tear gas and incense in the same half hour. Once more, everyone seemed to know my trusty guide. One, a middle-aged woman in a shawl, handed each of us a small chunk of fresh bread. Father Stransky told her I was an American priest. While he was not quite accurate, I knew his intentions were proper. She then turned to me and said excitedly in English, "Tell them to talk, talk, please, not shoot, shoot. Otherwise, dead." I thanked her for the bread and told her I would do my best.

"Her husband was killed during the Intifada," Tom said, "She's still a little unbalanced. Never really recovered."

I told him I thought her idea was about the sanest thing I'd heard all morning.

Tom smiled. Then he led me down a narrow stone staircase to the tiny grotto under the church where Jesus is said to have been born. I shelved for the moment the historical-critical thesis that Jesus was probably not born in Bethlehem at all and that the birth story was added later by people who wanted to build up his connection with the City of David. Still, I detected that I was becoming weary of all the shelving and bracketing of recent biblical research I had been doing since I arrived in the Holy Land. I was beginning to swim along with the current. Was the place working its spell on me after all? Even that thought I shelved for later reflection.

But now Tom was showing me something else that appealed to me much more. At the head of the right aisle near the Altar of the Manger is a stone with a directional arrow engraved in it. The arrow points to Mecca. It seems that when Omar, the Muslim general who conquered Jerusalem and Bethlehem in 704 c.e., first saw this church, it was described to him as a place where the Christians honored Mary, the mother of Jesus. Since Mary is mentioned respectfully in the Qur'an several times, he ordered that the church not be harmed and even asked that Muslims be allowed to pray in it. The Christian bishop, it is said, quickly granted his wish. But to orient the Muslim worshipers properly in a building that was not originally constructed to face Mecca, the stone with the arrow was laid in the floor so that they could pray with their heads in the mandatory direction. To this day, Tom told me, Muslims come in, walk to the stone, sit on their knees, press their foreheads to the floor, and say their prayers toward the other Holy City.

As Tom showed me through St. Catherine's, the Roman Catholic church that amicably shares a courtyard with the Church of the Nativity, I was still thinking about the stone with the arrow. I asked myself why religious people find it so hard to share their holy places with each other. Why do we have to possess the places we revere? I later checked several guidebooks to find out what they say about the stone, but I have not found one yet that mentions it. Maybe the authors think it is not important. But it seemed to me that in Jerusalem and Bethlehem, cities literally built on stones reeking with history, this could be the most important stone of all.

The return trip to Bethlehem was uneventful. Back at Tantur, after an ample supper prepared for the mostly Christian guests by a genial Muslim cook, I went to my room to pack for my early departure. After I crawled into bed, I couldn't sleep. I kept seeing puffs of tear gas, Arafat's photo, the pinched face of the woman who had given us the bread, the fawning face of the blessing merchant at the Wall, the sickening pictures in the *Jerusalem Post* of the charred bodies being carried out of the restaurant. I turned the pillow over uselessly. Then I suddenly wondered whether my passport was where I had placed it. I turned on the light and got up; it was there. But just next to it I saw a little book, *The Testing of Hearts*, written by Donald Nicholl, who had preceded Tom Stransky as the director of Tantur. Since I was not going to sleep anyway, I opened it.[12]

The book focuses on the "three circles" Nicholl thought about most during his years in Jerusalem. The first was Jerusalem itself, the second Tantur, and the third his own heart. Jerusalem, Nicholl says, is a "testing place for that which is deepest in any one of us." Which is why, he goes on, "this is the city of lies: men pile one lie upon another in a desperate, futile attempt to heap lies so thick that the truth relentlessly demanded of them by this holy city shall remain hidden."

Stern words. But I knew what he meant. Jerusalem, for all its glistening pink stone and air of sanctity, is a city filled with lies. Big ones and small ones, everything from the innocent fictions about the alleged holy sites to the constant propaganda of the Israelis and the Palestinians and the outside powers that traffic on these tensions for their own selfish purposes. It is the city, as Jesus said, "that murders the prophets." But I could not rid myself of the conviction that behind all the lies there was something true, even profoundly true, that this tortured city was trying to say to me, both as a Christian and as the husband and father of Jews. How could I uncover it?

Nicholl's little book helped. He describes his formula for knowing when your own heart is being infected by the lies. Note, he advises, your first reaction when you hear that the Israeli Defense Force has shelled an allegedly terrorist camp, or a Hamas suicide bomber has exploded his dynamite in a restaurant, and in both cases people die. Do you say to yourself, "Well, what do they expect if they are op- pressing people?" Or do you feel, first of all, that this is a human trag- edy? This test always works, he says, because even if your ideology is correct, if your first response is ideological, then your heart has be- gun to harden.

I am afraid I had not passed his test; what Nicholl calls ideology still clouded my perception. I had found myself thinking, "What do they expect if they bulldoze people's homes?" or "What do they think will happen if they blow up innocent people in restaurants?" What was making me do this? Was it ideology? Whatever it was, I wanted to lay it aside. I was sure that if I could, it would help me carry some- thing valuable away, along with the tear gas and incense of this most peculiar of all the Easter Sundays I had ever lived.

I went back to Nicholl's first insight about Jerusalem. It is, he says, "a testing place for whatever is deepest in us." Then I remembered, in the darkest part of the night between Easter Sunday and the follow- ing morning, that my own deepest intuitions in Jerusalem had been disturbingly ambivalent. I had been touched and revolted, inspired and enraged, overcome by both awe and abhorrence. As I digested this upsetting realization, I remembered that nearly every thoughtful Jew, Muslim, and Christian with whom I had ever discussed Jerusa- lem harbored virtually the same seething nest of contradictory emo- tions about it. Was this a negative or a positive? Does one have to feel unambiguously positive about one's holy places?

One of the greatest scholars of religion of the twentieth century, Rudolph Otto, in his classic study *The Idea of the Holy,* suggests that the most distinctive human response to the Holy is intense and per- vasive ambivalence. The Holy both fascinates and terrifies us, often at the same time. But most people want a "nice" Jerusalem, a Disney version. The trouble is that each of the three traditions that claims Je- rusalem as a holy city is itself soaked in a bloody history. The ques- tion for me is, Can Jerusalem remind us of these histories without perpetuating them? One lifelong resident of Jerusalem wrote a few years ago that whenever there is a stabbing or a bombing in the Old City, an Israeli sanitation vehicle with "Jerusalem: City of Peace" in block letters on the side arrives to clean up the blood. But there has been too much blood ever to clean it up completely, including — I am well aware as a Christian — the Jewish and Muslim blood that coursed through the city's streets "as deep as the horses' stirrups" when the Crusaders, their shields embossed with crosses, first conquered it.

Is it too much to hope that as a new millennium begins, the three kindred faiths that have striven with each for so long over the possession of Jerusalem can begin to see it, instead, as a place of penitence and hope? The city is, as Nicholl claims, a place of testing, but not just for individuals. It is the place where the three traditions that stem from Father Abraham are being put to their ultimate test. Remember that in one of its many symbolic interpretations Jerusalem is depicted as a microcosm, the place where human history began and where it will end. It is the whole cosmos in miniature. Even the Christian Zionists, like the evangelist in sunglasses I met on my first visit, in their own convoluted way, manifest some understanding of this. I realize that all this theology may be loading too much symbolism on what is, after all, not just a religious construct, but a city of human beings with all their frailties. But there is an odd sense in which it rings true. It is as though God were saying, "Look, here you are, all crowded into this tiny quadrangle of steeples and minarets and domes. What does it mean? If you can't find a way to live together here, then forget it. I have other peoples I can choose."

At last the religious understanding of Jerusalem I had not been able to formulate during my first visit began to take shape. It seemed suddenly clear to me how vastly important it is for Jews, Christians, and Muslims to recognize that according to tradition, Jerusalem is the city where *Abraham did not have to shed the blood of human sacrifice.* Biblical scholars often interpret the "binding of Isaac" as a powerful reminder that at that moment in human history, God showed us that there had been enough human sacrifice. It was now time for Abraham and Isaac to move toward the fulfillment of the divine promise that through them and their seed, all the clans of the earth would be blessed. In Jerusalem I came to see that, in addition to the Jews, we Christians and our Muslim cousins are also among the clans that are supposed to be blessed.

12

Death Among the Jews

Sitting Shivah

The day of death is when two worlds meet with a kiss;
this world going out, the future world coming in.

— Yose ben Abin, a Talmudic sage[1]

Human beings cannot be mature until they encompass a sense of
their own mortality. To recognize the brevity of human existence
gives urgency and significance to the totality of life. To confront
death without being overwhelmed, driven to evasions or dulling of
the senses is to be given life again as a daily gift.

— Rabbi Irving Greenberg[2]

A DEATH IN THE FAMILY is painful for many reasons. It
brings with it not only sadness but also spitefulness, not
only a sense of loss but also regret, fear, and resentment. At
no time is it more important for families and tribes to
cling together than when someone in the circle dies. But nothing
raises divisive issues or festering animosities more than deaths and
funerals. Mourning rites have evolved over many thousands of years
to help survivors find their way through these mazes. Even when
these rituals seem to be addressed to the deceased, like *The Tibetan
Book of the Dead*, which purports to guide the departed spirit into
the next incarnation, I believe mourning rituals are actually designed
for the living. They enable us to recognize the privation, and to face
the anger and guilt, that often erupt after a death. They help us begin
to reweave the torn fabric. During the years of my marriage to Nina

we have lost a number of close friends and relatives, and I have come to appreciate how well Jewish mourning practices fulfill these purposes. As my wife says, "We do deaths well." They do.

In my own tradition there is much talk at funerals and burials about the ultimate fate of the deceased. Prayers beseech God to receive the lost one into his presence. The body is returned to the soil "in the sure and certain hope of the resurrection of the dead." I had never attended a Jewish funeral before I married Nina. But when I did, I noticed right away that very little of this kind of language is used. In fact, almost none. Even the famous Kaddish, repeated by mourners for a year after someone's death, then once a year on the anniversary of the death, says nothing about either death or the deceased. It is a prayer that glorifies God, nothing more. This puzzled me at first, since I had sometimes heard the Kaddish referred to as the Jewish prayer for the dead. But now whenever I hear it or say it (using the transliteration of the Hebrew found in some prayer books), I think how wise and profound it is. In my experience at Christian funerals, when the priest or minister refers to the "sure and certain hope of the resurrection," you can almost hear the fingers crossing in the congregation. The eventual resurrection of all the dead is a hope. For many people, both Jews and Christians, it is a serious and heartfelt hope. But "sure and certain"? It is probably wiser on such occasions to remind ourselves of the infinite mystery and mercy of God, which is what the Kaddish does:

Let God's name be made great and holy in the world that was created
   as God willed.
May God complete the holy realm in your own lifetime,
in your days, and in the days of all the house of Israel, quickly and soon.
And say: Amen.
May God's name be blessed, forever and as long as worlds endure.
May it be blessed, and praised, and glorified, and held in honor,
Viewed with awe, embellished, and revered:
And may the blessed name of holiness be hailed, though it be higher
Than all the blessings, songs, praises and consolations
That we utter in this world. And say: Amen.
May Heaven grant a universal peace, and life for us, and for all Israel.
And say: Amen.
May the one who creates harmony above, make peace for us and
For all Israel, and for all who dwell on earth. And say: Amen.

Jews have never had as elaborately developed a doctrine of life after death, of heaven and hell, as Christians have. Before their exile into Babylon in the sixth century B.C.E., the Israelites had only vague notions of the fate of the dead. God's reward for a virtuous life was not paradise after death but long life on earth, sufficient worldly goods, and many children. Sometimes the word *sheol* is used to designate the abode of the dead, but its meaning is far from clear. It might simply mean "grave," or it could mean a kind of shadowy continued existence, not connected with reward or punishment. After the exile, however, the Israelites began to absorb more embellished pictures of the afterlife from the Persians and the Greeks. The former taught that after death there would be a judgment, and then the righteous would ascend to the realm of light and the wicked would be punished. Many Greeks believed the soul, not the body, was immortal. Consequently, in the later books of the Old Testament, after these influences have been felt, one finds the beginning of a belief in the resurrection of the dead, followed by their consignment to bliss or to shame. In the first century C.E. this belief was still considered novel and suspect by the more traditional Jewish teachers, but it was embraced by at least some of the pharisees, who were open to new ideas. We find echoes of this dispute in the Gospels in the accounts of Jesus' encounters with the pharisees.

The early Christians, in turn, absorbed the ideas of the pharisees on this subject (which they believed Jesus had also taught) and within a few decades had constructed a expanded depiction of both heaven and hell. (The idea of purgatory, an intermediate station where one undergoes the purification necessary to enter the presence of God, came much later.) But within a century debates broke out among early Christian theologians about just how literally the flames of hell and the eternity of the punishment should be taken. Origen (185?–254?), the first great Christian theologian, argued that these ideas should not be taken literally. He favored a symbolic reading, and was followed in his interpretation a century later by St. Ambrose (340?–397) and St. Jerome (c. 347–420?). Eventually the Catholic Church officially chose the more literal reading, but never without considerable dissent. The vivid portrayal of hell, purgatory, and heaven informing Dante's great classic, *The Divine Comedy*, which he wrote at the opening of the fourteenth century, draws on this representation, although the ingenious and often gruesome details of the torments of hell are of course Dante's own poetic invention.

Neither the Protestant Reformers nor the Counter Reformation Catholic Church altered this teaching substantially. Revivalist preachers used the fear of hellfire to push people toward repentance. A graphic example of how alive it still was in the early twentieth century can be found in the sermon preached to the boys' school in James Joyce's *Portrait of the Artist as a Young Man*. But in modern liberal Protestantism, in much of contemporary Catholicism, and even in many otherwise conservative Protestant churches, the whole idea of hell now seems to have fallen into disuse. Ministers and priests more often assure mourners that the departed one is now "with God" and leave it at that. Pope John Paul II said in 1999 that one should not think of hell as a place but as a spiritual condition, as separation from God and other human beings.

I love Dante's poetry, but I am happy to see the vicious theology that undergirds it go. Taken literally, it becomes a kind of moral terrorism that attempts to frighten people into being good or believing the proper doctrine. But such scare tactics have no moral validity. People will do anything to avoid torture, but the result is devoid of ethical worth. The twentieth-century Russian Orthodox theologian Nicolas Berdyaev may have overstated his case when he calls Dante "a genius of vengeance," but I agree with him when he says that hell is a symbol of "absolute self-centeredness . . . the final inability to love."[3] His view sounds like that of John Paul II, who has said that hell is a symbol of spiritual isolation. No flames, no little demons with tridents, just the pain of realizing that one is cut off from what makes life livable.

I welcome the demise of hellfire in my own tradition. More and more now, Christians dismiss the idea of a literal, eternal hell and speak with an element of respectful restraint about the afterlife. But I find it odd that this brings us back to about where the Israelites were before they began swallowing Persian speculations, which, unfortunately, Christianity then inherited. When it comes to what happens to us after we die, it is better to rely on the compassion of God than to imagine what it will be like.

When my wife's sister, Masha, died of leukemia at forty-nine, her death became the occasion for my first Jewish funeral. It was also my first experience of the humbling but strangely comforting week of *shivah,* the seven-day mourning period. (The word is the Hebrew for "seven.") We had both been very close to Masha, even though she lived in New York City. She was a sunny, handsome woman with a winning habit of leaning toward you and nodding her head when you talked. She supervised a school for teaching English as a second language to Russian immigrants. A courageous person, she had suffered throughout her adult life from the damage caused by a botched operation on her leg, which caused her to walk with a slight limp. But she was indefatigably cheerful and ebullient. She had two teenage sons from her first marriage. Shortly before she died she married again under a *chuppah* in her apartment on the Upper West Side. She remained an optimist until the final days of her illness, adopting a grain diet and hoping that a bone marrow transplant, or something else, might reverse her rapid deterioration. She died in St. Luke's Hospital on a cold day in March.

Masha's funeral was held at an undertaking establishment that specializes in Jewish funerals. It took place on Nina's birthday. The casket stood in the front of the hall, and a rabbi read prayers in Hebrew and English. Several people spoke, including one of her sons, her former husband, her widower, Nina, and myself. Her other son sang "Hush little baby, don't say a word," which Masha had sung to him as a child. Nina recounted how when they had shared a bedroom as girls and were unable to sleep, they used to talk about whom they would invite to their next birthday parties. But now, she said, somehow preventing the tears from stopping her, it was her birthday, and the only person she wanted to be there was Masha. Then, in a somewhat anticlimactic manner, I described how Masha had transformed the nondescript relationship of "brother-in-law" into something full of complex content. I noticed that people seemed to appreciate what I said but did not find it all that unusual. It was, perhaps, still too early in my discovery of all the reaches of Jewish family practices to know that although Masha did it with unusual gusto, the energetic splicing of in-laws, cousins by marriage, and distant aunts and uncles onto the larger family tree is not all that unusual.

At Masha's burial in a cemetery an hour's drive from the city, again the rabbi read a psalm, then recited the Hebrew prayer *Eyl mlay rachamin,* which simply asks God to receive this soul and grant it eternal rest in his presence. Then everyone dropped pieces of dirt into the grave. This sometimes happens at Christian burials as well, but often only by those closest to the deceased. Also, lamentably, some funeral directors have introduced the practice of scattering flower petals instead, another vain attempt, I assume, to prettify the stark reality of death. Afterward, we returned to the apartment of Nina's mother, Suzanne, where the family had decided to "sit shivah."

"Sitting shivah" itself is not complicated. Its purpose is to relieve the mourners of as many workaday responsibilities as possible so that the grieving can proceed with few interruptions. As soon as the family returns from the cemetery, they light a single candle as a symbol of the spirit of the departed person. Then the family is supposed to eat a small meal, which friends and neighbors prepare for them. Life, and therefore eating, must go on. During the week of *shivah,* the family does not leave the house, but friends and relatives come by to offer their sympathies and to bring gifts of food. Since the mourners are expected to recite the Kaddish every day (in some families, two or three times a day), friends gather at a convenient hour so that the ten people (the *minyan*) required to say prayers can be mustered. There are many other customs, some kept and some neglected in recent years, such as sitting on the floor or on low benches and covering the mirrors in the house.

I could not leave my teaching responsibilities for a whole week, but I spent as much time as I could with Nina's family. When I arrived on the Friday after her death, however, I noticed that everyone was preparing to leave the apartment even though the seven days were not yet up. It was then I learned that on the Sabbath that occurs during *shivah,* the mourning is interrupted for twenty-four hours. Sabbath must be a day of joy and celebration no matter what. So we all walked up the street to B'nai Jeshurun and were ushered into one of the front rows. We purposely arrived a bit late, after the more festive elements of the Sabbath celebration — the clapping and dancing — were done. The rabbi made special mention of Masha and her family in the prayers. On the seventh day, the rabbi came by the apartment, led those assembled in some prayers, including the Kaddish, and then led us out to the corridor, down the elevator, and outside the building. He then walked with us as we all headed up West End Avenue, turned left on Eighty-fifth Street, left again on Riverside Drive, and then came back along Eighty-fourth to West End. This, he explained, was an integral part of the ritual of *shivah.* It was time to begin going back into the world. It was not time to end the mourning completely, however. There would also be the *shloshim*, the prayers said after thirty days; the *matzevah*, the dedication of the gravestone; and the *yahrzeit*, the custom of saying prayers every year on the anniversary of the person's death.

I was fascinated throughout *shivah* with how psychologically wise these ancient customs are. The centuries have taught that we do need some special care right after the death of someone close. Gifts of food at such times are virtually universal. The first thing my mother did after she heard that someone had died in our town was to take out her cake pan and begin mixing eggs, flour, milk, sugar, and vanilla flavoring. But after a period of intense mourning we also need to be gently nudged back into the street, otherwise we can prolong it more than we should. I have also noticed that after a few weeks, when people have stopped offering condolences, a period of depression can set in. We begin to realize that the person is really gone for good. This makes the *shloshim* especially helpful. Everyone also knows that the anniversary of a death can be acutely painful; by then, most people except those closest to the deceased have forgotten just when the person died. So the *yahrzeit* ritual is also timely. I was impressed when I realized that the Jews evolved and systematized these rituals centuries before modern psychologists invented their theories of death, mourning, and how "grief work" needs to proceed.

The next death deprived us of our most trusted spiritual guide. Rabbi Marshall Meyer, the leader of B'nai Jeshurun and my old friend, who had comforted us after Masha's death and led our cautious sortie out into the world when *shivah* was over, died during the cold final days of December after an unsuccessful operation for liver cancer. This was an especially hard blow because Marshall had been "our" rabbi. We saw each other whenever we were in New York or he came to Boston. When he visited Harvard for a semester, we taught a course together, Contemporary American Theology. Marshall charmed the students as well as instructed them. That semester, he had been in our house several times a week. A large man with a huge presence, he seemed to occupy an enormous space in our kitchen, where he loved to sit, talk volubly, drink vodka-and-tonics, and sing. He had a fine voice, and the surgeons were astonished to hear him belting out an aria from *Rigoletto* as he was wheeled down the corridor into the operating room. When one of them asked why he was singing, Marshall said that as a rabbi he had tried to help people learn how to live, but if he couldn't show them how to die, then what good was he?

Marshall's funeral took place in B'nai Jeshurun. It was the first funeral I had ever attended in a synagogue. The casket was a stark wooden box with a cloth bearing the Star of David spread over it. It was closed, but I knew Marshall, who liked well-cut suits and silk ties, would be wrapped in a burial shroud as many observant Jews are and as he wanted. As I watched the box being wheeled down the aisle, I remembered the Sabbath when he had walked beside me as I carried the Torah, the people touching it with their prayer shawls and prayer books. I also remembered the Jewish adage he had once quoted to me when we were talking about money: "There are no pockets in a shroud." The synagogue was crowded to the doors, with latecomers standing in the aisles, the lobby, and on the front steps. Afterward, we followed the funeral procession the whole way to northern Connecticut, to the town where Marshall grew up. Again, after the prayers, we dropped pieces of the frozen earth into his grave. Then we all drove to his family's former home to eat and talk with the other mourners. Suzanne, my mother-in-law, had ridden with us to the burial. But we arranged for her to be taken back to New York by another guest, and we drove directly back to Cambridge. We said very little on the way home. We knew the loss of Marshall would leave a large gap in our lives.

Not long after that, Suzanne herself died. It was her death and funeral that provided me with my most treasured insight into what might be called the Jewish way of death. In the spring of 1994 Suzanne, who had continued to be remarkably healthy into her mid-eighties, was diagnosed with cancer. In a short time it had spread to several organs and she became noticeably weaker, no longer able to exercise or to drag large bundles of Nova Scotia lox, fruit, loaves of black bread, and dessert ingredients the four blocks from Zabar's to her apartment. Nina asked me how I felt about inviting her to move in with us for her last months or weeks. I welcomed the idea. So she did, arriving in early May with Nina, who had flown to New York on Mother's Day to help her pack and to accompany her on her last trip to our home. Suzanne looked thin and tired but had the same sparkle in her eyes. We rearranged the nursery next to our bedroom for her and, after several weeks, rented a hospital bed with an electric motor. The room had a chest of drawers and a rocking chair she could use when she felt able.

At first Suzanne would join us downstairs for part of the day and for our evening meals, but that soon required too much exertion. She ate less and slept more. She had never been hospitalized in her life and made us promise she would not be sent to one this time. She wanted no extraordinary measures taken. Between her naps, which grew still longer as the days passed, she remained alert and even held court. A sister flew in from Florida to say good-bye. Cousins and grandchildren flocked to her bedside. When one grown grandchild asked her how she was, her reply was entirely straightforward. "I'm fine," she said with an ironic smile. "I'm dying, of course, but I'm fine."

I asked her later what she had meant by that remark.

"Just what I said," she answered. "I'm exactly where I want to be. I am dying surrounded by people who love me. I am not afraid of death, though I am a bit scared of dying."

As we could see her slipping away, we relied heavily on the superb staff of Cambridge Hospice. They were unfailingly competent and thoughtful. They know how to help dying people, but just as important, they also know how to help those who live with dying people. I was especially taken with Marilyn, a Caribbean black woman whose unique combination of empathy and reserve carried us through the last days and hours. She treated Suzanne with immense respect and tenderness and answered our anxious questions firmly and quietly. She sat by Suzanne's bed all night the last three nights, closely monitoring her condition. But when there was nothing to watch she snatched a few minutes' glance at one of her small pile of *True Romances* magazines. I liked that about her, too.

We never left Suzanne alone. Even though she was now sleeping most of the time, Nina sat in the armchair by her bed hour after hour, watching and waiting. I relieved her now and then, sat in the same chair, and talked quietly with Suzanne when she seemed to want to. A friend of mine who is a rabbi and a professor of Jewish studies told me that we were performing a significant *mitzvah,* a righteous deed. I had not thought of it that way until he mentioned it. I found the times I sat quietly by her bed richly rewarding. I thought about the brevity of life, recognizing that one day I would be lying where she was, possibly in this very room, and someone — I hoped — would be sitting by me. I also thought about her. One night, sitting in the darkened room, I glanced at the piece of polished wood on which a map of Cape Cod had been painted, which hung next to her bed. It was no doubt a souvenir of summers long ago in Wellfleet, when Nina was a little girl. For years it had hung just outside the door to Suzanne's apartment, but she had recently given it to us. As I looked at it, I suddenly felt a sense of immense loss. I realized how much I was going to miss both Suzanne and her surroundings in New York. The surroundings — the paintings and books, the traces of three worlds (Russia, France, and America) piled on top of one another, the Upper West Side itself — all seemed so much a part of her. For years I had promised myself I would someday spend several days there with her. I would take her to Teacher's Restaurant at Eighty-second and Broadway for dinner, which I had done once or twice in the past and which she loved. I would get her to talk about the old days, which she would do only after some urging. I would also gorge myself on art exhibitions, films, and plays, taking her with me to the things she wanted to see. When I went to such events alone I would tell her about them because she always listened so avidly. But I had just not gotten around to it, and now it was too late. Now not only would Suzanne be gone but our outpost in Manhattan would be too. I wondered briefly if this was a selfish way to think about her, but I soon decided that it wasn't. Suzanne was not a disembodied spirit. She not only played the part of the skilled hostess, New York movie specialist, salon proprietor, and repository of memories well. That is who she really was. With her gone, in a sense Manhattan would be gone too. It would never be the same.

On my birthday in late May, just a few days before she died, Suzanne — who had not come downstairs for over a week — got up. She dressed, applied some lipstick, and made her way downstairs to join us for the birthday dinner and the blowing out of the candles. We helped her back upstairs right after dinner. It was the last time she came down. We knew it would not be long now. Nina had asked a rabbi to remind her what we should do at the actual moment of her last breaths. He said we should repeat the Sh'ma ("Hear, O Israel, the Lord our God, the Lord is One") close to her ear; this is what Jews have done for centuries, aware perhaps that the last sense to go is usually hearing. Then, just as she stopped breathing, we should open the window in the room. He explained that this was a very old custom that probably goes back to a folk belief that the soul can then fly, unimpeded, to God. It occurred to me that opening the window also has another sensible function: it gives the survivors something to do, something physical, at just the moment when everyone feels particularly awkward and inept.

At about three o'clock in the morning on the third day Marilyn was with us, she tapped gently on our bedroom door and told us that Suzanne's pulse had become almost inaudible and that the end would come soon. Nina and I both went to Suzanne's bedside. It was a singular moment for me. I had not been present at the death of either of my own parents. For reasons I may never understand, during the ten years I had known Suzanne, I had come to feel closer to her than I had to my own mother.

Suzanne's breathing became labored. A low rattle accompanied each inhalation. I noticed that her decision to eat very little during her last days made her appear thinner than I had ever seen her. But her face and especially her aristocratic nose retained their stately look. Marilyn watched closely, checking her pulse now and then with a stethoscope. Outside it was still dark, but a very slight ridge of gray hovered over the roofs of the houses to the east of us, along Prentiss Street and over to Somerville. After a while Nina took her guitar out and began to sing some of Suzanne's favorite songs in Russian. My throat was so full, I was amazed that she could summon her voice. But she did, clear and resonant, the sibilant vowels set off by the harsher *sks* and *chs* in the lyrics. Suzanne would have heard some of the songs as a girl in St. Petersburg.

Nina had been singing for about ten minutes when Suzanne's breathing became more sporadic, the intervals between breaths longer. Marilyn watched intently and listened through the stethoscope. "She's ready to go," she said quietly, undramatically but not casually. "She may take one or two more breaths." Nina leaned her guitar in the corner, knelt next to the bed, and, with my hands on her shoulders, said almost in a whisper, "It's OK, Mom. You can let go now. It's OK."

Then, in the same strong and resonant voice with which she had been singing the Russian songs, she intoned the Sh'ma, the prayer that is the heart of Judaism and surely one of the oldest prayers in the world. It begins: *"Sh'ma Yisrael, Adonai Eloheynu, Adonai Ehad."* It is a short prayer. But by the time she had finished, Suzanne had stopped breathing. Marilyn listened through the stethoscope, then took it out of her ears, looked at Suzanne's quiet face, turned to us, and said simply, "She's gone." We both kissed her on the forehead. I opened the window. It was only about five o'clock, but already there were traffic sounds coming from Beacon Street, and the gray finger over the houses had widened.

We had already planned the next step. At seven o'clock I awoke Nicholas, who was then seven. He knew that his grandmother was dying and that it was going to happen soon. While he was brushing his teeth, I told him that Suzanne had died and asked him to get dressed quickly because I was taking him out to the International House of Pancakes for breakfast. I told him we would be leaving that very day to accompany her body to New York. I gave him a big hug. He looked thoughtful, swallowed once hard, and then appeared to be ready for blueberry pancakes. Over the pancakes with maple syrup we talked about Suzanne and remembered some of the funny things she said, fondly imitating her Russian accent. As arranged, Nina received the undertakers after we left for the restaurant, and they took the body to the morgue. When we got back from breakfast we packed our bags. Later that morning we drove to the funeral parlor in Brookline. When the hearse stopped beside us, we drove behind it out the Massachusetts Turnpike and down through Connecticut, pulling over once for a bathroom break and once for lunch. Each time we stopped, Nina peeked through the old-fashioned parted curtains in the back of the hearse at the stretcher with the flowers the undertaker had placed on the covered body. Finally we turned south and drove along the glistening Hudson River into Manhattan.

As the river hove into view, I thought about the Sh'ma, the last words Suzanne heard. Maybe I thought about it just then because I remembered an appealing explanation of its meaning given by Rabbi Michael Lerner. The Hudson is surrounded on both sides by towering buildings, a mighty force of nature framed by the work of human hands. The Sh'ma is usually translated: "Hear, O Israel, the Lord our God, the Lord is One." By itself it seems to be a rather flat declaration of monotheism. Not particularly unique. But Lerner explains that, while *Adonai* refers to the aspect of God that "embodies the capacity for freedom and transcendence," *Eloheynu* refers to the aspect of God that created the universe, the God of nature. The Sh'ma means that the God of history, the realm of human freedom, and the God of nature's laws are one.[4] Like God, at least in some measure, human beings are free to change and create. We are not determined by instinct, like animals. But we change and create within the framework provided by God. The river and the skyscraper frame each other.

I am very attracted to this interpretation of the Sh'ma, even though I'm not sure how many Jews attach this meaning to it. I doubt that Suzanne did. To her it was the eternal mantra, the leitmotif of her people. It provided the bridge she crossed from life to death. But the power of a traditional prayer is precisely that it can carry several different meanings at several different levels.

Eventually we turned away from the river and into the busy streets of Manhattan. When we got to the Plaza Funeral Home at Ninety-first and Amsterdam Avenue, where the funeral was to take place, we stepped out into the warm sun. Almost immediately a woman dressed in a tattered fur coat, sequined gown, and bedroom slippers standing near the curb extended her hand and asked if I had any change. I handed her two quarters. We put the car in a garage, then ordered some takeout and carried it to the apartment where Suzanne had lived for nearly fifty years. We were silent as we took the elevator up and Nina let us in with her own key. It seemed strange to be coming into Suzanne's apartment without her being there. We munched on the tuna sandwiches, corn chips, and pickles. Nina's cousin Nick arrived, and he and I walked over to a grocery store at Eighty-seventh and Broadway and bought huge bags of food.

The funeral, according to Jewish custom, was scheduled for the very next day. B'nai Jeshurun had recently created a committee of lay members who performed the ritual washing of the body, the *tahara*, before it was wrapped in its shroud. One of the women on the committee described it to us. It seemed to me both a respectful and a tender human expression, so much better than simply turning the body over to a professional undertaker. The funeral itself had both its sober and its zany moments. It would have pleased Suzanne, I'm sure, especially the zany parts. Nina had arranged for a *shomer* to remain with the body all night. A *shomer* is a pious Jew who stays near the casket and reads from Psalms until the funeral begins. Another good custom, I thought. It must be a relief to the members of a family, who have often been with the person almost without interruption for days, not to fret over the body lying alone in a frigid morgue. Once again I saw how many mourning rituals are intended more for the survivors than for the dead.

But this was not your ordinary Conservative or Orthodox funeral. This was, after all, a thoroughly mixed family. Early that morning Nina's sister-in-law, Teresa, a pious Latin American Catholic, had called me at Suzanne's apartment, to ask if I thought it would be all right if she came to the funeral a little early to pray for Suzanne at the casket. I assured her, even without asking, that everyone would want her to pray for Suzanne and the family in her own way. Also, since Suzanne had been a devotee of Edith Piaf, Nina had dug out a tape on which Piaf sings her most famous song, "Je Ne Regrette Rien." The lyrics concern what is obviously an older woman near the end of her days who declares that she does not regret anything she has done, and Piaf sings it to the rinkydink background of 1930s Paris bistro music.

We arrived at the funeral home an hour before the service was to begin. We met with the rabbi in a side room, where he pinned a black ribbon on Nina's dress and on my lapel. Then he tore the ribbons as a symbol of mourning. We had also come early to make sure everything was ready. Nina took the Piaf tape into a room on the ground floor where the hi-fi system, which projected the sound to the different chapels in the building, was located so she could try it out. Meanwhile, I stepped into the room where the casket was already in place for the funeral. It was the one where Masha's funeral had occurred just the year before. I wanted to have a private moment with Suzanne myself. When I walked in, however, I found the *shomer,* complete with black coat, wide-brimmed hat, and side locks, seated in the first row, bending his head and murmuring softly over the prayer book, while Teresa was kneeling by the coffin, praying with her rosaries. I smiled because the scene defied all the careful logic of high-flown ecumenical dialogue. One person, one death, two outpourings of piety, both dignified. But before I could savor the moment, it was topped off by the voice of Edith Piaf suddenly issuing from the sound system, turned up just a shade too high. *"Je ne regrette rien,"* sang la Piaf, "*rien, rien, je ne regrette rien.*" Unfazed, Teresa and the *shomer* kept on praying. I looked at the closed casket; I was sure that if it were open, Suzanne would have been smiling.

Back from the cemetery, once again we began to "sit *shivah,*" this time without Suzanne or Marshall Meyer. The first evening the apartment was crowded with friends, neighbors from the building, and relatives who had flown in for the service. The prayers were led by a woman rabbinical student from Jewish Theological Seminary. The second night they were led by Rabbi Rolando Matalan, who had been Marshall's associate at B'nai Jeshurun and was now head rabbi. Nina and I had talked about what to do with Nicholas during *shivah.* We decided that we wanted him to be there for the prayers each evening but that requiring him to stay inside all day would be asking too much. So I was commissioned to take him around to some of the tourist sites in New York for part of the day, returning each evening. We took the ferry to the Statue of Liberty, walked around Battery Park, and strolled into the Hilton Hotel (where, to the amazement of both of us, a friendly waiter served us each a free glass of frosty lemonade). I told him that the next day we were going to visit the Museum of Modern Art. I said I just knew he would love it, even though I wondered how much appeal it would have for a seven-year-old. He did love it. I could hardly pull him away from the collection of photographs influenced by surrealism. He also liked the "found object" sculpture and immediately got the point of it. But most of all he liked the Jackson Pollock exhibition. For some reason the MOMA restaurant was not crowded, so we had lunch there and talked more about Suzanne. I had felt a little guilty about not sitting in the apartment all day, but after a few days with Nicholas in New York City, I knew it had been the right decision. Suzanne had so loved New York. Now, by exploring it with her grandchild, we were both honoring her in a way she would certainly have encouraged, perhaps even suggested.

As I had learned at the *shivah* for Masha, Jews are always expected to interrupt their mourning to participate in the Sabbath. We all donned our best clothes and walked the few blocks to B'nai Jeshurun. As a mourning family, we were again ushered in late and seated in an honored place at the front. I knew it was a relief to Nina to get out after two days of being in the apartment. I marveled again at how expert the rabbis had been at devising ways to help people get over the rough places in life, even though these rituals may seem so burdensome to outsiders. And I also admired how expert they were at devising equally important loopholes and exceptions. Being the kind of people we are, human beings need both.

I'm not sure how the classical rabbis would have felt about it, but Nina decided she wanted to hold part of the *shivah* in Cambridge, so our friends could come by to offer their condolences. The trip back was pleasant, even a little lighthearted. The hard part came when we arrived home, back into the house where Suzanne had been with us for the last weeks and where she had died. I called to explain what *shivah* is to our non-Jewish friends, all of whom seemed to understand it. The first night our living room was crowded, and our friend Rabbi Hillel Levine led the service by inviting us to talk with each other about the Jewish saying: "He who saves one life, it is as though he saved the whole world." He told us these were the words inscribed on a piece of paper inside the ring given to Oskar Schindler by the Jews he had rescued from death during the Holocaust. The following evening, with a somewhat smaller group, he led us in a kind of kabbalistic excursion into the Torah. He invited each of us to read a verse from Psalms that began with one of the letters of Suzanne's Hebrew name, Shoshana, and then to say what came to mind. At first this seemed a bit contrived. It reminded me of throwing the *I Ching*. But somehow it drew people into a strangely comfortable way of talking about Suzanne.

We now use some of Suzanne's dishes, her lithographs and paintings hang on the wall, and we often repeat some of her favorite expressions in her Russian accent. Every time I walk into the little room where she died, I think of her. We always light a candle at her *yahrzeit*. Almost three years after her death we finally got around to unpacking some of the items Nina had gathered up from her apartment before it was vacated. In one box I found a copy of a book called *An Interrupted Life*. It is the diary of a young Jewish woman named Etty Hillesum who lived in Holland during the war.[5] She was eventually picked up by the same agents who arrested Anne Frank and died in one of the death camps. I remembered noticing it on the table next to where Suzanne used to sit and read. I remembered because I had picked it up and glanced at it the last time we visited her there. Suzanne herself rarely mentioned the Holocaust, but I always suspected she thought about it often, and when this book turned up at our house I noticed it had a bookmarker in it two-thirds of the way through. Suzanne had been reading about this woman's interrupted life when her own life ended. In fact, I realized these women would have been roughly the same age had Etty not been killed. But what a difference. Etty's life had indeed been cruelly interrupted, while Suzanne had been granted a long and full life, and it was clear to me that when she died, she did not consider it an interruption but a final chapter, an ending. I was grateful I had been there for some of the last pages.

13

Lady Sings the Blues

Tisha B'Av

How lonely sits the city that was full of people!
How like a widow she has become,
She that was great among the nations!
She that was a princess among the cities
Has become a vassal.
She weeps bitterly in the night,
Tears on her cheeks;
Among all her lovers
She has none to comfort her.

— Lamentations 1:1, 2

I FIRST HEARD about the holiday of Tisha B'Av from a student some years ago, when I was teaching a course for undergraduates. One day I talked about the well-known incident in which Jesus overturns the tables of the money-changers in the Temple in Jerusalem. I mentioned that later, during his trial, Jesus was accused — falsely, I think — of threatening to destroy the Temple. Then I added that a few decades later the Temple had in fact been destroyed, not by Jesus or his followers, of course, but by the same Romans who had put Jesus to death. I told them that although both rabbinical Judaism and Christianity had come into existence shortly before the destruction of the Temple, it was only after it had been razed that they began to grow and spread — in part because, with the Temple in ruins and both groups expelled from Jerusalem by the Romans (for whom the two were indistinguishable), there was no longer a geographical or architectural center for their worship. Both

Judaism and Christianity needed to become "portable" or die. Jews responded by making the study of Torah, following the Law, and the Jewish home the new center. With no Temple for the priests to serve, the rabbis became the main religious leaders. The Christians believed that Jesus Christ, and the growing body of his disciples, had replaced the Temple. But both movements were highly portable, and both have survived and flourished, without a Temple, for two thousand years.

It was a straightforward lecture, and I had given it in previous years with little comment from the class. But that afternoon a serious young man wearing a black *yarmulka* appeared in my office. I recognized him as a student from the class. He was poised and polite but obviously upset. "I just want to know," he asked, "how you can talk so lightly about the destruction of the Temple. For us it was something terribly tragic. We have a whole holiday dedicated to mourning its loss. It is called Tisha B'Av."

I assured him that I was sorry if I appeared to take such a disaster lightly, but reminded him that there had been many Jews who were very critical of the Temple priesthood, whom they believed had sold out to the Romans. It had been rebellious Jews, not Romans, who had initially captured the Temple from this priesthood and thrown them out. He was apparently unaware of this piece of history, and when I promised I would be more careful of my intonation the next time I lectured on this topic, he thanked me. But the incident made me grateful once again that I teach at an institution where the students come from many different religious backgrounds and do not hesitate to challenge professors when they think it is appropriate. I also promised myself I would find out immediately both about the spiritual significance of the Temple and about Tisha B'Av.

When the Romans destroyed it, the Temple had a meaning for pious Jews which went far beyond anything I had imagined. Possibly the best treatment of this subject that I have found is a book by C.T.R. Hayward called *The Jewish Temple: A Non-Biblical Sourcebook*.[1] This volume is engaging because it asks a question that goes beyond the descriptions of the building and the sacrifices that took place there. It tries to uncover what they actually meant to the people at the time. Hayward suggests a number of answers, all of which explain why the loss of the Temple was so traumatic. Pious Jews, Hayward says, believed that the Temple service actually maintained the stability and order, not just of Jewish life, but of the whole cosmos. Without it, the universe itself could implode into chaos or nothingness. Likewise, the structure and arrangement of the buildings in the Temple complex provided a symbolic map of the universe. In this view, the universe included both heaven and earth; consequently, the actions of the priests harmonized with the worship of the angels around God's throne, and the high priest — while he was officiating — became more than just a representative of God. He became, temporarily at least, the embodiment of divine Wisdom itself. It's no wonder that when the Romans destroyed the Temple, it seemed like the end of the world. It was.

Tisha B'Av falls in August. It was probably the holiday I knew least about before my exploration of Jewish life. It is also one of the holidays I had most difficulty appreciating. But I have come to believe it is one from which those of us who are not Jewish have much to learn. I am not alone in my original ignorance. One rabbi remarked recently that if you stopped the first ten Jews you met in Brookline, Massachusetts (a heavily Jewish city), and asked them what it was, nine out of ten would probably say, "Oh, that's the one about the trees, isn't it?" It is not. (The "one about the trees" is Tu B'Shavat.) Tisha B'Av, on the other hand (the words mean the ninth day of the Jewish month of Av), is the holiday on which Jews mourn the destruction of not one, but two of their Temples. The first was the one built by Solomon, which the Babylonians destroyed on the ninth of Av 586 B.C.E. The second was begun by Herod the Great, who reigned as king under Roman auspices from 37 until 4 B.C.E. But it was still not fully completed when, in 70 C.E., also on the ninth of Av, the Romans razed it after putting down the Jewish revolt that eventually ended in the famous mass suicide at Masada. Whether the date was a cruel coincidence or the Romans consciously selected it to deepen the humiliation of the Jews is not known. However, ever since that second destruction (the Romans went on to demolish the entire city of Jerusalem), Jews have gathered on the ninth of Av to grieve the loss of the Temples, the two exiles that followed them, and the other tragedies that have haunted them throughout history.

Traditional Jews begin to prepare for the mourning rites of Tisha B'Av three weeks before by refraining from celebrations, weddings in particular. Then, for the nine days immediately preceding it, they do not eat meat or drink wine. The reading in the synagogue on the

Sabbath just before Tisha B'Av is a disquieting passage from Isaiah in which the prophet warns that if the people continue their unfaithfulness to God it will lead to terrible consequences. On the holiday itself the synagogue is sometimes lit by only a single candle and the people sit on low stools or on the floor. Since Jews do not wear a *tallit* (prayer shawl) when they are in mourning, they do not wear them on Tisha B'Av. While the congregation is crouched in semidarkness, Lamentations, the opening verse of which begins this chapter, is read or, more often, chanted. It is one of the most chilling texts in the entire Bible. Verse after verse repeats the themes of abandonment and despair:

> I called my lovers, but they let me down:
> my priests and my elders perished in the city
> while seeking food to keep themselves alive.
> Lord, see how sorely distressed I am.
> My bowels writhe in anguish
> And my heart within me turns over (Lamentations 2:19, 20).

The effect is almost unrelievedly sorrowful, but as the awful drama draws to a close in the afternoon, the worshipers pull their *tallits* on. At least, they seem to be saying, we can still hope and pray for something better.

At first it was hard for me to make any connection with Tisha B'Av or to think of anything in Christian worship or tradition that corresponds to it. I got some help the first time I attended a Good Friday and then a Holy Saturday service in a Russian Orthodox church. There the liturgy assumes the form of a funeral. The dead Jesus, whose body is believed to have replaced the Temple in worship, is symbolically present in a real casket that lies at the front of the church. The prayers and liturgies of a Christian funeral are recited. The mood is one of sorrow and mourning. Late Saturday night, the congregation processes around the outside of the church, then comes back inside at about midnight. Then the priest announces, "He is risen!" and the congregation responds, "Risen indeed!" The music, which so far has been plaintive and in a minor key, suddenly turns joyful. Clearly, there are both similarities and important differences between this powerful liturgy and Tisha B'Av.

But even after making this connection I was still uneasy about this holiday. My appreciation of it came only by overcoming two serious reservations. The first arises from the awkward fact that the spot on the Temple Mount where the Temple once stood is now the location of the Haram al-Sharif, the Noble Sanctuary, one of Islam's holiest sites. On the Haram stands the gilded Dome of the Rock, which shelters the huge boulder from which, in Muslim belief, the Prophet Muhammad ascended to heaven. It was built under the great caliph Abd al-Malik (685–705), who employed Christian craftsmen and architects from Byzantium, hoping to make it the most beautiful religious building in the world. Some people believe they succeeded. Near it stands the Al-Aqsa Mosque, which the Prophet is believed to have visited on his "night journey" from Mecca.

The location of these two Muslim shrines on the site of the destroyed Temple obviously creates serious problems. According to Jewish tradition, the Temple has to be built on that spot, where — according to legend — Abraham's near-sacrifice of Isaac took place. It can never be anywhere else. But this means that if mourning for the loss of the Temple slides into a yearning to rebuild it, then real troubles begin. And these troubles are not merely theoretical. There are religious Jews, in Israel and elsewhere, who devoutly believe the Temple should be rebuilt, even though it would entail the removal of the Dome of the Rock and Al-Aqsa.

The fear that "Al-Aqsa is in danger," whether it has any basis in fact or not, continually gnaws at the Muslim soul, not just in Israel and the territories but in many other places as well. My Israeli friends and colleagues assure me, whenever I ask, that there is no realistic possibility of any tampering with the Temple Mount, let alone the removal of Al-Aqsa. They insist that the vast majority of Jews oppose any such move, pointing out that the government of Israel not only guards the Temple Mount against it but disallows Jews from even praying in the vicinity of the Mosque. But Muslims do not seem to be reassured. Consequently, when the Israeli political leader Ariel Sharon walked there in the autumn of 2000, escorted by several platoons of police and soldiers and with helicopters hovering overhead, Palestinians launched what has been called the Al-Aqsa Intifada. That upsurge of anger and violence and the massive Israeli military response seem, at this writing at least, to have dissolved, possibly for a long time, the hopes of the Palestinians and Israelis who believed a just and peaceful settlement between the two peoples could be worked out.

I also have a hard time believing that even an Israeli government controlled by conservative religious parties (not an impossibility) would do something as foolish as trying to dismantle the Noble Sanctuary. But it is also easy to understand why Muslims continue to worry. There are Israelis who not only fervently believe the Temple should, and will, be rebuilt; they are actively preparing for it. I have visited Jewish religious schools in Jerusalem that are training students in the techniques of resuming animal sacrifice, interrupted in 70 C.E. There is also a workshop devoted to the manufacturing of the holy garments and implements that would be needed if such rituals were resumed. The students and teachers tried to assure me, when I asked, that of course they had no intention of tearing down the Dome of the Rock. "God will do his part," one teacher told me, "and we will do ours."

The trouble is that even if no Israeli administration would ever make such a radical move, it does not take much to fan Muslim suspicions. It would not require a majority, only a tiny handful, of zealots to destroy the Mosque in order to clear the way for the reconstruction of the Temple. This is not merely a conjectural possibility. During the early-morning hours of an August day in 1969, an Australian tourist named Denis Michael Rohan somehow found his way through the guards and into the Mosque. He stuffed a bundle of wadded cotton soaked in gasoline under the pulpit, lit it, then strolled out and began snapping pictures of the blaze with an Instamatic camera. Amos Elon describes the scene vividly in *Jerusalem: City of Mirrors.*[2] The fire quickly spread to the dome at the southern end of the mosque, near the site of the Court of the Gentiles, and licked up into the aged wooden beams, which began crashing down. Assuming that the fire was the result of an Israeli plot, a crowd of infuriated Muslims swarmed onto the mount and hampered the work of the firemen trying to extinguish the blaze because someone had told them the firemen were pumping gasoline on it instead of water. When, after five hours, the flames were finally put out, it was clear that the Mosque had suffered terrible damage. A historic pulpit, most of the dome, and the ceiling had all been destroyed. Incensed nearly beyond words, some Jerusalem Muslims insisted that the firemen had been lackadaisical and that the city had deliberately cut off the water supply. In response, an Israeli cabinet minister publicly suggested that the fire had been set by an Arab provocateur.

How convenient it would be to attribute Rohan's provocative act of arson to his having taken Tisha B'Av too literally, thereby making it the act of a Jewish religious fanatic. But Rohan was not Jewish. He adhered to the beliefs of a Christian Zionist group called the Radio Church of God, which taught that the Temple had to be rebuilt in order to prepare for the Second Coming of Jesus Christ. Therefore the Mosque had to be destroyed. Rohan did not succeed. If he had, it would have been an irony of ruinous proportions: a frenzied Christian sparking a crisis of calamitous dimensions, thus igniting something like the Armageddon he was anticipating.

Some Jewish groups have attempted the same tactic. Amos Elon reports that since Rohan's failed attempt, "more than twenty religious fanatics have been caught in the act of preparing one or another violent outrage on the Temple Mount."[3] Sadly enough, not all were members of fringe sects. In 1984 police arrested twenty-eight students from a respected rabbinical college in Jerusalem when they found them at the foot of the Temple Mount carrying ropes and ladders. Less than a year later, members of a Jewish underground organization were seized for plotting to blow up all the Muslim shrines on the Temple Mount. Two of them actually had explosives in their hands when they were caught.

It is understandable that people who know the meaning of Tisha B'Av, and who also know the distressing facts about Christians like Michael Rohan and Jews like the arsonists apprehended by the police, should sometimes wonder if there is any connection between the two. I continue to hope, however, that although in the literalistic minds of some misguided zealots such a connection may indeed exist, these amount to very few people, and their misplaced fervor does not diminish the underlying spiritual value of the holiday.

I had a second reservation about Tisha B'Av. In reading about the history of Jerusalem, I was shocked and angered to learn that when Byzantine Christians controlled the city, they barred Jews from entering it except on one day of the year. They were allowed to come in on the ninth of Av so they could cry and wail at the Western Wall while the Christian residents watched. Then they were sent out again. I can understand that for the Jews who engaged in this annual ritual, one day in Jerusalem might have seemed better than none. And if only one day, then why not the ninth of Av, when they could bewail the loss of the Temple standing at its only remnant?

That part makes sense. But the motivation of the Byzantine rulers had nothing to do with respect for the Jews or their religion. Quite the opposite. For them, the ninth of Av had become a scene in a demeaning morality play. The Christians taught that God was punishing the Jewish people for being so stubborn and wicked that they had rejected their own Messiah. Heretics had to recant or be exterminated. Infidels were to be conquered. But Jews were neither heretics nor infidels. They were meant to serve a different purpose: they were allowed to live but only as a miserable object lesson, condemned to wander without a home and to pine and moan for their lost Temple for the rest of history. It was during this period that the Western Wall became known as the Wailing Wall. It was where the Christians of Jerusalem gloated with callous satisfaction as the Jews acted out (or seemed to be acting out) the very scenario in which the Christians had cast them. There is little worse than one religious group exploiting the rituals of another to ridicule and demean it. But this was exactly what happened year after year on Tisha B'Av in Byzantine Jerusalem. Reading about it left a bad taste in my mouth, and I approached learning about the present meaning of the holiday with suspicion and discomfort.

What I discovered about its current significance helped rid me of the bad taste. First, it was valuable to find that many thoughtful Jews were struggling with the same question: namely, since the vast majority of Jews today are not longing for the actual rebuilding of the temple and the reinstitution of animal sacrifice, then just what are they longing for? A startling answer came from a rebbe and scholar in Jerusalem named Mordechai Gafni, who reports that according to the teaching of at least some of the rabbis, it all has to do with sex. It seems that when the Temple was destroyed, the enjoyment of sex was taken away from married people and given to adulterers. "Stolen waters taste sweeter," as the old saying puts it. The yearning for the Temple turns out, in this reading, to be the yen for erotic dalliance.

As winsome as this theory may be, I doubt that even one Jew in a thousand thinks of eros in connection with Tisha B'Av. So I kept looking for another explanation. Rabbi David Hartman was more helpful. He describes returning to his Orthodox synagogue in Canada on Tisha B'Av, fresh from the jubilant celebrations in Israel after the victory of the Six-Day War, only to find his congregants sitting downcast on the floor, mourning for Jerusalem. They seemed uncomprehending when he asked them why they were crouched there when their fellow Jews, at that moment, were dancing in the streets of the city whose loss they were lamenting. It took a few years for the rabbi to answer his own question, but his resolution was helpful to me as well. It has to do with how we handle the sadness and loss that eventually come to all of us.

There are many jokes about why, as a people, Jews sometimes seem to cling to the memories of suffering. I had sometimes wondered myself, along with many other people influenced — often against our wills — by the recent deluge of New Age psychology, why Jews could not achieve "closure." How long should mourning continue? When does healthy "grief work" become a neurotic obsession? But now I wonder if popular ideas about standard stages of grieving and closure are no more than a modern therapeutic myth. When a tragedy strikes, we are constantly told "to do the grief work," then "to put it behind you" and "to get on with your life." But there is another way of looking at it. The afflictions that assail us as individuals, as families, and as peoples become part of us. Like the scars we carry from physical injuries, they eventually heal, but they are still present, reminding us of who we are and where we have been. We move ahead, but we never put them completely behind us. Indeed, I do not think we should.

I learned a bit of Jewish wisdom on this difficult subject of remembering and forgetting one Saturday morning in August when I attended the Sabbath service called Shabbat Zakhor at Temple Beth Zion in Brookline. The Torah reading for that week contains dozens of regulations, covering everything from how to treat women captives after a military victory, to how to keep the camp clean of human waste, to why one should allow the mother bird to fly away before taking eggs from a nest for food. In the middle of the passage, Deuteronomy 25:17–19, however, stands a brain-racking admonition. It speaks of Amalek, the collective name for the desert tribe that harassed the Israelites as they were trudging across the wilderness. It was the Amalekites who cruelly killed off the old people and the stragglers who had a hard time keeping up with the march. "Remember what Amalek did to you on the way as you came out of Egypt," it begins, "how he attacked you on the way, when you were faint and weary, and cut off at your rear all who lagged behind you; and he did not fear God."

Up to this point, the text seems to endorse bitterness and resentment, the seething sentiments that fuel blood feuds and cycles of recrimination. But then it takes a surprising turn: "Therefore when the Lord your God has given you rest from all your enemies round about, in the land which the Lord your God gives you for an inheritance to possess, you shall blot out the remembrance of Amalek from under heaven; you shall not forget."

I immediately wondered about the apparent contradiction in this final verse. How can anyone both "blot out" the memory and also "not forget"? As it happened, someone else raised this question with Rabbi Waldoks during the discussion period. "That's exactly it," the rabbi responded. "You have to remember something in order to forget it. But how you do it . . . that's the question."

His answer not only clarified this wise but puzzling text; it also struck me as exactly true to my own experience. As human beings we need times and spaces to return to both the saddest and the happiest moments of our lives. We recognize this about the happy ones; that is why we celebrate birthdays and anniversaries. The trouble is that in secular life we have fewer occasions, if any, to remember the sad ones. But Jews mark yahrzeits, the anniversary of the death of a loved one, and they have both the raucous festivity of Purim and the gloomy drama of Tisha B'Av. Christians have both the horror of Good Friday, the jubilation of Easter, and the joy of Christmas. Tisha B'Av is a reminder that the therapeutic orthodoxy of our current culture may be superficial and even downright wrong at points.

Just after my encounter with the Deuteronomic insight I ran across Timothy W. Ryback's *The Last Survivor*.[4] In this wrenching account, an elderly Polish Jew named Martin Zaidenstadt tells Ryback — and anyone else who will listen — that he was a prisoner in the death camp at Dachau, but he survived and stayed on in the nearby village of Dachau. Zaidenstadt's name does not appear on the camp register, but this does not mean his claim is false. There is no doubt that he has lived in Dachau since the camp was closed, married there, apparently did well, and eventually retired. But as he approached his nineties, he began to engage in what the other villagers thought to be bizarre, or least somewhat eccentric, behavior. Every morning he would walk to the camp's brick crematorium and stand there all day, telling the streams of visitors not to believe those who say the ovens in this particular camp were never used. They were used, he insists, and he can remember the screams. On this point historians differ, and the record is not entirely clear. But he also tells the guests that he has been standing there every day for fifty years, which — though it may be true in his own mind — is not accurate. He sometimes asks for money from the visitors, and he threatened Ryback, who tried to understand his story, with a gun. As Steve Dowden writes insightfully, Zaidenstadt is "haunted by a past too painful to remember and too painful to forget."

At a certain point in reading Zaidenstadt's story, the empirical question of whether he is in fact a survivor of Dachau, which seems important at the beginning, becomes much less so. In one sense, every Jew in Europe who was alive at the time is a survivor. And the screams he says he heard, though they were muffled for years after the Holocaust, are still reverberating, or should be, in everyone's ears. Whatever else he is, Martin Zaidenstadt stands as a reminder that there are some things we must remember to try to forget and some we must remember never to forget.

Remembering and forgetting: we need them both. We live in an era that threatens to erase memory in a deluge of triviality but, at the same time, nurses ancient grudges and vendettas. We can never annul them completely. But like the brutality of Amalek — and of Amalek's numerous successors — we need to remember in order to forget. How can we do it?

Classical drama and literature, folk songs, and historic liturgies stand as fragile dikes against the flood of today's psychological fads and the manipulation of bygone animosities by ambitious ideologues. I can think of nothing that better meets our innate need to remember and forget than crouching uncomfortably in a darkened house of worship and listening to Lamentations being chanted in melancholy tones. Though not read very often, Lamentations is one of the most moving and profound books in the entire Bible. It ruthlessly portrays the decimated city, sparing the reader few details of the horror. The children are all gone, dead or in exile. Passersby mock and ridicule those in torment. Mothers search vainly for bread for their infants. But although it skirts despair and nihilism, Lamentations never falls into them. It is at once painful to read, brashly iconoclastic in its open anger at God, and — in the end — strangely hopeful. Lamentations, as the name suggests, is a classical example of an enduring human cultural expression called the lament. This is a form as old as primitive keening and the wails for the dying Sumerian god, Tammuz, in the *Gilgamesh* epic. But it is as contemporary as the classical blues of Bessie Smith and her successors. The black American author Ralph Ellison once wrote: "The blues is an impulse to keep the painful details and episodes of a brutal experience alive in one's aching consciousness, to finger its jagged grain, and to transcend it, not by the consolation of philosophy but by squeezing from it a near-tragic, near-comic lyricism."[5]

Both blues and the lament merge our personal grief with our social grief. The two sources of pain draw on and reverberate with each other. In Lamentations, the agony the prophet once suffered as the representative of his nation is now the lot of everyone. As in the black American anguish, from which the blues emerged, personal pain and the pain of one's people are sometimes indistinguishable. Also, as blues adepts always say, you don't just sing the blues when you are blue, you sing the blues to "get blue," that is to recall, deepen, and struggle with intimate and corporate loss. This invocation of a mood is as old as human history. In earlier times most societies relied on paid mourners, usually women, who might not even know the deceased person, to evoke the appropriate spiritual energies that would enable people to mourn.

Lamentations grows out of this tradition. There is hardly a more wrenching opening line in any book of the Bible. "'*Eikhah*," it cries, "*yashvah badad ha'ir*" ("How doth the city sit solitary!"). Recalling the anguish that pulsates in hundreds of blues songs, it depicts Jerusalem as a woman who has been abandoned by all her lovers. Once a princess, full of joy and the center of God's loving care, now "there is none left to comfort her." I am sorry that Billie Holiday never recorded a version of this text. It would have been a natural for her, for it mixes equal measures of despondency about the city's pitiful condition with fury at the God who allowed this to happen. But the grim picture it paints of the destitute wreckage of the most proud and beautiful capital goes beyond most blues. There is so little food, mothers must eat their own children because they cannot give them suck. Mourners, smeared with mud and ashes, lie on the ground and groan. And God is being blamed: "Thou hast slain them in the day of thy anger" (2:21). Worst of all, since God has allowed the Temple to be despoiled and the priests to be murdered at their altars, now the devastated people have nowhere to turn for solace. It is hard enough to cope with shipwreck when the familiar symbols of meaning are still in place. But when they too are lost, calamity becomes catastrophe. This is the blues raised to a tragic level. Not only are the people reeling, but every landmark that might have brought them comfort is gone. The festivals have been forgotten and — a nightmare of unfathomable depth — even the Sabbath is not being observed. Chaos threatens. Nothing, literally nothing, is left.

But as the third chapter unfolds, a curious and spiritually cogent change begins to take place. The author of this lament has vehemently insisted that since God no longer hears prayers, it is futile to pray. But now he begins to pray anyway.

> But I called, Lord, on your name
> from the depths of the pit;
> you heard my plea: "Do not turn a deaf ear
> when I cry out for relief."
> You came near when I called to you;
> you said, "Have no fear" (Lamentations 3:55–57).

This seeming contradiction cannot help but remind someone familiar with the New Testament of the paradoxical plea of the forlorn father of a young man said to be possessed by demons who, when Jesus asks him if he believes his son can be healed, cries out, "I believe. Help my unbelief!" Both the book of Lamentations and this encounter between the rabbi from Nazareth and a despondent father expose the superficial notion held by many secular and many religious people as well: that there is a clear line between belief and unbelief. It is a baseless idea, and one that virtually all the greatest mystics, rabbis, scholars, and theologians reject. This has particular relevance for spirituality in our time, when so-called believers are often assailed by doubts and agnostics sometimes begin to doubt their skepticism.

The vast majority of gentiles have never heard of Tisha B'Av. Even among Jews it is often considered a minor holiday, and some believe that since Jerusalem is now back in Jewish hands, there is no reason to continue the mourning. But over the centuries Tisha B'Av, like holidays in all religions, has developed a life of its own and has come to embrace something more than its original meaning. Among all the Jewish holidays, it may have more to teach us than any other. I became especially aware of its value when a former student of mine, Rabbi Yehezkel Landau, who now lives and teaches in Jerusalem, sent me some reflections on Tisha B'Av that he, in turn, had received from his friend and teacher Michael Kagan. I not only prize the thoughts, I also appreciate the way they have been handed on to me in a typical "rabbinical" fashion.

Kagan points out that (at least in the Middle East where it arose), Tisha B'Av takes place during the hottest weather, when the sun often blazes down without mercy. But he also reminds us that *av* is the Hebrew word for "father," and that during our early formative years, for many of us — maybe most of us — the anger of our earthly fathers is the thing we find hardest to bear. I know this was true in my own childhood. Although my father was almost always a gentle and considerate person, he did occasionally become angry with me, and when he did it was devastating. This was especially true if that anger took the form of a temporary withdrawal, if not of his love, then of his presence. It took me years — even after he had died at an early age — to outgrow the fear of his anger. I suspect that, like most people, I have never fully outgrown it. Kagan says this is the meaning of the phrase about God "hiding his face," which recurs often in the Old Testament. Somehow the most painful expression of a father's anger is not a scolding or even a spanking. It is withdrawal. The same is true in Lamentations and in the mood of Tisha B'Av. It is not only that God has punished his children — or so they believed — by letting appalling things happen to them. This would be terrible, but endurable. But God has also withdrawn. He has hidden his face.

I also remember that during those rare times when I felt my father's rejection, I needed my mother even more. Mostly I could rely on her. But sometimes I could not, and these were the worst times. What makes Tisha B'Av particularly intense is that, while it lasts, this compensatory love of the mother is — symbolically — exactly what is not available. This holiday is the one day in the entire year that Jews do not wear the *tallit* because, Kagan says, it symbolizes the sheltering closeness of the *Shekhinah,* the feminine side of God. Without it we must, as it were, bear the full blast of the sun-father's heat with a bare head. During Tisha B'Av, says Kagan, we have the opportunity to take another step toward maturity by symbolically reliving this harrowing but important inner wound.

There is still another layer in this remarkable holiday. The Bible says that the Children of Israel who left Egypt were condemned to die in the wilderness. Only their children would ever reach the Promised Land. Kagan recounts a Jewish legend that every year during the forty years of wandering, the entire people would dig their own graves and lie in them all night. Each year fifteen thousand failed to arise, and their graves were covered over by the survivors, who would then shove on toward their goal. This continued, it is said, until all those who had left Egypt were dead and only their offspring remained. It is a harrowing picture, especially in view of all the records that indicate how many times during the Nazi years Jews, and others, were forced to dig their own graves, only to be shot and pushed into them.

Sleeping in a grave is not a custom that commends itself to many people today. But I do not believe we should dismiss it as bizarre or morbid. For thousands of years religions have evolved rituals that help people to come to terms with their own mortality, not to make them morose but to enable them to embrace the full amplitude of life. Once a year, as I noted earlier, Tibetan Buddhist monks sleep all night in a cemetery. Saint Francis, one of the most life-loving saints, taught his followers always to keep a human skull in their rooms as a memento mori. Baptism in Christianity, especially in those denominations that practice full immersion, is interpreted as dying, being buried, and being raised to a new life by God's grace. On Ash Wednesday many Christians appear at work or school with a dark smudge on their foreheads, a reminder to them — and to anyone they meet who wants to consider it — that we all eventually return to dust. These various practices all suggest that only a full and uncompromising awareness of our death allows us to live life fully. Yet today, despite violent video games, serial murderers, wars, massacres, and famines, most people still manage to avoid dwelling much on their own death. They think of it mainly as something to be postponed as long as possible. Longevity in years rather than the intensity of a life has become the goal.

Maybe the reason Tisha B'Av is not a particularly popular holiday among Jews, and virtually unknown by others, is that it brings to mind things none of us likes to think about. But we should think about them more than we do. There is a wisdom enshrined in both Tisha B'Av and in these other rituals that our generation — both death dealing and death denying — needs to recover. They remind us that life and death are both part of the human venture and that they are complementary, not contradictory. By denying one we also short-circuit the other. Death, after all, is a kind of loss that is relentlessly foreshadowed by the other losses we encounter in life. Early or late, we lose parents, friends, spouses, sometimes even children. We lose anticipated opportunities, jobs, and rewards. Eventually we lose our vitality and alertness. Life, it would seem, along with all its rich bene-fits, is also made up of a series of little deaths. For many of us, our first response to any loss is to try to rearrange our psychic armor so that we will not be shattered by the next one. But since life means loss, that armor also defends us from life. It becomes a wall between us and those with whom we live. The wisdom of Tisha B'Av is that we need times when we can safely allow that armor to be penetrated so that our hearts are once again exposed to both pain and joy.

14

Under and After the Canopy

Wedding and Marriage

Then God said to Noah, "Go forth from the ark,
you and your wife and your sons and your sons' wives with you.
Bring forth with you every living thing that is with you
of all flesh — birds and animals and every creeping thing that
creeps on the earth — that they may breed
abundantly on the earth,
and be fruitful and multiply on the earth. . . ."
And God said, "I will never again destroy every living creature
. . . and this is the sign of the covenant which I make between me
and you and every living creature
for all future generations:
I set my bow in the cloud, and it shall be a sign of the covenant
between me and the earth."

— Genesis 8:15–17, 21, 9:12–14

LITTLE OR NOTHING in my life had prepared me for the pic-ture-book day in August 1986 when I found myself standing under a *chuppah*, the traditional Jewish wedding canopy, hearing Hebrew prayers said over my bride and myself and smashing a champagne glass under my polished white shoe. Little, I suspect, had prepared Nina for standing under the same *chuppah* and hearing the reading of a portion of the Sermon on the Mount at a wedding presided over by a woman minister. It was the second marriage for both of us. I had three grown children; she had none. As it turned out, both of us were elated with our wedding ceremony, as were the friends and family gathered around us. We knew, of course, that there were people in both our traditions who would not have liked it one bit. But somehow, on such a splendid day, that did not make much difference to us. Still, it took a lot of effort for us to make it to the *chuppah*, and there were moments when we thought we might never get there.

Not that we had any doubts that we loved each other and wanted to marry. It was just that when a Jew marries a Christian, there are not that many models of the kind of ceremony it should be, at least not many that we found acceptable. Eventually, with the patient help of a wise and tactful rabbi, we composed our own ceremony, incorporating elements from both traditions and including touches that would be recognizable by both sets of relatives, at the same time trying to avoid a mere superficial mishmash. But the conversations and negotiations it required taught me something important, not just about Jewish-Christian weddings, but about the marriage itself that, as the saying goes, "begins when the wedding is over." I learned that the wedding, in effect, becomes a kind of microcosm of the new phase of life it initiates.

As soon as we began to talk seriously about marriage, we knew we would have to face a range of issues. First, we realized there would be people who would not approve of our decision. Every year more and more Americans marry across religious lines. It happens even though most of the leaders of our faiths continue to discourage "mixed marriages," as do some of the families and friends of a couple that is considering one. However, fewer and fewer couples seem to be dissuaded by such advice, and for the thousands who actually enter such a marriage, the issue of approval or disapproval immediately becomes moot. They, like us, face a different set of questions.

The first one, voiced by each questioner as though we had never heard it before, was: "Yes, but what about the children?" The second question, which was rarely asked but we did ask ourselves, was — and is — how to create a genuinely shared approach to all the varied facets of married life, including the religious ones. The third, as much an ethnic as a religious question, was how to cope with quite different attitudes toward time and space, home and family, and a host of other things that seem to be taken for granted by Jewish and gentile families. (I had to learn, for example, that it is entirely normal for Jewish women to talk to their mothers on the telephone four or five times a week, which might seem a bit excessive for those from my background.) Finally, we would have to think carefully about how to approach holidays and home rituals, another matter in which there is little symmetry between the two traditions since so many Jewish rituals occur in the home. We knew all these issues would emerge eventually, and we thought we were ready to face them. What we had not anticipated was that they would appear as soon as we started preparing for the wedding ceremony itself.

We should not have been surprised. Rituals, including weddings, are always occasions at which the most indelible, though often unspoken, beliefs and assumptions of the participants are sure to come to expression. It is not just the bride and groom who stand under the *chuppah*. They carry with them their life histories, with all the loyalties, stories, and memories that have shaped them. And they bring along the ingrained traditions of preceding generations. When they take each other as husband and wife, they not only begin to weave a new fabric, they weave into it the differently tinted threads of those lives and traditions.

We already knew many happy couples who had entered into marriages across religious lines. We talked with many of them, not just about the ceremony, but mainly about what came after. Each one seemed to have devised its own way of handling the issues such marriages raise. But there are some common patterns, and we found four major strategies:[1]

1. Some couples adopt a kind of live-and-let-live modus vivendi toward each other's religions. They tolerate, respect, maybe even appreciate the other's faith, but they stand back at a safe distance and try not to comment or criticize. This might be called a "passive interfaith marriage," and it often works well, up to a point. But we think that as the years go by, the husband and wife will come to notice that they are — perhaps unintentionally — depriving each other of something that, rightly handled, could add real *frisson* to their marriage. "Don't ask, don't tell," may be appropriate for some situations, but hardly in a marriage.

2. Sometimes one spouse will embrace the other's faith, or both will affiliate with a third tradition that feels like a kind of halfway house. A Roman Catholic and a Lutheran may join an Anglican church. A Reform Jew and a liberal Methodist might become Unitarian-Universalists. These arrangements frequently work well too. But

in this strategy, the marriage ceases to be an *inter*faith one and misses both the hazards such a marriage poses and the rewards we have come to think a genuine interfaith marriage can provide.

3. To our dismay, for many couples, in order to head off any trouble, both the husband and the wife had simply ceased to practice their respective faiths. To avoid Scylla or Charybdis, they opted not to set sail at all. The result is what someone has wryly referred to as an "interfaithless marriage." We both came to feel that this is a sad solution and, in the end, is no solution at all. When the various holidays roll around — Passover, Christmas — even the most determined partners in such a sterile arrangement feel an inner tug. Something seems to be missing. What, no Seder at all? Not even a tiny tabletop Christmas tree? But the inner tug may be difficult to bring up with the other spouse, who might view it as a sign of backsliding from a previous agreement. Also, more seriously, when relatives and parents die, or especially if one of the partners dies, having chucked it all in order to avoid tension will, we fear, come to seem like a dreadful mistake. There must be a better way, and we think there is.

4. This fourth approach is the one we have chosen and, as it seemed to us, is the strategy chosen by an increasing number of interfaith couples. It is the path for the couples who fall in love, wish to marry and have children, and for whom each faith tradition is respected and followed. For these people, "none of the above" strategies will do. Neither wishes either to convert to the other's faith, to join a *tertium quid*, or to abandon both ships.

This whole book has been, at least in part, a case study in this fourth strategy. We believe it has worked well for us. Still, we realize that all these other scores for orchestrating a mixed marriage have worked — more or less — for others. We only hope that any couple choosing one of them reflects, well in advance, about the main question most of their families and religious leaders will already have asked them, usually many times over: "But what about the children?" In our observation, even the most secure couples who have adopted one or another of the strategies mentioned above cannot avoid having at least some second thoughts when a child is born. Sometimes they are hesitant to raise this "second thought" even with their own spouses. But sometimes they do. "I know I'm not formally religious, but couldn't we at least have her baptized? It would make my parents so happy." Or, "I know I'm not observant, but I somehow think we ought to have him circumcised. They can do it in the hospital." And that is only the beginning.

The question those parents, ministers, and rabbis raise so persistently may seem tiresome and repetitious. But it is not pointless. The word "tradition," as in "faith tradition," means "handing over," and the core of any religion concerns what stories and values we hand on to succeeding generations, including the little representatives of those generations who are born into our own families. It is especially troubling, if understandable, to realize that some couples who may have wanted children are tempted not to have them just to avoid the fracas that may ensue. This nonsolution sounds, as it were, like quite literally throwing the baby out with the bath water (in this case, the *mikvah* or the baptismal font).

Clearly, all the questions we would eventually face came up — in embryo — when we began to prepare for the wedding ceremony. We did not have to wait for years to cope with a measure of disapproval of our decision; or "what about the children?"; or how to cooperate fully with each other in planning the ceremony; or how to handle the feelings of our families, the scheduling of the event, and its location. At first they seemed like a series of awkward obstacles we would have to clamber over. But we now see that they provided us with indispensable training for what was to come. Preparing for the wedding became preparing for the marriage, although we only recognized that later.

We both decided not simply to brush off the disapproval of mixed marriages that is sometimes aired by families (though, in our case, in a very muted way) and by both Christian and Jewish leaders, but especially by the latter. We would take them seriously and try to understand them. This exercise helped me to understand Judaism better than I had before. It began, of course, with the question of who would conduct the ceremony. It was clear to both of us that there was no question of either of us abandoning our own faith. Neither of us wanted a perfunctory city hall ceremony or a justice of the peace officiating. From the outset I was happy to have a rabbi do the honors, and of course Nina wanted a rabbi too. With what now seems to me astonishing innocence, I assumed this was all that we needed.

Not so. Even those rabbis, some of them our friends, who told us they were delighted we were getting married and who offered wise counsel on many subjects, all respectfully declined to officiate. Each explained that, whatever his personal feelings might be, he was empowered by his rabbinical ordination to officiate only at the wedding of one Jew to another. The reasoning is very straightforward. A Jewish marriage is recognized under Jewish law when two witnesses see the bride accept a ring from the groom and hear him say, "*Haray aht m'kudeshet lit'baba'at zu k'dar Moshe v'Yisrael*" ("With this ring, you are consecrated to me according to the laws of Moses and Israel"). But if one of the parties does not consider himself, or herself, bound by these laws, then the marriage, which is traditionally viewed as a formal contract, is devoid of meaning.[2] Consequently, these friendly rabbis wished us well, but they did not want to stand under the *chuppah* and declare us husband and wife according to the laws of Moses. One rabbi even told us that although he could not do it, he knew there were a few rabbis who would, but that in any case he would suggest we find some other way to manage it.

We were disappointed, but we understood. We had done some reading about Jewish opposition to marrying outsiders. It expresses the underlying belief, still held if only in a residual way and even by nonobservant Jews, that Jews are different from other peoples. Religiously expressed, it says that Jews have been called by God to a special task in the world, a responsibility that no one else has in quite the same way. They are called to be "a light to the nations," a living example of God's will for all the peoples of the world. The nonreligious Jews have abandoned the theological basis, but they still retain an innate sense that there is a difference, that the difference is terribly important, and — given the enormous centrality of the family among Jews — marrying "outside" endangers the specialness.

It does not help much to point out that this disapproval, though enshrined in Jewish law, has not always been vigorously applied. The Israeli archaeologist and historian Magen Broshi, who served for a number of years as the director of the Shrine of the Book in Jerusalem (where the Dead Sea Scrolls are housed), recalls a list of prominent Israelites who married non-Israelites. The roll includes King David himself, whose favorite wife, Bathsheba, sprang from pagan parentage. Indeed, when their son was born, David wanted to give him a good Israelite name, Jedidiah, but Bathsheba insisted on calling him Solomon, after the pagan god and legendary founder of Jerusalem, Shalem. It was not the last time that a domestic controversy would arise about child naming, and surely not the last that would eventually be won by the mother. But in taking a non-Jewish woman to wife, David had many Israelite predecessors. These included Judah, Simeon, Joseph (who was admittedly in exile in Egypt at the time and presumably did not meet many "nice Jewish girls"), Moses, Gideon, and Samson. It's an imposing catalogue. It would seem that the marital choices of these Israelite worthies greatly diversified the gene pool, and the practice can hardly have been restricted to the ruling class. Later, however, especially after the return of the Israelite elite from Babylonian captivity, severe restrictions on intermarriage began to be decreed.

Today, after many centuries of living in the diaspora and after the Nazis made a serious attempt to annihilate every last one of them, Jews are understandably wary of even the most innocent-looking threat to their continuity as a people. The "as a people" is what Christians, at least at first, have a hard time understanding. Christianity in most of its branches is both individual and universal. Technically, no one is born a Christian, rather every individual must become one, even though in practice most Christians (though hardly all) are the children of Christian parents. Also, since Christianity began by insisting that gentiles could also share in the mission and the promises to which God had first called the Israelites alone, Christianity is by definition (though, again, not always in practice) universal.

The bottom line is the question, "What about the children?" In short, many Jews fear that since they constitute a minority in most places in the world, every mixed marriage puts the next generation's Jewishness at risk. These fears are hardly groundless. Statistics show that the children of mixed marriages are far less likely to think of themselves as Jewish than are the children of marriages between two Jews. The grandchildren of mixed marriages are even less likely to do so. Christians need to understand why Jews view this prospect with such dread. At some level, most Jews feel very intensely that something of immeasurable importance would be lost, not just to them but to everyone, if all Jews were to disappear from the earth. I agree, and many of the pages of this book have demonstrated why. Of course, many Christians feel the same way about their own faith, but here a stark demographic reality looms into view. There are only about fourteen million Jews on earth. Furthermore, the number of Jews has stabilized, and in some parts of the world it is even in slight decline. In contrast, there are an estimated two billion Christians in the world, and the number continues to grow. So the fear on the part of Jews, which I think Christians should understand and share, is hardly without basis. But I believe that Christians must go beyond merely sympathizing. We need to reassure Jews by words and actions that we are also committed to a future for the Jewish people.

This commitment carries a special resonance for those of us who marry Jews. It means that taking the faith of the Jewish partner seriously begins with the determination that the children born to such a marriage will not be lost to the Jewish people. They will be considered Jewish and will be nurtured and educated to grow up with that realization. I feel so strongly about this that I have come to view many of the apologetic statements about Jews made by Christian churches in recent years as largely pious verbalizing because this central issue — the question of children — is never addressed. I am waiting, not always with total patience, for both Catholics and Protestants to emerge from the present period of breast-beating and begin to change their actual practices in regard to Jews. This means respecting the particularity of Judaism and its continued place in God's economy and taking every measure possible to ensure that Jews — as a people — will continue to be numbered among the peoples of the earth. This in turn means respecting one of the most basic of all Jewish beliefs — that the child of a Jewish mother is a child of the covenant, a Jew, and should be recognized as such.[3]

"What about the children?" also reminds the non-Jewish spouse, if it had somehow escaped notice, that a marriage such as ours is not just a mixed religious one. It also mixes cultures and ethnicities. To most Jews (as opposed to most Protestants, for example), "being Jewish" means more than belonging to a particular spiritual tradition. There are many Jews, in fact, who disclaim any religious identity at all yet proudly insist on being Jewish. And people who have embraced Judaism as a religious tradition have sometimes told me that after many years they still do not "feel Jewish." This complexity is real, and it can be very puzzling to the non-Jewish partner. But it is one of the areas in such a marriage that requires patience and good humor. The Jewish spouse has to learn to sympathize with the partner's bafflement. And the non-Jewish one must learn to live with an element of ambiguity.

But why should this question come up as soon as the couple de-

cides to marry? Maybe there won't be any children, so the issue becomes moot. Isn't it something that can be settled when the preg-
nancy test comes back positive? My answer to that is "absolutely not."
In fact, if there is any chance that children will come, it is probably
the first question that should be asked. And the couple can be sure
that if they do not ask it of themselves, and ask it right away, they will
hear it, and they will hear it time and time again. They should understand that it is — at least from the Jewish perspective — not just one
question among many. For Jews, having children, continuing the life
of the covenant people, and contributing to succeeding generations
is what marriage is all about. This was always the question the rabbis
who told us they were happy we were getting married but could not
officiate themselves asked. And I strongly suspect they would not
have been so happy with our plans if we had not assured them that
we had decided that we would raise whatever offspring came as the
Jewish children of a Jewish mother and a Christian father.

When, eventually, Nicholas was born, we were ready. I had no objection to his being circumcised. Instead of a *bris,* the traditional
ceremony, we followed Nina's preference in the matter, so the circumcision took place in the hospital. Three months later we invited
friends and family to our home for a Jewish naming ceremony, con-
ducted with verve by Lewis Mintz, the same rabbi who had helped us
prepare the wedding ceremony. Nicholas Tumarkin Cox, who was
named for his paternal great-grandfather, received his Hebrew name,
Nisson. Nina wore a blue and green ankle-length dress, and I wore
my best suit. Nicholas slept through the entire ceremony. Unlike
some Jewish-Christian parents, we did not even have to discuss
whether to have him baptized, both because we had already decided
he was to be raised as a Jewish child and because in my own branch
of Christianity (Baptist) there is no infant baptism. A few weeks later
Nina and I took Nicholas, wrapped in a tartan blanket, to the regular
Sunday service at the church I attend. There the congregation offered
prayers that he would grow up to be a strong man of faith and make
a contribution to the coming of the Kingdom of God. No water was
sprinkled, no oil administered. We did it because Nina thoughtfully
recognized that I wanted us to dedicate our child to God in a setting I
was familiar with. It did not seem like a compromise to her; before
and since, she has accompanied me to church on special occasions,

and Nicholas, as he grew older, has accompanied us. But all three of us recognize that they come as welcome guests, just as I feel I am a welcome guest at synagogue services.

The wedding ceremony Nina and I crafted would not have been to the liking of purists on either side. It was an adaptation of a ceremony called "the Children of Noah," originally prepared by three rabbis — Arthur Waskow, Rebecca Alpert, and Linda Holtzman. We chose it in part because the covenant God made with Noah is the only one recorded in the Hebrew Scriptures that God explicitly makes with all of humanity. Also, everyone knows the story of the ark, and since we had chosen to exchange our vows on the shore of Lake Waban on the campus of Wellesley College, where Nina teaches, and the writers of the ceremony strongly recommend that it be held out of doors, the epic of the flood and the rainbow seemed exceptionally fitting. Nina also wanted the seven traditional Hebrew wedding blessings said, and I gladly agreed. I wanted a reading of Jesus' Beatitudes from the Sermon on the Mount, and Nina readily agreed to that. She also wanted to ask a woman friend whose maiden name was Cohen (and is thus technically descended from the priestly Israelite line) to give a blessing.

At last everything seemed ready. Nina wore a street-length white Afghan dress with an intricate red, gold, and black design on the front of the bodice and around the cuffs. I was attired in a splendid white tuxedo, white tie, and white shoes. We asked four people — a close colleague of Nina's, her oldest woman friend, one of her nephews, and my closest faculty colleague — to hold the four poles that supported the *chuppah*.

Naturally, my theologically inclined colleague wanted to know what the *chuppah* symbolized. That sent me off to reference books. The official explanation is that it represents the house into which the groom is inviting the bride to join him in establishing a new family.[4] But another thought also occurred to me when I saw the actual awning fluttering in the soft August breeze. Faithful people in many different traditions have for centuries erected either temporary or permanent shelters over places meant to be thought of as sacred. In the East, statues of the Buddha are often sheltered by an umbrella. In Catholic and Orthodox churches, a canopy often covers the altar. The one in St. Peter's Basilica in Rome may be the largest in the world. As a people who were nomadic for long stretches of their history, Jews became accustomed to fashioning temporary shelters, the most famous of which was the tabernacle that sheltered the Tablets of the Law. But even a temporary shelter leaves a mark on the place it stands. Nina and I have been back many times to visit the lakeside where we were married. The *chuppah* is long since gone, but the spot still seems holy to us.

As the ceremony itself started, two friends played incidental music and a short processional on keyboard and string bass. We repeated our vows and exchanged rings. The woman minister of my Baptist church gamely took on the responsibility of officiating at what was, I am sure, the most unusual wedding she had ever seen. She did it with genteel taste and, near the end of the proceedings, called my three grown children to stand under the *chuppah* to share in the blessing. At the conclusion, not just the minister but everyone present joined in declaring us husband and wife. Then I kissed Nina and smashed the glass. Everyone applauded. We both felt quite married — if not precisely "according to the law of Moses," then in the spirit of Noah and the rainbow sign.

As soon as the ceremony was over, Nina and I put into practice an old Jewish wedding custom we had learned about from Anita Diamant's book called the *yichud* ("seclusion"). Instead of greeting friends immediately, we stole away for twenty minutes to the second floor of a cottage overlooking the wedding site. I suspect that in former days this custom had something to do with the actual consummation of the marriage. Nowadays it gives the bride and groom a welcome opportunity to catch their breath, have a bite to eat (since they won't have time to eat much at the reception), and let the promises they have just made to each other sink in before they start saying "So glad you could come" to all the guests. I think it is an admirable tradition, especially for the harried bride and groom, and should be adopted immediately by all religions and denominations!

At the reception, several of my family and friends asked about the smashing of the wineglass. I had wondered about this too and had heard several interpretations. One rabbi confided to me that it probably derived from an old custom about breaking the bride's hymen; he declined to elaborate further. Another said it signified the groom's resolution to discard forever the wanton ways of bachelorhood. A more religious interpretation says that it represents the destruction of the Temple and reminds the couple and all those present that even at such a joyous moment the tragedies of life should not be forgotten. No doubt all of these explanations, and many more, have been held at one time or another. What is beyond a doubt, however, is that if the groom does not break the glass today, no Jews present will believe they have attended a Jewish wedding.

We had a short honeymoon at a little resort on Cape Cod. Then we returned to take up the strenuous privileges and responsibilities of being official members of two large families with strikingly different histories. Nina's parents were both born in St. Petersburg, Russia, and came from highly "russified" Jewish families descended from many generations of merchants and tradesmen. One of her grandfathers was the macaroni mogul of the czarist era, the purveyor of pasta to the imperial army. The family had been quite wealthy, and the children (Nina's mother and her mother's brothers and sisters) benefited from French governesses, Russian peasant nannies, and a retinue of household servants.

But St. Petersburg in 1917, as the Bolsheviks seized power, was not a good place to be either Jewish or bourgeois, so the whole family fled. But their exile was not entirely unpleasant, at least not at first. They merely moved to their ample summer home in Finland, then a part of the Russian empire, taking some of the household staff with them. Nina's mother still remembered the rush to the train station and the hurried trip to Helsinki. No one expected to be gone more than a few weeks — a few months at worst. But they never returned. When World War I ended, they found themselves in Finland, now independent. Later the family fanned out to Paris and other parts of Europe. When the Nazis came and World War II loomed, they had to emigrate again. This time Nina's mother and father came to New York, where they married and eventually rented an apartment at Eighty-fourth Street and West End Avenue, where Nina was born. She grew up on the Upper West Side speaking Russian, French, and English. Her father died when she was a young girl. When her mother died, some years after we were married, we inherited a treasure trove of Toulouse-Lautrec lithographs, paintings, and books in four or five languages.

My family has quite a different history. On my father's side, we stem from the Friends (Quakers) who followed William Penn to Pennsylvania in the early 1700s to escape religious persecution. On my mother's side, my forebears were Rhineland pietists who, because they were pacifists, fled to avoid military conscription. They settled in Chester County, Pennsylvania, in the southeastern part of the state, which also became the haven for the Mennonites and the Amish. For generations they were mainly farmers. My mother's father was the chief herdsman for a wealthy cattle breeder. As the generations passed they became less devout, but on both sides they maintained some of the basic ideals of the Friends and the pacifists. They would not bear arms during the American Revolution (although they buried the Continental soldiers who were killed by the British during a skirmish fought near their farm). One of my great-great-great-grandfathers was the founder of the Chester County abolitionist society. My own grandfather left school after third grade but was a deacon in the Baptist church. As a young man, he started a house painting and decorating business that grew and prospered; he eventually turned it over to my father. No one from either side of my family ever went to college or traveled to Europe. The only Jews we knew were the family of Dr. Jacob Sherson, who lived across the street. Dr. Sherson himself attended my father while he was dying of cancer and gained the lifelong affection of my mother.

There may be mixed couples whose lineages are even more disparate, but ours was divergent enough to present us with a number of intriguing challenges. I cannot answer for Nina, but I have never regretted becoming a thread in the vast network of time and space in which I found myself by marrying her. In fact, I am still learning what it is like to be grafted into a Jewish family tree. Family, as Jews always say, is what it is all about. There are hundreds, maybe thousands, of jokes about Jewish family life and probably ten thousand about Jewish mothers. I had heard a lot before we were married. I heard many, many more afterward, because Jews love to tell them themselves. But after a while I had to ask myself, what is so funny about these gags, and why is family life such a recurrent theme in Jewish humor?

I don't know how to answer this question. However, a fascinating book on ethnicity and family life edited by three psychotherapists — Monica McGoldrick, Joe Giordano, and John K. Pearce — helps a little. In the chapter on Jewish ethnicity, the first heading is, not surprisingly, "Centrality of the Family." I think it should be required reading for any gentile contemplating marriage to a Jew. "The family's centrality," say the authors, "cannot be underestimated in looking at Jewish cultural dynamics." They attribute this "familism" to the idea that it is a violation of God's law not to marry. Marrying and raising children are "core values." Asceticism is not approved of, and celibacy is condemned out of hand. These core values are reinforced by other factors. Children and grandchildren are considered "the very essence of life's meaning." In the face of discrimination and exile, the family became in many instances the last place of refuge. The authors point out that after marriage, close connections and obligations with the extended family continue to be important. They warn that this can at times feel a bit "stifling," but is a "source of much joy as well as pain."[5]

I had some idea about this "familism" before Nina and I married. But I had little idea of just how strong it was until I became a part of the family. I have to add, however, that although it has been the source of much joy, only seldom has it been the source of pain. Perhaps this is because I myself grew up in a large extended family in a small town. My youth, therefore, had more of the connectedness Jewish families maintain even though so many live scattered around the world. This became evident to me long before Nina and I were married when I noticed how many of her relatives she was eager for me to meet. I could understand her wanting me to get to know her sister, to whom she was very close, and her mother, who was her only living parent. But why was I being introduced to cousins and the cousins' wives and children in what sometimes appeared to me an endless latticework of *mishpocha*? At none of these encounters did I feel as though I was being "looked over" (although I probably was), but I was not always relaxed. This was in part because I knew I did not have to reciprocate in kind. I could not imagine introducing Nina to my cousins, many of whom I had not seen or heard from for decades, even though I had played with many of them almost daily throughout my childhood. Having her meet my immediate siblings and their wives seemed quite enough. In the culture I grew up in, when children reach maturity they are encouraged to go it alone, albeit with occasional emergency interventions. But I soon lost count of how many of Nina's aunts and second cousins I had met, sometimes confused them, and often needed to ask her to explain one more time who was the nephew of whom.

Furthermore, since we have been married I have continued to learn more and more about her ancestors. They keep popping up in faded brown photographs and dog-eared letters in Russian, French, and German, an endless portrait gallery of Russian-Jewish lumber barons, grain importers, ballet dancers, archaeologists, lawyers, and physicians. One great-aunt was exiled to Siberia when she was a youthful revolutionary for her involvement in an attempt to assassinate the czar. Getting to know this genealogy was no easy task. When Nina and I began to travel to other countries, I was constantly astonished to discover she had relatives and old family friends to contact almost everywhere we went, whether it was London or Paris or Rio de Janiero. The network I was now part of turned out to be considerably larger and more fascinating then anything I had anticipated. There is something to be said for Jewish "familism," especially if, instead of being born into it, you have married into it, which may make it somewhat less problematic.

There are other ethnic qualities we both had to learn about. Even before we got married we received some valuable advice. "Remember that for Jews, worrying is constructive work, so share her worry, never minimize it!" an astute friend advised me in Nina's presence. "And you," he continued, as he turned to Nina with a serious gaze, "you need to appreciate that for WASPs, denial is a useful and effective tool for coping with life's difficulties. It is nothing to smirk at!"

These tidbits have come in handy over the years. On other matters it is hard to know whether the differences that enliven our marriage are ethnic, or the varying habits of someone reared in a city versus someone who grew up in a small town, or the child of sophisticated European immigrants compared to a tenth-generation American, or a matter of divergent personalities, or that we are a man and a woman. But we both believe that differences add a tang that has given our marriage and our family life more zest. We believe we have not only made an interfaith marriage work but that it has deepened our separate commitment to our own traditions while making us more appreciative of our spouse's.

Still, we do not believe such marriages are for everyone. The questions we had to answer for ourselves were all worth asking. Our only advice to others considering the same decision is: *do not avoid these questions.* They are real, and these issues will come up. Some people who are considering such a marriage may ask them and then decide it is not a step they wish to take. Others will ask them and decide to go ahead. We welcome them to a growing company of those who, in small but significant ways, may be creating a whole new way of being Jewish and of being Christian in a world in which, one way or another, we must all live together.

15

The Boy Becomes a Man

Bar Mitzvah

The Lord said to Abram, "Leave your
Own country, your kin and your father's house,
and go to a country that I will show you.
I shall make you a great nation.

— Genesis 12:1, 2

WITH THE POSSIBLE EXCEPTION of death rituals, it is hard to think of any rite found so consistently from one religious tradition to another than ceremonies marking the passage from childhood to adulthood. Adolescent boys among Australian aboriginal peoples cringe for days in a dark, sweltering, steam-filled sweat lodge while their elders make terrifying noises outside. Then the boys crawl through the legs of adult men and are pulled out into the daylight head first, in a simulation of birth. Native American adolescents used to be sent off alone for days or weeks into the forest on a "vision quest," to wait for a vivid dream to seize them. With the exception of modern American culture, where a young person gets the keys to the station wagon at sixteen, may vote at eighteen, and can order a Budweiser at some age determined by state laws, in few societies does this passage go so strangely unnoticed.

Still, rites of passage are important. Like punctuation marks — a period, a semicolon — they signal the end of one phase and the beginning of another. They focus and amplify the vague feelings we all have at such moments of change that something significant is happening. What is often overlooked in the study of these rituals is that they are not just important for the young person, they are also milestones in the life of the community of which he or she is a part. The twice-told tales are told yet again for all to hear, the founding myths are recited, the old songs are sung, the gods and spirits are invoked. The community recalls the past in order to step into the future. The whole people, as well as the youth, begins a new stage of life.

In the Jewish tradition, the bar mitzvah ceremony is not an ancient one but emerged in the medieval period. It does not have its own special service but takes place during the regular Sabbath worship, usually in the morning, though sometimes in the late afternoon as well. Still, it has gradually assumed a place of larger and larger importance, and for some barely observant Jews, it may be one of the few times they find themselves in a synagogue. If only intuitively, everyone seems to sense its importance. In a secular or religiously pluralistic culture like ours, with only rare occasions for invoking traditions and few clear clues to personal identity and markers of life transitions, the bar mitzvah can be a powerful and memorable event. No doubt, it has sometimes been cheapened by appalling taste and excessive expenditure, especially in recent years — lush parties in swank hotels, fish sliced to look like shrimp (which is not kosher), a disk jockey, and a magician for the smaller kiddies. There is even a Jewish joke about a bar mitzvah reception featuring a bust of the bar mitzvah boy molded in chopped liver, which I am sure has never happened. Still, despite it all, the occasion somehow retains its spiritual power.

I never imagined that I would be as intimately involved in a bar mitzvah as I was in the one that culminated at Temple Beth Zion in Brookline on October 16, 1999. It was one of those gold and blue autumn days in New England that make bearable the seemingly interminable winters that follow. It was also 6 Heshvan 5760 in the Jewish calendar. And it was the day I took my longest step toward feeling at home in the Jewish community while remaining in the Court of the Gentiles. It was the day Nicholas officially became "bar mitzvah," a "son of the commandment." It was his vision quest, his new birth, his rite of passage from childhood into young manhood. And it was my passage from being the father of a Jewish child to being the father of a young Jewish man.

Strictly speaking, according to Jewish tradition Nicholas had already become bar mitzvah when he reached the age of thirteen years and one day. He was already eligible to be counted among the ten who form a *minyan*, to be called to the front to read the Torah (*aliyah*), and to fast on Yom Kippur. Technically, no ceremony is really necessary, and certainly no party or reception, but try telling that to a Jewish parent today, or especially to Jewish grandparents. I learned early in my marriage that a bar mitzvah is not to be taken lightly. If you are part of the extended family, no matter where you live, you show up. However important weddings and funerals may be, I quickly discovered that they are no more so than bar or bat mitzvahs. There is no equivalent command performance in Christianity; confirmations cannot compare. But it is not difficult to see why the bar mitzvah has become so central to Judaism. Among a people who have been banished and exiled, whose families have been decimated time and time again, in which parents have had to say good-bye so often to their children with little hope of seeing them again, the bar mitzvah ritual becomes far more than the welcoming of another member into the community. At every bar mitzvah Jews say to the world and to each other, "Look, despite it all, here we are!" And the party that follows says, "And we're still eating and drinking and dancing!"

We began preparing for Nicholas's bar mitzvah event four years before it would happen by enrolling him in a twice-weekly Hebrew and Judaism class. I had studied Hebrew many years before but had never taken to it, so I signed up for a weekly elementary class, made up — it seemed to me — mainly of uncomfortable parents who were embarrassed that their young children would soon know more Hebrew than they did. The school also ran a religious education program in which the children learned the Bible and Jewish history. For his project, Nicholas chose to construct a shoebox model of the story (found in a Midrash, not in the Bible itself) of the young Abram (later Abraham) smashing the idols in his father's store. He took considerable glee in filling the box with splinters and shards. I was pleased to see a promising young iconoclast in the making, but he may simply have been exhibiting that sense of power many eleven-year-old boys feel when they can smash something.

Eventually, with the event itself little more than a year away, we engaged a bright college junior to guide him in learning the prayers, also in Hebrew, that he would be expected to lead at the service.

Nicholas took on the task cheerfully and seemed to enjoy the sense of mastery he got from learning what those curious letters that march from right to left actually say. As I watched him progress, soon outdistancing me completely in his knowledge of the language of Isaiah and Jeremiah (and the one in which Jesus undoubtedly prayed), I had mixed sentiments. I was proud that he was taking to it so well, but I felt some regret that in my own faith no such command of the original sources was required of children his age. I saw again how deep the tradition of learning is in Jewish spirituality.

The centerpiece of the bar mitzvah ceremony itself occurs when the bar mitzvah boy-becoming-a-man (or bat mitzvah girl-becoming-a woman) reads the portion of the Torah assigned to him or her and then offers a D'var Torah, a comment on it, known familiarly as a "drash" (short for *midrash*). He does not choose the passage. The Jewish year follows a calendar of readings, specifying a part of the Torah to be read each week. Since the ceremony must come shortly after the thirteenth birthday, the passage is the luck of the draw. Some adolescents are not so lucky. We once heard a determined young woman struggle gamely with a puzzling passage from Leviticus about how long a woman's impurity remains after menstruation. Nicholas was one of the favored ones: his passage was Genesis 12–17. In the Jewish year, it is read on the Sabbath that takes its name from the key phrase in the text, *lech lekha*, which means, in effect, "leave this place." It describes God's calling of Abram, telling him to leave his family and his homeland and to travel to a country "that I will show you." It is an exciting and affecting passage in itself, but it is also hard to imagine a more appropriate one for a bar mitzvah: it's about leaving things behind and pushing on into the future. And it features the iconoclast who as a youth had pulverized his father's idols, the same Abram who appeared in the shoebox full of stone fragments. It all seemed so right, I was sure that in the cosmic lottery of who gets what passage, Nicholas had won the jackpot.

Nicholas himself, however, was not so sure. I found out quickly because, although it was the tutor's job to teach him the Hebrew he would need to read his Torah passage, I had assumed the responsibility for helping him to think through and write his commentary. I tried to use a Socratic method but could see it was going to be a daunting assignment nevertheless. The first thing Nicholas wanted to know was why Abram was so sure this was indeed God who was asking him to do this strange and unprecedented thing. Had he discussed it with anyone before he packed the camels? "If a voice came to me," Nicholas said, "and told me to leave everything behind — family, friends, and all the rest — and just head off for who knows where, I don't think I'd do it." He eventually decided that Abram must have had some previous encounter with God. After all, where had he gotten the idea to granulate all those idols?

So far so good. Then, however, in reading the passage together, we came upon a little nugget that I had almost forgotten. It pops up in the latter part of Chapter 12 when Abram, because of a famine in the land, has taken his family to Egypt.

> As he was about to enter Egypt, he said to his wife Sarai, "I know what a beautiful woman you are. If the Egyptians see you, and think, 'she is his wife,' they will kill me and let you live. Please say that you are my sister, that it may go well with me because of you, and that I may remain alive thanks to you."

Apparently Sarai went along with the deception. As the text tells it, when they arrived in Egypt, the pharaoh's courtiers did indeed notice her and praised her comeliness to the pharaoh. She was taken into the pharaoh's palace. "And because of her," the passage continues, "it went well with Abram, he acquired sheep, oxen, asses, male and female slaves, she-asses and camels."

Nicholas looked puzzled. Was his idol-splintering hero now not only lying but surrendering his wife to the pharaoh's lust and getting rich in the bargain? It seemed sneaky and deceptive — hardly a model of family values. It was time for a frank discussion, to me quite refreshing, about how the Bible — especially the Old Testament — is not a saga of moral virtue and chivalrous heroes. It is about flawed human beings trying to cope with the curve balls and sinkers life throws at all of us. Nicholas was disappointed in his champion. But he soon came to accept that no one is perfect; even Father Abram was not an exception. I was pleased. Studying this passage together had already spared him the burden of the traditional Protestant compulsion to read the entire Bible as a series of morality tales, a bad habit I was exposed to in Sunday school (where we never heard of Abram's little deception about Sarai).

Next Nicholas read a long entry on Abraham in a Bible dictionary I gave him and learned that he is considered to be the ancestor not only of Jews but also of Arabs and — since Jesus was Jewish — in a sense also of Christians. He was also impressed by the way Abram, once he had decided he was going to go, did not allow anything to stand in his way. I knew it would turn out to be a good D'var Torah, a thoughtful commentary.

Meanwhile, as Nicholas and I talked about the passage, Nina — with advice from Rabbi Moshe Waldoks of Temple Beth Zion — worked for weeks with consummate creativity to craft a *siddur,* the special prayer book to be used at the service. Consulting with Nicholas, she picked out appropriate drawings, many from the work of Marc Chagall, and inserted them throughout. She included a whimsical picture of the infamous "wise men of Chelm," engaged in one of their incessant ridiculous arguments. She also included some songs, poetry, and some favorite family recipes. The whole thing was assembled in a three-ring notebook, with two more Chagall prints on the front and back covers, one of a traveler setting out on a journey, and one of Aaron surrounded by a Torah and a menorah. It was a true work of art, and every guest was invited to take it home as a souvenir of the event.

A few weeks before the day itself, Nina wrote a letter to the people who had already been invited — especially to my relatives, most of whom had never attended a bar mitzvah — explaining its purpose. We also planned to entertain all the out-of-town guests at home on the evening before the ceremony and to hold a brunch on Sunday for everyone who was still in town. All this, of course, was in addition to the party in the basement social room of Beth Zion on Saturday evening, right after the service. We expected about one hundred and forty guests, evenly distributed between our families and our mutual close friends. I was gratified that all three of my siblings and their spouses, as well as many of their children, came from upstate New York, rural Pennsylvania, and South Carolina. They must have caught the note of urgency in my voice when I invited them, nearly a year earlier, and told them in no uncertain terms how important this occasion was. Nina's extended family also showed up in impressive strength (but I had expected that).

After the Sabbath dinner at our home, with the traditional blessing of the candles, the wine, and the bread, I passed out the *siddurs* and took everyone through it page by page, explaining just what would happen. Then I asked them to take it back with them to their hotels, glance through it again, and bring it with them to Beth Zion the next afternoon. Later, several of my relatives and non-Jewish friends told me this was the main thing that helped them feel at home. Some confessed that they had been apprehensive about getting lost in the Hebrew of a book that starts at the back.

The sun was still shining brightly as we all gathered at Beth Zion for the late afternoon Sabbath service, called *mincha*. Nicholas was in high spirits. Although we had not asked him to, he stood on the broad front steps of the Greek Revival building and welcomed the guests as they arrived. When it was time to begin the service, he climbed confidently onto the *bimah*, the raised platform at the front. The rabbi welcomed everyone and explained what a bar mitzvah is. Then Nicholas began to lead some of the prayers he had learned. I was immensely proud. Relatives and friends came forward to read portions of the Torah. My own grown children and their spouses read selections we had picked out from Albert Einstein, Saint Francis of Assisi, and Rabbi Nachman of Bratslav. At one point Nicholas led the congregation in singing the psalm "By the Rivers of Babylon" in the reggae version made popular by Jimmy Cliff in the film *The Harder They Come*. When it was time for Nicholas to deliver his D'var Torah, I stirred in my seat. I had listened to him rehearse it several times and given him some tips. I knew he was capable of presenting it clearly and with feeling. But would he do it?

He did. He even seemed to relish his moment at center stage. When he finished, the rabbi (as planned) asked him some questions, then opened the floor for questions from the congregation. "Why did Abram change his name?" someone asked. "What does the fact that Abraham is the progenitor of three faiths tell us about how they should be relating to each other today?" Nicholas seemed unfazed by any of it. Then Nina and I both spoke to him briefly. She reminded him of the long line he was joining. I told him, and the congregation, that I was glad I had learned the Yiddish word *kvell*, which expresses the special pride a parent feels for a child. I also passed on to him a verse from the Bible that had been given to me when I was about his age and was being made a part of our little Baptist congregation. They were the words, I said, of "the rabbi from Nazareth": "Let your light so shine before men that they may see your good works and glorify your Father in heaven." I had wondered how this explicit reference to my own tradition would be heard in a bar mitzvah service.

I had not asked in advance, so when I was finished I was gratified to see the rabbi smiling broadly and giving me a thumbs-up.

For many guests, the high point of the afternoon came with the procession of the Torah around the inside of the synagogue, with Nicholas, and then others, carrying the ornate old scrolls. While they wound up and down the aisles, many people reached out to touch the Torah with their prayer books, then kiss the book. Later that evening, three of my relatives said they found this the most moving part of the whole afternoon. I was puzzled at first, but now I think I know why. Almost all of them, like me, were raised in the Baptist tradition. In many Baptist churches, the only sacred object is the Bible, which occupies a central place on the pulpit in the front. In some Baptist churches there are no crosses, no statues, and no stained glass windows. Even for my relatives who had not been to church recently, and who probably rarely opened the pages of a Bible, it was still — deep in their subconscious — the holy book. Even though this "Bible," an ornately decorated and rolled scroll, did not look like the big black leather one on the pulpit, they knew full well what it was. They had seen the pictures in the Sunday school books. Besides, the one Nicholas was carrying looked like the real, original article. Whatever Baptists do not know about Jews, they do know that it was the Jews who gave us the Bible, or at least that big first part of it. Seeing a real Torah and watching Nicholas carry it made the connection for them.

For the beginning of the last part of the service (called the *havdalah*), the rabbi invited the whole congregation to gather outside on the front steps. The sun was just beginning to sink toward the horizon. Cars whirred by on Beacon Street, rushing from the center of Brookline toward Cleveland Circle. When we filed back into the synagogue, it was getting dark enough to be able to see the reflection of the candles on our fingernails, the customary Jewish way of determining if the Sabbath is indeed ending. It was time to remember the departed members of our families — Nina's parents and her brother and sister, my parents — by saying the mourners' Kaddish, then receiving the benediction.

As soon as the formal service ended, Nina's cousin Alex Hasilev, a professional musician who sings with a well-known group called the Limeliters, perched on a stool and began to lead the congregation in singing "Those Were the Days." (The Limeliters sang the famous jingle "Things Go Better with Coke," something Alex would like to forget.) I chimed in on my saxophone. People sang along happily as we did two or three more old favorites that Nina had placed at the end of the *siddur*. It was a nice touch. And it served the important secondary purpose of filling in a few minutes until the caterers, who did not work on the Sabbath, could get the food on the table and the dance band — made up of friends of ours — could start playing. There was no molded chopped liver bust, no disk jockey, and no magician.

The rabbi asked everyone to form a human energy chain for the prayer before the meal. Everyone waded into the Middle Eastern feast (kosher and vegetarian). The band played. The guests made toasts and danced. One cousin, an aspiring soprano, came to the microphone and belted out a song. The rabbi interrupted at one point to announce that the Red Sox were trouncing the Yankees in the third game of the American League East playoff at Fenway Park. Mostly, friends and family from both sides mixed amicably, although some preferred to sit with people they already knew. As the guests dribbled out I noticed the bar mitzvah boy, dressed in the best suit he had ever donned, trying out some chords on a guitar one of the musicians had allowed him to strum. His tie was a bit askew, and his *yarmulka* sat crooked on his head. Maybe he had become a man today, but to me he still looked a lot like a kid.

Psychologists correctly remind us that one reason we are moved by rites of passage, even when we are not the one undergoing the passage, is that they call to mind similar transitions in our own lives. Weddings make us think about our own wedding, either the one we had or the one we hope to have someday. Funerals remind us of our own mortality. Inevitably, Nicholas's bar mitzvah reminded me of the comparable ritual I had experienced at the same age, albeit in a different tradition. I was also thirteen at the time, growing up in Malvern, a small town in southeastern Pennsylvania. It was 1942. Years before, my grandmother had taken me to the First Baptist Church, where I attended Sunday school, joined the youth group, and, when I got a little older, faithfully attended Sunday morning services. Since my parents were not churchgoers, I was not obligated to go, so never considered it an onerous duty. If anything, it was a chance to get away, if only briefly, from the tight family circle and participate in the adult world. I also liked the music — even sang in the senior choir when I reached the proper age — and listened attentively to the sermons. Since ours was a small, impecunious congregation, our ministers were usually young men, often fresh out of seminary, energetic, and full of the latest ideas. I believe every adolescent is a secret theologian, asking the big questions before learning to stifle them in the interests of social propriety, and I was no exception.

It was the custom in that church for boys and girls at about the age of thirteen to attend a six-week pastor's class and prepare for baptism, which, in the Baptist tradition, is only permitted at the "age of consent" and is done by complete immersion in a baptismal pool placed just behind the pulpit. Six weeks of learning a few Bible stories and "what it means to be a Christian" certainly does not compare to spending three years learning Hebrew and preparing a thoughtful commentary on a Torah passage. But the ritual of baptism by immersion is immensely powerful. To believe that you are going to die and be buried with Jesus and then, like him, rise to a new life is potent stuff, even for an adult. It even has its frightening aspect, perhaps like the first time you fling yourself down a ski trail or when some people (not me) leap out of a plane to sky dive. Of course, I had been underwater many times before; I was a fair swimmer. But this was qualitatively different. You were dressed entirely in white, and you had to wade in up to your chest and place yourself in the hands of the pastor, who lowered you into the water, like lowering you into a grave, and then pulled you up again. Meanwhile, the whole congregation is gathered around the pool and singing a hymn like "Just as I Am" or "My Faith Looks Up to Thee."

It is hard to forget such an experience. Even though my theology has changed and evolved in ways my thirteen-year-old self could never have anticipated, my baptism stands out as a real *rite de passage*. Water is a symbol in almost every religion — as a cleansing power, a threat to life, a beneficent gift, or a challenging obstacle to overcome. I am glad my own "passage through Jordan" took place when I was old enough to appreciate it but young enough to feel its full impact. I understand the theological rationale of those churches that baptize babies. They claim it symbolizes the love of God that reaches out to us even before we are aware of it, and there is a point to that. But I am still grateful that I grew up in a church where what seems to some people a primitive and even laughable ritual remains. After all, to outsiders, most rituals must appear a little ridiculous. The proverbial man from Mars would surely be just as puzzled or bemused by people who kneel at a railing and nibble small wafers or who cut a small piece of skin off the penis of baby boys.

I also realize that, like many things in life, my baptism has meant different things to me as I think back to it at various stages of my life. Reading Saint Augustine taught me that it sometimes takes decades for the full significance of an experience to sink in. He wrote his *Confessions* many years after the events he recalls in it; only in retrospect does he find the presence of God in some of them. I remember trying to make a joke just after my baptism, as I was drying off and putting on my clothes with the help of the deacons. I said something about not needing a bath that night. They did not laugh. But they did not scowl either. They knew, I think, that a thirteen-year-old can only appreciate a fraction of what the experience would mean in years to come.

I am sure the same thing will be true for Nicholas. He made a little joke at the beginning of his D'var Torah. He got involved in plucking a guitar when he might have been saying farewell to the guests. But he will never forget that, at one time in his life, family and friends flew across an ocean and traveled across a continent to be with him the first time he was called to the Torah. He will not forget that we all listened while he continued the timeless Jewish tradition of interpreting and reinterpreting what those enigmatic letters say. He will remember that he was not only welcomed into one of the oldest continuing human communities in the world but was expected to take some responsibility for its health and nurturing. These things will mean something different when he is twenty-five, and fifty and seventy-five. Some of it may dim in his memory; some may become more vivid. But what happened at Temple Beth Zion on 6 Heshvan 5760 will be a part of him forever.

Afterword

In the Court of the Gentiles

A FEW YEARS AGO, I borrowed a video for a course I was teaching that showed a computer-generated full-color reconstruction of the ancient Temple of Herod in Jerusalem. Based on the latest archaeological evidence, it was a remarkable feat. With just a tad of suspension of belief, my students and I could approach the towering stone walls, just as thousands of pilgrims and visitors, including Jesus, might have in the first century c.e. We could walk past what is now called Robinson's Arch, pass through the Huldah Gate, then pause in awe as the intricate facade of the central edifice came into view. But just as we paused it occurred to me that at that moment I was standing, virtually if not quite literally, in the Court of the Gentiles. After that, much of the rest of the fascinating visual reconstruction was lost on me. I lingered in the Court of the Gentiles. I rather liked it there.

After two thousand years of history and my fifteen years of marriage to a Jewish wife, I am still in the Court of the Gentiles. I still like it here. I have no intention of trying to enter the inner courtyard, where only male Jews are permitted. But I also have no inclination, having trod on the holy ground, to leave and go somewhere else. I appreciate the fact that many of the psalms refer to the Temple, not just as a place to worship or visit, but as a "dwelling place." That suits me. I prefer its in-between, fluid, somewhat elusive character. I would not like a dwelling place that is too definitively demarcated. True, high stone walls surrounded the old Court of the Gentiles. But its gates opened on all sides, and I suspect no one paid much attention to who strolled in and out. That is the kind of space I value.

I realize full well, however, that although I am still in the Court of the Gentiles, the court itself is not the same. Both in stone and in metaphor, it is a different place. It is different because as the landscape around a location changes, the location itself changes as well. And the world around the Court of the Gentiles has shifted. When the Romans razed the Temple in 70 C.E., they also, of course, destroyed the Court of the Gentiles. Then the Jewish people, deprived of their central symbol and driven into exile, responded with dazzling spiritual creativity. They created an intangible Temple positioned within the ongoing life and prayers of the people, a Temple that could never be destroyed as long as this people survived. But if a spiritual Temple still exists, then presumably the Court of the Gentiles, with the generous space it allotted to people like me, still exists as well. But just where, in this eternal Temple, is the Court of the Gentiles now?

During the twenty centuries that have passed since the stone court was demolished by the legions, Jews have answered this question in many different ways. A final and definitive response has never been given, and probably never will. Jews have always insisted that they are different. There is "us" and there is "them." That much is clear, but not much else. The Talmud is full of disputes about where the borders should run. Should Jews patronize a Roman bath that displays a statue of a goddess? If a pagan temple shares a wall with a synagogue and the wall falls down, should the Jews rebuild it, and thus presumably provide shelter and indirect support for the worship of idols? The debates go on and on. Nothing much changed, in this regard at least, when Israel was founded in 1948 or when the Israelis occupied the Temple Mount at the conclusion of the 1967 war.

That was an ambiguous victory. After 1967, the huge structure on which the Temple — and the Court of the Gentiles — had stood was back in Jewish hands. But the area was now surmounted by the glistening golden Dome of the Rock, a site sacred to Islam. In the interest of civil peace, the Israeli authorities turned the administration of this area over to the city's Muslims and enforced a prohibition against Jews praying there. Orthodox Jews, in any case, are forbidden to pray there because in order to do so, they might inadvertently step on the site of the Holy of Holies, where only the high priest could enter. I have visited the Dome of the Rock, one of the most dazzling religious buildings I have ever seen, and since no one has ever warned me not to pray in or near it, I once did (albeit silently and standing, not moving my lips).

But none of this answers the question: Where, for Jews, is the Court of the Gentiles today? Exactly where do we gentiles stand in the Jewish religious view of the world? I do not expect a single answer to this question. Jews have no pope to issue teachings applicable to all of Judaism. Consequently, I have looked at it from the other side. How do gentiles define their relationship to Jews? To this I regret to say there have also been many varied answers, and from the earliest decades of Christianity most of them have been negative. Depending on time and circumstance, various gentile nations have ignored, expelled, forcibly converted, married, taxed, segregated, murdered, caricatured, made friends with, and lived next door to Jews. There is no Court of the Jews in the various temples of the gentile faiths. Muslims come closest to having one. They define Jews, along with themselves and Christians, as "people of the Book." But Christianity has no such category. Of course neither does Buddhism nor Shinto nor many other traditions. But that is understandable; until quite recently Jews were not part of the experience of these religions as they were, from the beginning, for Christians.

The way different faiths define their relationship to others, including Judaism, is not fixed. It changes from time to time, and sometimes a particular event can change the whole focus. I think just such an event took place in March 2000 when a frail, bent old man, clothed in white vestments, shuffled painfully across the rough cobblestones of Jerusalem, prayed quietly at the Wall, and then placed a scrap of paper with his prayer into one of the cracks that have received so many thousands of prayers for so many years. The pope's simple, silent gesture said more than a thousand encyclicals or a million words. I am not sure what or how much it said to Jews. But to hundreds of millions of Christians — and I think many others around the world — it said something like this: whatever our attitude toward the Jews has been in times past, from now on it will be one of profound respect. The pope, in effect, created a symbolic place of esteem and affinity for Jews in the Christian worldview, a sort of Court of the Jews. And he did so in a display, not of pomp and power, but of weakness and vulnerability. I do not think the importance of his gesture should be underestimated.

But the pattern of the pope's movements on that day also demonstrated something else. Just before he prayed at the Wall, he had visited the Dome of the Rock. Whether he prayed there or not, no one knows for sure. But, mystic that he is at heart, I believe he did, maybe as I did, without moving his lips. Then, after he prayed at the Wall, he stopped at the Church of the Holy Sepulcher, where he led an ecumenical Christian prayer service. Thus, within one short hour, the bent old man in white indicated that there is an ineradicable triangularity involved. He demonstrated that Jewish-Christian relations will mean very little unless they include Muslims. I would only add that once that principle is established, we must go on to quadrangles, pentagons, and hexagons. The other faiths must also have a place at the table. The much-touted Jewish-Christian dialogue cannot continue as a duet. It must become a trio, a quartet, and eventually a whole choir. This is not to say that as Christians and as Jews we do not have our own special issues. We do. So do Jews and Muslims, and so do Hindus and Muslims; the list could go on. But as Jews and Christians, we can no longer engage in dialogue as though we were the only performers on the stage.

One of the most attractive features of the original Court of the Gentiles is that the Jews made no distinctions among "the nations." We were all "them." From one perspective this may seem narrow, but from another it makes the Court of the Gentiles a wonderfully open space. There were, of course, no Muslims when it still existed in stone, and not many Christians (and most of them were Jews). But there were Hindus and there were Buddhists even then. It is tempting to fantasize about a dusty camel caravan of traders arriving in Jerusalem in those days, perhaps from India or China. They would surely have been welcome in the Court of the Gentiles.

As I write these concluding lines, I have recently returned from taking part in a modern scenario in Jerusalem that was similar, but not quite the same, as this fantasy. This time I joined six other teachers at what used to be a monastery only a few hundred yards from the Old City and, therefore, not that far from where the Court of the Gentiles once stood. My colleagues included two rabbis, a Jesuit scholar, a Hindu, a Buddhist, and a Muslim. Our caravans gathered in stifling 100-degree-plus heat under the auspices of something called the Elijah School, where we spent three weeks teaching students from several countries who wanted to explore the frontiers of interfaith relations today. Like previous encounters of this sort, the experience was both rewarding and difficult. Such a multifaith meeting inevitably raises questions that rarely come up when representatives of only two or even three traditions meet. There is, of course, also value in one-on-one dialogues. For example, when I, as a Christian, speak with Muslims, I get a sense of what Jews must feel about the claim Christians have often made, that we have absorbed and gone beyond them, for this is just what Muslims often say about us. I also realize, in conversations with Muslims, that Christianity has not yet developed a way to appreciate what I call postcanonical prophets, those like Muhammad, who arrived after the Bible was written. But I have also noticed that when the three "Abrahamic" faiths — Judaism, Christianity, and Islam — meet, they often tend to underline their common "monotheism." This, however, opens a gulf between us and hundreds of millions of Buddhists and Hindus. Conversations with these Asian faiths, on the other hand, tend to evoke from Christians their conviction, awkwardly formulated in the idea of the Trinity, that the one God has many faces. This, in turn, sometimes convinces Jews and Muslims that, as they suspected all along, Christians are not really monotheists after all. And so it goes. Perhaps what we need now are not just duets or quartets but a full oratorio that includes all these plus a complete orchestra and a mighty chorus, joining not just as background, but as full-voiced participants.

Nevertheless, I am still drawn to the idea of the Court of the Gentiles. It symbolizes something I wish every religion had. It has three essential components. First, it stands near, but separate from, a central sanctuary that is highly particular in its rites and its vision, a place that can make real sense only to those who share in its history. But its second component, the court itself, is a wide-open space, still sacred but in a different way, in which all the children of God can enter, mix with one another, and benefit in whatever way they can from its atmosphere. Third, there is the whole outside world, acknowledged as outside, but the gates are wide open. This three-tiered model of how a specific religious tradition presents itself — a central sanctuary, a spacious surrounding court, and an openness to the world — is one we especially need in our new epoch of global religious heterogeneity.

I started this book by saying that my personal gateway into the Court of the Gentiles and into the abundant legacy of the Jewish tradition began when I married a Jewish woman. I know I will never be able to appreciate that legacy in all its fullness. As the psalm puts it, "My cup runneth over." Like the gentile woman Ruth's famous words, "Whither thou goest, I will go," I have faithfully journeyed with my Jewish partner, and I have become, insofar as I could, a part of her people. Such a marriage can be a demanding and rewarding crash course in interfaith relations for both parties. It has been for us. But such a marriage is not for everyone. (Indeed, marriage itself is not for everyone.) Still, you do not have to be married to a Jew to enjoy the full benefits of the Court of the Gentiles. Its many gates remain open, and the traffic is heavy. Also, as we all speed into a truly global world, and religions that used to be distant phantoms are now neighbors, the spiritual open space symbolized by the Court of the Gentiles has become an ever livelier place. I like dwelling in it. I am here to stay.

Notes

Introduction

1. The issue of interfaith marriage seems to have opened a rift between the rabbis and Jewish officials on the one side and an increasing number of Jewish people on the other. In September 2000 the American Jewish Committee took a survey that found that most American Jews now accept marriages between Jews and non-Jews, even though most rabbis, both Orthodox and otherwise, oppose them. Forty percent of the respondents said they were neutral about such marriages, while 16 percent viewed them as "a good thing." Twelve percent said they strongly disapproved of interfaith marriages. As recently as 1990, however, a mail survey of 2,170 rabbis, synagogue presidents, Jewish agency officials, and Jewish laypeople asked what they would do if they were a rabbi asked to marry an interfaith couple. Sixty-two percent said they would not officiate. See Gustav Niebuhr, "Marriage Issue Splits Jews, Poll Finds," *New York Times,* October 31, 2000, page A18.

2. One excellent example of such a book is *Christianity in Jewish Terms,* edited by Tikva Frymer-Kensky, David Novak, Peter Ochs, David Fax Sandmel, and Michael A. Singer (Boulder, Colo.: Westview Press, 2000).

3. See Arthur Green, *The Language of Truth: The Torah Commentary of the Sefat Emet* (Philadelphia: Jewish Publication Society, 5759/1998). In the venerable Jewish tradition of commentary on commentary, this volume includes both the wisdom of the revered Rabbi Yehudah Leib Alter of Ger and thoughtful comments on his comments by Rabbi Green. I have relied on it heavily throughout this book (pp. 341, 342).

1. A Cathedral in Time

1. See Chapters 10 and 11 for a further discussion of the significance of "the land" in Jewish thought.

2. The information in the following paragraph is based on my notes from an unusually informative lecture, "First Century Jews, Christians, and the Sabbath," given by Professor Weiss on November 20, 1999, in the Early Jewish-Christian Relations Section at the Annual Meeting of the American Academy of Religion in Boston.

3. See especially Gershom Scholem, *The Messianic Idea in Judaism and Other Essays on Jewish Spirituality* (New York: Schocken Books, 1971) and *Major Trends in Jewish Mysticism* (New York: Schocken Books, 1995).

4. Quoted in Karen Armstrong, *Jerusalem: One City, Three Faiths* (New York, 1997), p. 336.

5. See also Armstrong's fine description of Luria's interpretation of the Sabbath, ibid, p. 338.

2. Starting Over at the Right Time of Year

1. As in so many other matters, there is much disagreement among Jews about how to spell the holidays in transliteration, and also, as in many other matters, many variant spellings flourish. In general, I have stayed with the spellings found in Michael Strassfeld's very useful *Jewish Holidays: A Guide and Commentary* (New York: Harper and Row, 1985).

2. Rudolf Otto, *The Idea of the Holy*, trans. John W. Harvey (New York: Oxford University Press, 1958).

3. Strassfeld, *Jewish Holidays*, p. 104.

4. One can find this bit of creative exegesis, written by the late Walter Russell Bowie, in Volume I of *The Interpreter's Bible* (New York: Abingdon-Cokesbury Press, 1952), p. 642.

5. Søren Kierkegaard, *Fear and Trembling* (Princeton, N.J.: Princeton University Press, 1941).

6. Quoted from Kierkegaard's *Point of View of My Work as an Author* in Claude Welch, *Protestant Thought in the Nineteenth Century*, Vol. I (New Haven: Yale University Press, 1972), p. 295.

7. See Emmanuel Levinas, *Collected Philosophical Papers*, trans. Alphonso Liugis (Pittsburgh: Duquesne University Press, 1998), and *Nine Talmudic Readings* (Bloomington: University of Indiana Press, 1990).

8. Green, *Language of Truth*, pp. 344, 345.

3. Closing the Big Book

1. *High Holiday Prayer Book*, compiled by Rabbi Morris Silverman (Hartford: Prayer Book Press, 1948), pp. 222–24.

2. Strassfeld, *Jewish Holidays*, p. 105.

3. Irving Greenberg, *The Jewish Way: Living the Holidays* (New York: Summit Books, 1988), p. 213.

4. Ibid., pp. 207–8.

5. See Arthur Green, *These Are the Words: A Vocabulary of Jewish Spiritual Life* (Woodstock, Vt.: Jewish Lights Publishing, 1999), p. 139.

6. There is a much-discussed text in the Bible, Genesis 5:1, which says that in the time of Noah, "The Lord saw how great was man's wickedness on earth, and how every plan devised by his mind was nothing but evil all the time." *The JPS Torah Commentary* section on this passage, however, states that it is not about the eternal human condition but God's "judgement on the moral state of man at that specific time." New York: The Jewish Publication Society, 5749/1989, p. 47.

7. Also, for centuries Christian theologians were misled by what amounts to a mistranslation by Saint Jerome in his Latin translation of the original Greek version of Saint Paul's Epistle to the Romans. Whereas the Greek text states that we have all sinned *since* Adam, Saint Jerome made it clear we all sinned *in* Adam. There is quite a difference.

8. In Strassfeld, *Jewish Holidays*, p. 120.

9. Herman Melville, *Moby-Dick; or, The Whale* (Chicago: Encyclopaedia Britannica, 1952), p. 419.

4. The Strength of Fragility

1. Strassfeld, *Jewish Holidays*, pp. 125f.

2. Lynn White, Jr., "The Historical Roots of Our Ecological Crisis," *Science* 155 (March 10, 1967), pp. 1203f. The essay has been reprinted numerous times since.

3. Theodore Hiebert, "The Human Vocation: Origins and Transformations in Christian Tradition," in Dieter T. Hessel and Rosemary Radford Ruether, *Christianity and Ecology* (Cambridge: Harvard University Press, 2000), pp. 135f.

4. Ibid., p. 139. Hiebert also contends that the word used in the second creation account to describe the role God prescribes for man's relation to the soil is not "to subdue" but *'abad,* which he thinks means "to serve." But other scholars say *'abad* can have many different meanings and Hiebert may be reading too much into it.

5. Ibid., p. 141.

6. See Ruether's essay "Ecofeminism: The Challenge to Theology" in *Christianity and Ecology*, pp. 97f. See also Ivonne Gebara, *Teologia a Ritmo de Mujer* (Madrid: San Pablo, 1995).

7. Ruether, "Ecofeminism," p. 108.

5. Gamboling with God

1. Quoted in David Hartman, *A Heart of Many Rooms: Celebrating the Many Voices Within Judaism* (Woodstock, Vt.: Jewish Lights Publishing, 1999), p. 53.

2. For my information on the "dual Torah" I have relied heavily on Jacob Neusner's chapter on "Judaism" in Arvind Sharma, ed., *Our Religions* (San Francisco: Harper, 1993), pp. 319f.

3. Jacob Timerman, *Prisoner Without a Name, Cell Without a Number* (New York: Vintage Books, 1981).

4. I say "humanity" here rather than the Israelites alone because there is a Jewish *midrash* that says God gave the Torah to all the people at the same time, but only the Israelites accepted it.
5. Hartman, *Heart of Many Rooms*, p. 45.
6. Ibid., p. 49.
7. Ibid., p. 50.
8. Ibid., p. 39.
9. Paul Tillich, *A History of Christian Thought*, ed. Carl E. Braaten (New York: Simon and Schuster, 1968), pp. 46, 47.
10. See his three epoch-making books: *Paul and Palestinian Judaism* (Philadelphia: Fortress Press, 1977); *Paul, the Law, and the Jewish People* (Philadelphia: Fortress Press, 1983); and *Jesus and Judaism* (Philadelphia: Fortress Press, 1985).
11. Terence Donaldson, *Paul and the Gentiles: Remapping the Apostle's World* (Minneapolis: Fortress Press, 1997). I am grateful for this thoughtful book and have used it extensively in this discussion of Paul.

6. December Madness

1. Leslie Kaufman, "On Web, Season's Greetings Are Sent in One Size Fits All," *New York Times*, Dec. 7, 1999, p. 1.
2. Strassfeld, *Jewish Holidays*, p. 167.
3. Ibid.
4. Ibid.
5. Note the compact disk *Canticles of Ecstasy*, a collection of Hildegard's medieval music performed by Sequentia, a women's vocal ensemble directed by Barbara Thornton and accompanied by medieval fiddle and medieval harp. Deutsche Harmonia Mundi (New York: BMG Music, 1994).
6. University of St. Thomas, Proceedings of the Center for Jewish Christian Learning, 1991 Lecture Series, Vol. 6, Spring 1991, p. 35.
7. Kaufman, "On Web," p. 1.
8. Quoted in Karal Ann Marling, *Merry Christmas: Celebrating America's Greatest Holiday* (Cambridge, Mass.: Harvard University Press, 2000), pp. 160–61.

7. Funny Masks and Texts of Terror

1. The rabbi in question is Moshe Waldoks, who, among his many accomplishments, is the editor, with William Novak, of *The Big Book of Jewish Humor* (New York: HarperCollins, 1981). This could explain why his ensemble may have been a bit more frolicsome than that of some other rabbis.
2. René Girard, *Violence and the Sacred* (Baltimore: Johns Hopkins Press, 1972).
3. Ze'ev Chafets, "Dump Shas Now!" *Jerusalem Report*, April 10, 2000, p. 20. A few months later, in another televised sermon, the same rabbi referred to the Palestinians as "snakes."

4. A. David Napier, *Masks, Transformation, and Paradox* (Berkeley: University of California Press, 1986), pp. xv, xvi.

8. A Night Different from All Others

1. See Gayraud S. Wilmore, *Black Radicalism and Black Religion* (Maryknoll, N.Y.: Orbis Books, 1973), especially ch. 2.
2. New York: The Free Press, 2000, p. 70.
3. Rabbi Liebowitz's ideas are explicated in David Hartman, *A Heart of Many Rooms* (Woodstock, Vt.: Jewish Lights Publishing, 1999), p. 288.
4. The words Jesus uttered were "This bread is my body" and "This wine is my blood." Christians have argued for centuries over exactly what he meant. At a minimum, he probably wanted to link his entire life, his "flesh-and-blood" and not just his words to his disciples, and through them to those who come later. See Chapter 1 for my remarks about the Christian Eucharist, which grew out of this "Last Supper."
5. I look somewhat more positively on the Jewish-Christian Seders that have begun to appear in the past few years, in which a Jewish congregation cooperates with a Christian congregation in holding an "interfaith" Seder. Even in this instance, however, I believe Christians should approach the Seder with a careful respect for its Jewish meaning.
6. See the informative discussion of this issue in Donald Harman Akenson, *Saint Paul — A Skeleton Key to the Historical Jesus* (Montreal: McGill-Queen's University Press, 2000), pp. 35, 36.
7. Reinhold Niebuhr, *The Nature and Destiny of Man: A Christian Interpretation* (New York: Scribner's, 1951), Vol. II, part 1. The term Niebuhr actually uses in his distinction between cultures that "do expect" or "not not expect" is "Christ." But the word "Christ," though it is now often thought of as part of Jesus' name, is simply an English rendition of the Greek *christos*, which means "messiah" or "anointed one."
8. The importance of the prophets in both Judaism and Christianity inevitably raises the question of the religious significance of Mohamet for Jews and Christians. Muslims accept Abraham, Moses, and Jesus as prophets, but insist that Mohamet was also a prophet sent by the one God. This poses an urgent theological question that, in our present pluralistic religious world, both Jews and Christians must address. See L. E. Goodman, *The God of Abraham* (New York: Oxford University Press, 1996).
9. Gershom Scholem, *The Messianic Idea in Judaism* (New York: Schocken Books, 1971), p. 48.
10. Ibid.
11. Elsewhere in this book I show why even Trinitarian language about God is not as foreign to all Jewish usages as many Jews and Christians have claimed. See Chapter 5.
12. Irving Greenberg, *The Jewish Way* (New York: Summit Books, 1988), Ch. 10. See also Eva Fleishner, ed., *Auschwitz: Beginning of a New Era?* (New York: KTAV, 1977).

9. After All the Apologies

1. Elie Wiesel, *Legends of Our Time* (New York: Holt, Rinehart and Winston, 1968), p. 56.
2. Irving Greenberg, *The Jewish Way* (New York: Summit Books, 1988), pp. 315–16.
3. Strassfeld, *Jewish Holidays*, p. 57.
4. Volume 7, *The Catholic Encyclopedia* (Nashville: Thomas Nelson, originally published in 1913).
5. Ibid., p. 30.
6. Volume 10, *New Catholic Encyclopedia* (New York: McGraw-Hill, 1967), p. 30.
7. Quoted by James W. Douglass, *The Non-Violent Cross: A Theology of Revolution and Peace* (New York: Macmillan, 1968), p. xvii.
8. Just as I was writing this chapter, I stumbled onto a vestige of the Reproaches still being used in a Roman Catholic church on Cape Cod. In a pamphlet entitled "The Way of the Cross," published by the Liturgical Press in Collegeville, Minnesota, in 1978, the portion beginning, "My people, what have I done to you" and continuing with "I brought you out of Egypt, and you have led me to the gibbet of the cross," appears on page 27 as a meditation for the Ninth Station of the Cross ("Jesus Falls a Third Time").
9. Examples of such statements include the document issued in 1965 by the Second Vatican Council entitled *Nostra Aetate;* the *Resolution on Anti-Semitism* made in 1961 by the Third Assembly of the World Council of Churches; the one entitled "The Christian Church and the Jewish People," adopted by the Faith and Order Commission of the World Council of Churches in 1966; and the "Declaration of the Evangelical Lutheran Church in America to the Jewish Community," adopted in April 1994.
10. I am grateful to my Harvard colleague Professor Kevin Madigan for his thoughtful comparison of the Vatican statement with that of the French bishops given during a meeting of the Religion, Holocaust and Genocide Group at the American Academy of Religion on November 22, 1999.
11. For a sweeping historical account of how the Catholic Church's attitude toward Jews has shaped so much else in its life, including its claim to unique authority over all Christians, see James Carroll, *Constantine's Sword: The Church and the Jews* (Boston: Houghton Mifflin, 2001).
12. I am grateful to my friend and colleague Hillel Levine for allowing me to consult his unpublished article on Deggendorf.
13. Grover A. Zinn, "History and Interpretation: 'Hebrew Truth,' Judaism, and the Victorine Exegetical Tradition," in *Jews and Christians*, ed. James H. Charlesworth (New York: Crossroads, 1990), pp. 100f.
14. Rosemary Ruether, *Faith and Fratricide: The Theological Roots of Anti-Semitism* (New York: Seabury Press, 1974).
15. Van Buren has published a series of three volumes on this issue with the collective title *A Theology of Jewish-Christian Reality:* Vol. I, *Discerning the Way* (1980); Vol. II, *A Christian Theology of the People of Israel* (1983); Vol. III,

Christ in Context (New York: Harper and Row, 1988). Although I affirm his idea of the extension of the covenant to the Gentiles, I do not agree with the way he applies his theological formula to the state of Israel, since he seems to imply that Israel should become a Torah state and apparently sees little grounds for sharing the land with the Palestinians. See the thoughtful critique of Van Buren in Rosemary Ruether's essay "The Holocaust" in Gregory Baum, ed., *The Twentieth Century: A Theological Overview* (Maryknoll, N.Y.: Orbis Books, 1999), pp. 76–90.

16. In George B. Grose and Benjamin J. Hubbard, eds., *The Abraham Connection: A Jew, Christian and Muslim in Dialogue* (Notre Dame, Ind.: Cross Cultural Publications, n.d.), p. 167.

17. Richard L. Rubenstein, *After Auschwitz* (Indianapolis: Bobbs-Merrill, 1966).

18. Greenberg, *Jewish Way*, p. 319.

19. Peter Novick, *The Holocaust in American Life* (Boston: Houghton Mifflin, 1999).

20. Judith H. Dobrzynski, "Giuliani Won't Move on Art Show," *New York Times*, March 10, 2000, p. 19.

21. Michael Dintenfass, "Truth's Other: Ethics, the History of the Holocaust, and Historiographical Theory After the Linguistic Turn," *History and Theory*, Vol. 39 (1), 2000, p. 1.

22. John Cornwell, *Hitler's Pope — The Secret History of Pius XII* (New York: Viking Press, 1999), presents a sweeping indictment of Pius XII, contrasting him unfavorably with his predecessor Pius XI and suggesting that his near-obsession to centralize all authority in the church in the papacy and in his own person distorted his views on everything else. However, in October 2000, a team of Catholic and Jewish historians reported that after investigating the available documents, they were unable to come to a clear decision about the pope's culpability. They also complained that some of the Vatican archives they wanted to examine have not yet been made available to scholars and requested that they be opened. See "Jewish and Catholic Scholars Seek Pius XII's Files," *New York Times*, Oct. 27, 2000.

23. Suki John, "Making the Holocaust Real for Inner-City Youths," *New York Times*, Sept. 5, 1999, Arts and Entertainment Section, p. 28.

24. Harvey Cox, *The Secular City* (New York: Doubleday, 1965).

25. Greenberg, *Jewish Way*, p. 320.

10. The Meaning of the Land

1. See Amos Elon, *Herzl* (New York: Holt, Rinehart and Winston, 1975).

2. Ibid., p. 197.

3. For the most comprehensive treatment of the history of this term and its complexity, see Robert L. Wilken, *The Land Called Holy* (New Haven: Yale University Press, 1992).

4. Josef Yerushalmi, *Zakhor: Jewish History and Memory* (Seattle: University of Washington Press, 1982). See also Elisheva Carlebach, John Efron, and David Myers, eds., *Jewish History and Jewish Memory* (Hanover, N.H.: University

Press of New England for Brandeis University Press, 1998). This is an excellent collection of essays on Yerushalmi's thought.

5. William E. Blackstone, *Jesus Is Coming* (first ed. 1878; third ed., Chicago: Fleming H. Revell, 1908).

6. Quoted in Paul C. Merkeley, *The Politics of Christian Zionism 1891–1948* (London: Frank Cass, 1998), p. 68.

7. Ibid., p. 69.

8. Quoted in ibid., p. 68. The entire "Blackstone Memorial" is reprinted in *Christian Protagonists for Jewish Restoration* (New York: Arno Press, 1977), pp. 1–23, under the title "Palestine for the Jews."

9. Quoted from Clark Clifford, *Counsel to the President* (New York: Random House, 1991), p. 8 in Merkeley, *Politics of Christian Zionism*, p. 160.

10. For an account of Truman's friendship with Jacobson, see Merkeley, *Politics of Christian Zionism*, pp. 180–91.

11. Lou Cannon, *President Reagan, The Role of a Lifetime* (New York: Simon and Schuster, 1991), p. 288.

12. Ibid., p. 289.

13. William A. Orme, Jr., "Succoth in Israel, and Here Come the Evangelicals," *New York Times International*, Sept. 29, 1999, p. 6.

14. Ibid.

15. Arthur Green, *These Are the Words* (Woodstock, Vt.: Jewish Lights Publishing, 1999), pp. 220, 221.

11. "Next Year in Jerusalem"

1. The text was originally part of Bernard's *De Contemptu Mundi* ("On Contempt for the World"). It was on it that John Mason Neale based his well-known hymn "Jerusalem the Golden."

2. Arthur Green, *The Language of Truth* (Philadelphia: Jewish Publication Society, 1998), p. 100.

3. Peggy Rosenthal, *The Poets' Jesus: Representations at the End of a Millennium* (New York: Oxford University Press, 2000), p. 113.

4. Peter Berger, *The Homeless Mind: Modernization and Consciousness* (New York: Random House, 1973), p. 94.

5. Quoted in Josef Yerushalmi, *Zakhor* (Seattle: University of Washington Press, 1996), p. xi.

6. Charles Maier, "Consigning the Twentieth Century to History: Alternative Narratives for the Modern Era," *American Historical Review*, Vol. 3, June 2000.

7. For a charming and well-informed guide to these and many more Jerusalem sights, see *Jerusalem Walks*, by Nitza Rosovsky (New York: Henry Holt, 1981).

8. See Kati Marton, *A Death in Jerusalem* (New York: Pantheon, 1994), for a troubling but highly readable account of the stormy and violent history of the city before independence.

9. See Martin Gilbert, *Jerusalem in the Twentieth Century* (New York: John Wiley, 1996). His references to terrorism are scattered throughout the book.

10. Ibid.
11. Quoted in Gilbert, *Jerusalem*, p. 331.
12. London: Lamp Press, 1989.

12. Death Among the Jews

1. Quoted in Wayne Dosick, *Living Judaism* (New York: HarperCollins, 1995), p. 314.
2. *Jewish Way*, p. 184.
3. Nicolas Berdyaev, *The Destiny of Man* (London: Geoffrey Bles, 1937), p. 277.
4. Michael Lerner, *Jewish Renewal: A Path to Healing and Transformation* (New York: Putnam's, 1994), p. 67.
5. Etty Hillesum, *An Interrupted Life* (New York: Henry Holt, 1996).

13. Lady Sings the Blues

1. C.T.R. Hayward, *The Jewish Temple: A Non-Biblical Sourcebook* (London: Routledge, 1996).
2. Amos Elon, *Jerusalem: City of Mirrors* (Boston: Little Brown, 1989), pp. 97f.
3. Ibid., p. 101.
4. Timothy W. Ryback, *The Last Survivor* (New York: Pantheon, 1999).
5. Quoted in Gerald Early, "Devil in a Blue Dress," *Books and Culture: A Christian Review*, Vol. 5, No. 5, Sept./Oct. 1999, p. 12.

14. Under and After the Canopy

1. It is my wife, Nina, who originally thought of this fourfold typology of mixed marriages. It is not the only idea I have adopted from her in this chapter and in this book.
2. Anita Diamant, *The New Jewish Wedding* (New York: Summit Books, 1985), p. 36.
3. I will not at this point comment on the dispute among Jews today about the status of the child of a Jewish father and a non-Jewish mother. I have my own views on this matter, but it seems to me a good example of something Jews should settle among themselves.
4. Wayne Dosick, *Living Judaism* (San Francisco: Harper, 1995), p. 296.
5. *Ethnicity and Family Therapy* (New York: Guilford Press, 1996), p. 613.

Bibliography

Akenson, Donald Harman. *Saint Paul: A Skeleton Key to the Historical Jesus* (Montreal: McGill-Queen's University Press: 2000). An immensely informative book that places Jesus within the various Jewish currents of his day.

Armstrong, Karen. *Jerusalem: One City, Three Faiths* (New York: Knopf, 1996).

Baum, Gregory, ed. *The Twentieth Century: A Theological Overview* (Maryknoll, N.Y.: Orbis Books, 1999).

Berdyaev, Nicolas. *The Destiny of Man* (London: Geoffrey Bles, 1937).

Berger, Peter. *The Homeless Mind: Modernization and Consciousness* (New York: Random House, 1973).

Blackstone, William E. *Jesus Is Coming* (1st ed., 1878; Boston: Little, Brown, 1989). Now a curiosity, this book was a best-seller in its time and an important text in the development of Christian Zionism. Valuable discussions on the pivotal thought of Josef Yerushalmi.

Cannon, Lou. *President Reagan, The Role of a Lifetime* (New York: Simon and Schuster, 1991).

Carlebach, Elisheva, John Efron and David Myers, eds. *Jewish History and Jewish Memory* (Hanover, N.H.: University Press of New England for Brandeis University Press, 1998).

Carroll, James. *Constantine's Sword: The Church and the Jews* (Boston: Houghton Mifflin, 2001).

Catholic Encyclopedia, The, Vol. 7 (Nashville: Thomas Nelson: 1913).

Chafets, Ze'ev. "Dump Shas Now!," *Jerusalem Report*, April 10, 2000.

Charlesworth, James H. *Jews and Christians* (New York: Crossroads, 1990).

Clifford, Clark. *Counsel to the President* (New York: Random House, 1991).

Cornwell, John. *Hitler's Pope: The Secret History of Pius XII* (New York: Viking Press, 1999).

Diamant, Anita. *The New Jewish Wedding* (New York: Summit Books, 1985).

Dintenfass, Michael. "Truth's Other: Ethics, the History of the Holocaust, and

Historiographical Theory After the Linguistic Turn," *History and Theory*, Vol. 39 (1), 2000.

Dobrzynski, Judith H. "Giuliani Won't Move on Art Show," *New York Times*, March 10, 2000.

Donaldson, Terence. *Paul and the Gentiles: Remapping the Apostle's World* (Minneapolis: Fortress Press, 1997). Sets a new tone in the study of Saint Paul and the earliest relationships between Jews and Christians.

Dosick, Wayne. *Living Judaism* (New York: HarperCollins, 1995).

Douglass, James W. *The Non-Violent Cross: A Theology of Revolution and Peace* (New York: Macmillan, 1968).

Early, Gerald. "Devil in a Blue Dress," in *Books and Culture: A Christian Review*, Vol. 5 (5,) Sept./Oct. 1999.

Elon, Amos. *Herzl* (New York: Holt, Rinehart and Winston, 1975). An absorbing biography of the colorful founder of political Zionism.

Fleishner, Eva, ed. *Auschwitz: Beginning of a New Era?* (New York: KTAV, 1977).

Frymer-Kensky, Tikva, David Novak, Peter Ochs, David Fax Sandmel, and Michael A. Singer, eds. *Christianity in Jewish Terms* (Boulder: Westview Press, 2000).

Gilbert, Martin. *Jerusalem in the Twentieth Century* (New York: John Wiley, 1996).

Girard, René. *Violence and the Sacred* (Baltimore: Johns Hopkins Press, 1972).

Goodman, L. E. *The God of Abraham* (New York: Oxford University Press, 1996).

Green, Arthur. *The Language of Truth: The Torah Commentary of the Sefat Emet* (Philadelphia: Jewish Publication Society, 5759/1998). This book stands in the old Jewish tradition of commentary on commentary. It includes both the wisdom of the revered Rabbi Yehudah Leib Alter of Ger, and thoughtful comments on his comments by Rabbi Green. It is among other things, a wonderful commentary on the Jewish holidays.

Greenberg, Irving. *The Jewish Way: Living the Holidays* (New York: Summit Books, 1988). This was the most useful and one of the most readable of all the sources I utilized in writing this book. Rabbi Greenberg is also one of the most active participants in the Jewish-Christian dialogue.

Grose, George B., and Benjamin J. Hubbard, eds. *The Abraham Connection: A Jew, Christian and Muslim in Dialogue* (Notre Dame, Ind.: Cross Cultural Publications, n.d.).

Hartman, David. *A Heart of Many Rooms: Celebrating the Many Voices Within Judaism* (Woodstock, Vt.: Jewish Lights Publishing, 1999).

Hiebert, Theodore. "The Human Vocation: Origins and Transformations in Christian Tradition," in *Christianity and Ecology*, ed. Rosemary Ruether and Dieter Hessel (Cambridge, Mass.: Harvard University Press, 2000).

Hillesum, Etty. *An Interrupted Life* (New York: Henry Holt, 1996).

Horsley, Richard, and James Tracy, eds. *Christmas Unwrapped: Consumerism, Christ and Culture* (Harrisburg, Pa.: Trinity Press International, 2001).

John, Suki. "Making the Holocaust Real for Inner-City Youths," *New York Times*, Sept. 5, 1999.

Kaufman, Leslie. "On Web, Season's Greetings Are Sent in One Size Fits All," *New York Times*, Dec. 7, 1999.

Kierkegaard, Søren. *Fear and Trembling* (Princeton, N.J.: Princeton University Press, 1941).

Lerner, Michael. *Jewish Renewal: A Path to Healing and Transformation* (New York: Putnam's, 1994).

Levinas, Emmanuel. *Collected Philosophical Papers*, trans. Alphonso Liugis (Pittsburgh: Duquesne University Press, 1998). The profound and original insights of the most significant Jewish thinker of the late twentieth century.

———. *Nine Talmudic Readings* (Bloomington: University of Indiana Press, 1990). I find the late Emmanuel Levinas one of the most timely and relevant of Jewish thinkers.

Maier, Charles. "Consigning the Twentieth Century to History: Alternative Narratives for the Modern Era," *American Historical Review*, Vol. 3, June 2000.

Marling, Karal Ann. *Merry Christmas: Celebrating America's Greatest Holiday* (Cambridge, Mass.: Harvard University Press, 2000).

Marton, Kati. *A Death in Jerusalem* (New York: Pantheon, 1994).

McGoldrick, Monica, Joe Giordano, John K. Pearce, eds. *Ethnicity and Family Therapy* (New York: Guilford Press, 1982). Includes an excellent section on the dynamics of Jewish "familism."

Merkeley, Paul C. *The Politics of Christian Zionism 1891–1948* (Portland, Ore.: Frank Cass, 1998).

Napier, A. David. *Masks, Transformation, and Paradox* (Berkeley: University of California Press, 1986).

Neusner, Jacob. "Judaism," in *Our Religions*, ed. Arvind Sharma (San Francisco: Harper, 1993). This volume includes the present author's section on Christianity.

New Catholic Encyclopedia, Vol. 10 (New York: McGraw-Hill, 1967).

Niebuhr, Gustav. "Marriage Issue Splits Jews, Poll Finds." *New York Times*, Oct. 31, 2000.

Niebuhr, Reinhold. *The Nature and Destiny of Man: A Christian Interpretation* (New York: Scribner's, 1951). The single most influential work in American Protestant theology in the twentieth century.

Novick, Peter. *The Holocaust in American Life* (Boston: Houghton Mifflin, 1999).

Orme, William A., Jr. "Succoth in Israel, and Here Come the Evangelicals," *New York Times International*, Sept. 29, 1999.

Otto, Rudolf. *The Idea of the Holy*, trans. John W. Harvey (New York: Oxford University Press, 1958).

Rosenthal, Peggy. *The Poets' Jesus: Representations at the End of a Millennium* (New York: Oxford University Press, 2000).

Rosovsky, Nitza. *Jerusalem Walks* (New York: Henry Holt, 1981).

Rubenstein, Richard L. *After Auschwitz* (Indianapolis: Bobbs-Merrill, 1966, 1992).

Ruether, Rosemary. "Ecofeminism: The Challenge to Theology." In *Christianity and Ecology*, ed. Rosemary Ruether and Dieter T. Hessel (Cambridge, Mass.: Harvard University Press, 2000). This is part of a series that includes volumes on the relationship of other religious traditions to ecology.

——. *Faith and Fratricide: The Theological Roots of Anti-Semitism* (New York: Seabury Press, 1974).

Ryback, Timothy W. *The Last Survivor* (New York: Pantheon Books, 1999).

Sanders, E. D. *Jesus and Judaism* (Philadelphia: Fortress Press, 1985).

——. *Paul and Palestinian Judaism* (Philadelphia: Fortress Press, 1977).

——. *Paul, the Law, and the Jewish People* (Philadelphia: Fortress Press, 1983).

Scholem, Gershom. *Major Trends in Jewish Mysticism* (New York: Schocken Books, 1995).

——. *The Messianic Idea in Judaism* (New York: Schocken Books, 1971). This book remains a classic and should play a larger part in Jewish-Christian dialogue.

Sharma, Arvind. "Judaism" in *Our Religions* (San Francisco: Harper, 1993).

Silverman, Morris. *High Holiday Prayer Book* (Hartford: Prayer Book Press, 1948).

Strassfeld, Michael. *Jewish Holidays: A Guide and Commentary* (New York: Harper and Row, 1985). For a thoughtful guide to the Jewish holidays, including lively dissenting views by a variety of rabbis, I recommend this lively book.

Tillich, Paul. *A History of Christian Thought,* ed. Carl E. Braaten (New York: Simon and Schuster, 1968).

Timerman, Jacob. *Prisoner Without a Name, Cell Without a Number* (New York: Vintage Books, 1981).

Van Buren, Paul. *A Theology of Jewish-Christian Reality,* Vol. 1, *Discerning the Way* (1980); Vol. 2, *A Christian Theology of the People of Israel* (1983); Vol. 3, *Christ in Context* (1988) (New York: Harper and Row).

Waldoks, Moshe, and William Novak, eds. *The Big Book of Jewish Humor* (New York: HarperCollins, 1981).

Welch, Claude. *Protestant Thought in the Nineteenth Century,* Vol. 1 (New Haven: Yale University Press, 1972).

White, Lynn, Jr. "The Historical Roots of Our Ecological Crisis," *Science* 155 (March 10, 1967). The essay has been reprinted numerous times since then.

Wiesel, Elie. *Legends of Our Time* (New York: Holt, Rinehart and Winston, 1968).

Wilken, Robert L. *The Land Called Holy* (New Haven: Yale University Press, 1992).

Wilmore, Gayraud S. *Black Radicalism and Black Religion* (Maryknoll, N.Y.: Orbis Books, 1973).

Yerushalmi, Yosef. *Zakhor: Jewish History and Memory* (Seattle: University of Washington Press, 1982).

Zinn, Grover A. "History and Interpretation: 'Hebrew Truth,' Judaism, and the Victorine Exegetical Tradition." In James Charlesworth, ed., *Jews and Christians* (New York: Crossroads, 1990).

Index